WORD HUSTLE:

Critical Essays and Reflections on the Works of

Donald Goines

WORD HUSTLE:

Critical Essays and Reflections on the Works of

Donald Goines

EDITED BY

L. H. Stallings

AND

Greg Thomas

INPRINT EDITIONS
Baltimore

For Mary Elizabeth Walker (Aunt Liz) who read Donald Goines and
Toni Morrison...and loved them both.

L.H. Stallings

For the late Dr. Lattimer, Chief Counselor of the Wretched
and For Aunt Libby the Ancestor, Eldest of the Superheroes.

Greg Thomas

CONTENTS

ACKNOWLEDGMENTS

The editors would like to thank *M.E.L.U.S.*
Journal for granting us permission to reprint
Andrew Sargent's "Representing Prison Rape: Race,
Masculinity, and Incarceration in Donald Goines's
White Man's Justice, Black Man's Grief. Thank
you Scott Michaelsen and *CR: The New Centennial
Review* for allowing us to republish L.H. Stallings
"I'm Goin' Pimp Whores!" for this collection.

Word Hustle

An Introduction to the Street and the Literary Legacy of Donald Goines

L.H. Stallings

I play the street life, because there`s no place I can go
Street life – it`s the only life I know
Street life – and there`s a thousand parts to play
Street life – until you play your life away.
RANDY CRAWFORD, *"Street Life"*

On any street (Woo)
Any street corner (Oh...oh...oh...)
They try to pick me up and take me for a ride
I tell 'em, "No, the girl is satisfied"
They say, "I've got the stuff that really turns you on"
I tell 'em, "No, this little girls is grown."
ASHFORD AND SIMPSON, *"Street Corner"*

This is the street
Nigga eat
where the bird don't tweet
the birds grow cheap
and niggas don't sleep
You may have heard of MLK
But I know a gang of niggas with they own street
The street life (Uh, uh).
LIL WAYNE, *"Street Life"*

During the 1970s, for the first time in their history, African Americans became a predominantly urban people, whether living in the South or the North. With urbanity forming the given condition of black social life, claims to racial representation could no longer be objectively grounded on organic models of community.

MADHU DUBEY, *Signs and Cities*

Word Hustle is the first scholarly treatment of fiction writer Donald Goines, and thereby the first serious consideration of what has been termed "street literature," "ghetto literature," "street fiction," or "urban fiction," etc. It is not a literary biography, but an edited collection that seeks to make room for new models for how we study Black literature and culture. Taking the street as its model, thus, it is an appraisal of Goines's legacy as well as an examination of a tradition and a model of writing – *a literary hustle* whose longevity has outlasted literary movements such as the Harlem Renaissance, the Chicago Renaissance, and the Black Arts Movement. Precisely because it resists periodization and geographical pinning, I would call it a "literary hustle" as opposed to a "literary movement."

Donald Goines was the son of a dry cleaner; a military man; a brother; a heroin-addict; an incarcerated felon; a "pimp, professional gambler, car thief, armed robber and bootlegger" (Matthews 321). Most importantly, he was a writer; a hustler of words who served as the "founding father" of a literary tradition – street literature or fiction, which rarely receives any scholarly attention. There are all kinds of hustles in the world. Some can lead to imprisonment, death or murder. Then there is this one, the "word hustle" that can set you free. For Donald Goines there were all kinds of hustles in which he sought proficiency. However, his most beneficial hustle was the word hustle in which he produced numerous works of fiction that remain in print some thirty years after most of them were published. Word hustle seems the most apt description for what Goines was able to do with ink, paper, and words.

Goines liberated himself by making the page his body, the ink his mind, and the words his spirit that could be set free every time someone read his work. In a country that has consistently used paper, ink and words to control and dehumanize Black bodies and minds in ways that chains never could, it is certainly an extraordinary word hustle for anyone who finds a way to use literature and writing to re-imagine self and community – using their oppressor's language while still maintaining their own values and ideas. Black writers have been word hustling for years in almost every genre. Some writers receive book awards, monetary rewards, and intellectual canonization for their efforts; others garner disdain and disrespect. Goines hustled words but, as discussed throughout this collection, it was his literary representation of other hustles that critics use to marginalize his legacy and impact on the African American literary landscape.

Goines did not begin the contemporary movement of street literature alone. Other critics have assessed that Iceberg Slim *a.k.a.* Robert Beck, like Goines, constitutes the beginning of the form. A mentor to Goines, Beck has been described as the "most prominent author of the street genre, which emerged in the 1960s" (Oliver 379); and, while several authors in this collection discuss Beck in the context of Goines, Beck also warrants a book-length study focused on his own six works. Other authors forging the path of establishing street literature as a form in the late twentieth century include authors of the Holloway House Publishing Company: Odie Hawkins, Eric Priestly, and Joe Nazel. All are equally in need of book-length studies. However, as opposed to simply settling on doing a collection focused on an amalgamation of various authors of street literature, the editors of this collection decided that an extensive study of one particular author would best exemplify how rich, complex, and profound street literature has been.

Personal admiration was not the sole deciding factor, although it was one reason. For Goines's level of production is more than double that of Iceberg Slim; and his influence globally, and historically, as indicated by the number of his texts translated into other languages, not to mention his importance to contemporary Black popular culture, all surpasses those of his other Holloway House contemporaries. A few of his books have been made into movies, and there is talk that more will follow. Undoubtedly, anyone who has produced this much work deserves more than a chapter in a collection. Typically, writers and texts need institutions or institutional apparatuses to garner such scholarly appraisal. To date, street literature has none. While there are numerous publishers willing to make fast money off of the fiction, there are no publishing presses pushing for critical attention to these works. There are no writing workshops, classes, or retreats that push for one to become a writer of this type of fiction. Coffeehouses, libraries, or book clubs often promote other types of popular fiction instead. *Word Hustle* is intended to break with such exclusionary traditions by theorizing about street literature and the legacy of Donald Goines for African American literary tradition.

Although *Word Hustle* is a collection of essays focusing on the novels of Donald Goines, it is not a work that could be classified under literary studies merely. Because Goines's work exceeds geographical, political, chronological and cultural locations due to its intersecting themes and representations of gender, sexuality, class, and racial politics within the sphere of the popular, the collection challenges African American studies, African American literary and cultural studies specifically. It steps outside of their traditional comfort zones. The challenge derives from three major concerns: form, purpose, and audience. Content alone is not the only reason Goines's work has received so little attention, for *written* texts in Black *popular* culture receive little to no sustained study in the context of Black cultural studies. Furthermore, the organizing principle of Goines's work (as well as other writers in the tradition of street literature, as Dubey alludes to at the opening of this introduction) is not grounded in "organic" models of community but in the *crisis* of forming and maintaining racialized communities in the post-Civil Rights era. Finally, an assessment of audience becomes a challenge here when the street, rather than academic or publishing institutions, determines audience.

In the past, any attempted assessment of street literature and Donald Goines in popular culture has been stymied by the fact that African American cultural studies has not engaged the broad proliferation of contemporary popular culture that is focused on the written word. Whether it's Amiri Baraka's use of the Blues to challenge Ron Karenga's opposition to Black popular culture, bell hooks's explication of "outlaw culture," or Stuart Hall's notes on how to deconstruct the popular, written texts aren't broached as subjects as much as they should be. Similarly, African American literary critics still cling to traditional notions of working class and underclass Black communities as illiterate or semi-literate, when the current truth is so much more complex. African American literary theory has historically, with some exceptions, assumed a general middle class readership with bourgeois values embedded in many of the novels selected for criticism.

There are minor studies on Black popular fiction that are published as essays in journals or edited collections on African American fiction. Herman Beavers examines gender and popular fiction in his essay "African American Women Writers and Popular Fiction: Theorizing Black Womanhood," which is included in an edited collection, *The Cambridge Companion to African American Women's Literature*. Bernard Bell in *The Contemporary African American Novel: Its Roots and Modern Literary Branches* comes closest to exploring the importance of Black popular fiction, despite the absence of a thorough assessment of street literature within the text, when he examines the works of Barbara Neely and E. Lynn Harris.

Garnering their own book-length edited collections, detective novelist Walter Mosely and science fiction writers Octavia Butler and Samuel Delany have produced novels that, for certain, have crossed over to be considered literary fiction. In the end, such crossover has made them worthy of study. To date, African American literary studies offer few critical collections on popular fiction produced by Black writers, or Black popular fiction writers, whose characters and plots concern Black underclass representation.

For decades Black music has paid homage to the city, the ghetto, and the street. As we will see throughout this collection, African American writers have done the same work. In theorizing about these tropes and traditions in Black music and literature, most of the work has examined the city. There have been plenty of literary studies of the city and African American literature or urban spaces and African American literature. Yoshinobu Hakutani and Robert Butler's edited collection *The City and African American literature* examines the diversity of visions of the city presented in Black literature. Essays in the collection look at texts by writers such as Frederick Douglass, Richard Wright, Ann Petry, Langston Hughes, Claude McKay, James Baldwin, John A. Williams, Claude Brown, Ralph Ellison and Charles Johnson. Farah Jasmine Griffin's *Who Set You Flowing* takes a look at the importance of urban landscape in migration narratives written by African American writers. What's more, one of the most recent and powerful explorations of the city in African American writing is Madhu Dubey's *Signs and Cities: Black Literary Postmodernism*. Dubey theorizes about print literacy and representations of urban Black identity in African American literature.

While these academic treatises do not exhaust the wealth of scholarship on the city and African American literature, they do by far demonstrate the importance of the macrocosmic entity of the geographical space of urban locations. Iceberg Slim, Donald Goines, and a host of other writers classified as writers of street literature or street fiction are not discussed in any of these works, significantly, even though their novels are set in the city. This lack of discussion is a form of chauvinism that can be best traced to an unacknowledged distinction between conceptions of the street and the city, with ideologies of the city being elevated over those of the street.

Defining Street Literature and Recognizing Its Importance

Detroit labor organizers James and Grace Lee Boggs's theories of the city and Black people provide some evidence as to why the city is glamorized in African American literary studies. But they also provide some reasons why street literature can offer an important form of representation and critique as well as an expression of pleasure and power for the Black underclass. In the now classic essay "The City Is the Black Man's Land," the Boggses postulate that the key to producing a revolutionary society lay in Black people's action, or their successfully gaining and maintaining political control over the cities in which they live:

America has already become the dangerous society. The nation's major cities are becoming police states. There are only two roads open to it. *Either* wholesale extermination of the black population through mass massacres or forced mass migrations onto reservations as with the Indians. (White America is apparently not yet ready for this, although the slaughter of 32 blacks in Watts by the armed forces of the state demonstrates that this alternative is far from remote.) *Or* self-government of the major cities by the black majority, mobilized behind leaders and organizations of its own creation and prepared to reorganize the structure of city government and city life from top to bottom. (36)

The Boggs note a third option in opposition to those which might be imposed by white supremacist structures. Operating under the thesis that majority might rule, the majority being African Americans, the city with all of its technological and industrial possibilities becomes a bright economic and political future for Black people if they can obtain control. Yet, the Boggs also submit the unlikelihood of the third solution, asserting:

> But because the American racist tradition demands the emasculation of blacks not only on the economic and sexual but also on the political level, the perspective of black self-government in the cities cannot be posed openly and frankly as a profession and perspective towards which black youth should aspire and for which they should begin preparing themselves from childhood. (38)

Undoubtedly, the ways in which the Civil Rights Movement was and is unable to alleviate the problems of the Black underclass suggest the need for cultural mechanisms that confront the (im)possibility of Black self-government in the city. The writers of street fiction, Goines and Beck especially, illustrate the Boggses' theory at a micro-level—the street. Street literature provides the dialogue that other social, political, and cultural texts were failing to do as they represented African Americans in the city.

Streets can exist in urban or rural areas. They are mapable terrain. Yet, contemporary constructions of the street as a site of cultural production remain tied to urbanity, and despite the fact that it is literally a piece or a part of the city and the ghetto, the street produces its own ideologies, languages and functions that are quite different from the city. The street, unlike the city, is representative not so much of "modernity" or the "high culture" of a "metropolis" or "cosmopolitan" area, but of a configuration of people's individual desires and the popularization of these desires. Critics engaged in theories about the city and the ghetto inevitably construct theses around collective racial identity. Authors of street fiction do something quite differently. In street literature, individual identity centers the text because the author of street literature texts is operating from the view that ideologies about collective identity and ownership in white America have not fed the hungry and poor.

Streets are dividing lines that can separate or segregate various families, ethnicities, races. They are markers of sexual, racial, and class communities. They become the border where "the gay neighborhood" begins and "the Black neighborhood" ends, or in the case of modern gentrification where blurring of spatial lines occur. Plots and themes revolving around characters who are drug dealers and users, pimps and prostitutes, hired guns and hustlers, these are not simply sensationalized representations of violence; rather, they reflect creative commentary on the crisis of community in urban locations as dictated by sexual desire, class diversity, and individual aspirations. Ironically, the street is not simply a border or boundary, but a liminal space, an "interzone" as Kevin Mumford might note, where binaries of moral/immoral, male/female, homo/hetero, and rich/poor may converge and dissipate. In addition to deconstructing notions of a unified and organic racial community, the street also forms the basis of what might be considered popular in urban Black communities. Like the city, the street is also an important metaphor and organizing principle for global, transnational, Pan-Africanist and diasporic considerations of Black people and writers.

Although it does not address Black popular print texts, Dubey's *Signs and Cities* provides a starting point for discussing the importance of street literature and Donald Goines for African American literary studies. Whereas Dubey examines the trope of the book and cities in representing the "difficulties of imagining racial community within contemporary urban conditions" (4), this introduction and the rest of the collection serves as evidence that the street has also acted as one of the tropes in which the difficulties of imagining racial community have been broached. For African American literary and cultural studies to critically engage the motif and metaphor of the street, as opposed to the city, it should remedy this inattention to the popular in general and street literature in particular. Such work is exactly what Dubey contends must occur:

> In response to this perceived crisis, literary and cultural critics are recalling and refurbishing models of community and of racial representation developed earlier in the century. For this reason, an encounter between postmodernism and African-American literary and cultural studies seems particularly urgent, and may at the very least occasion some rethinking of prevailing models of black literary production. In the two most influential critical paradigms that have governed African-American literary studies— revolving around uplift and vernacular tradition—print literature is imbued with broad-based representative powers. (Dubey 5-6)

Word Hustle allows writers in the collection to rethink prevailing models of Black literary production through the work of Donald Goines and the concept of Black street literature. Goines is the most influential writer to pose a problem for these two paradigms. In African American literary studies, critical essays on so-called popular fiction writers are rare. They are rare because "the popular" resists notions of communities emerging over the singular notion of race or the history of a racialized experience. If Beavers is correct when he argues, "popular culture has always been where black people theorize blackness in America. It has always constituted the sphere where black people produce narratives of pleasure, oppression, resistance, survival, and heroic performances" (356), then this collection is more than justified. Goines and other writers, up until now, have been ignored by African American literary and cultural studies because they used the street to highlight the crisis at a time when critics and scholars were invested in presenting a unified racial community to those outside.

Years ago, Harlem Renaissance critic Alain Locke's essay, "Self-Criticism: The Third Dimension in Culture," suggested a third dimension for cultural representation and cultural criticism of Black America. He closes with a burning question that still consumes scholarship on African American literature and culture:

> Why, then, this protective silence about the ambivalences of the Negro upper classes, about the dilemmas of intra-group prejudice and rivalry, about the dramatic inner paradoxes of mixed heritage, both biological and cultural, or the tragic breach between the Negro elite and the Negro masses... These, among others, are the great themes, but they molder in closed closets like family skeletons... To break such taboos is the crucial artistic question. (60)

Street literature, urban literature, or ghetto literature forces us at this particular moment to either break such taboos or simply belittle the form. *Word Hustle* suggests that we break the taboos and examine the economic and literary politics of the street literature genre and its dichotomous relationship to African American literary studies. According to Locke, the full potential of African American culture can only be realized through consistent and fearless self-criticism. While Locke's own literary work was (officially, here, at least) about self-criticism, the development of African American literary theory and studies has developed counter to even a Locke's call for one reason: the ignoring of class difference. Rather than dissecting major squabbles between critics, this introduction posits the urban or street fiction genre as a theoretical trope that disrupts the continuity of a stabilized canon of African American literature and a unified field of African American literary theory. Essays in the collection also explore the ways in which gender, sexuality, and class are represented outside the modalities of uplift visions. This collection also chooses to focus on Goines rather than Iceberg Slim or other writers because he really stands at the precipice of past and present debates about African American literature. He compels us to consider new ways of "imagining community" and liberation. He intuits the struggle between collective agency and individual aspirations. He is rife with the knowledge that the imagined collective is more important than the individuals who comprise the communities. The modes by which his work, and other writers of the tradition, is distributed, consumed, and produced also disturbs long-held assumptions about political publishing models of Black fiction.

The Street, Ann Petry, and African American Literature

Most of the recent production of street literature begins with a model of cultural self-determination, known in Black American as hustling. Street fiction literally starts in the street, with authors hustling and hawking their self-published novels long before publishing companies see the value. What began, literally, as fiction sold on the street corners, flea markets, and barbershops has become a packaged product for mainstream America. Street literature can be literary, popular, or formulaic. Its characters usually consist of hustlers, pimps, prostitutes, thieves, cops, wardens, and other "criminals," but its plots and themes vary. And while some would characterize it as a masculine space, there are historical texts that suggest the genre has not been dominated by a particular gender – in terms of authorship, for example.

One of the earliest forays into representing the street in African American literature comes to us via the 1950s: Ann Petry's novel *The Street*.[1] Petry had shown previous interest in urban themes focused on the city when she wrote the short story "The Winding Sheet." But here the focus was on collective racial identity. Published by mainstream presses, Petry doesn't produce enough work on the street to be called a street writer, but with her novel she does initiate the formula of representing the street as a separate entity from the city. In doing so she exposes how writing or representing the street can adhere to Dubey's paradigmatic approach, even if it eventually or potentially poses conflicts:

> The uplift paradigm casts the writer as an agent of social advancement and cultural improvement, thereby affirming the tangible value of print literacy for the masses. In the vernacular paradigm, writers may speak for distinctively black communities insofar as they can inflect their texts with the accents and idioms of black oral culture. (Dubey 6)

In street literature, no one really wants to "escape" the city, merely move to a different side of town or another street. The city is still seen as a place of unlimited possibility and modernity. But as Petry shows, certain streets dash such hope. In 1946, she disturbed the notion of collective identity and the city with the question of gender. In her construction of Lutie Johnson, a woman abandoned by her husband, harassed as a domestic worker by her white employer, and preyed upon by Black men as she seeks to take care of her son and preserve some sense of self, Petry provides one of the most powerful literary productions of street literature ever written. She wrote of the concrete path and roadway in urban spaces, not simply as a geographical space, setting, or location, but as a living, breathing force.

The street becomes a character, an antagonist to foil her protagonist Lutie Johnson's personal goal toward her own individual Black uplift. After violently killing a criminal, Junto, Lutie finds herself on a train with a one-way ticket to Chicago, since as she tells the ticket man: "I've had one since the day I was born" (434). It is on the train to Chicago that Petry uses her female heroine to acknowledge the literary form and art she has been participated in making:

> She remembered that when she was in grammar school the children were taught to get the proper slant to their writing... Once again she could hear the flat, exasperated voice of the teacher as she looked at the circles Lutie had produced. "Really," she said, "I don't know why they have us bother to teach you people to write." The woman's statement was correct, she thought. What possible good has it done to teach people like me to write? (436)

The texts of street literature act as narratives about literacy, literary form, and the erasure of self for a collective racialized community. Petry uses the act of writing as a metaphor for identity formation influenced by class, race, and gender: Lutie's inability to get the "proper slant" to writing and the teacher's comments expose that, in America, becoming literate in writing and reading means adjusting one's self to the ideals of a dominant society (be it white or Black middle class). Later, as Lutie tries to figure out how she murdered a man and landed on a train with a one-way ticket, "all she could think was, it was that street. It was that god-damned street" (437).

The street becomes a murderous force for Lutie; however, Petry's word hustle about the street actively insists upon constructing a liberatory voice and discourse for the masses of marginalized men and women who might be victims of the street, worldwide; a voice and discourse that does not become pathologized by sociologists; a voice that can emphasize the ultra-humanity of street people despite the inhumanity placed upon their daily lives. By the end of the novel, Petry has not simply produced a fictional "sociological work" that feeds the theories of "Black pathology" in inner cities, she has contributed to and helped define a literary form, its readers, and the writers who will continue to produce and evolve the form. Why this eruption of the street before the post-Civil Rights era? The most obvious reason has to do with gender. Black women writers recognized early on the ways in which less nuanced understandings of collective community could wreck havoc on their daily lives. Though representations of urbanity and city life have existed in African American fiction and literature for decades, the cultural construction of the street (rather than the city) as an organizing principle of the individual versus the community resurfaces during the 1970s alongside the Black Arts Movement.

Street Literature, Donald Goines, and Black Arts Movement Exclusion

With the 1967 publication of Iceberg Slim's *Pimp*, street literature begins to take shape right near the early beginnings of the Black Arts Movement (BAM). Goines's novels are published at the beginning of the 1970s when BAM is in full effect. Still, his popularity and influence far exceeds that time period. Despite the fact that these works are literally located between Addison Gayle's "The Black Aesthetic" and Trey Ellis's "The New Black Aesthetic" manifestos, there is rarely a critical mention of a Black Aesthetic that includes the street or Black underclass representation. Neither text or writer actually ever acknowledges the existence of the form or its importance to a Black Arts or Black Power Movement. I mean this facetiously since it is likely that members of BAM and BPP did daily encounter prostitutes, pimps, drug users, drug dealers, or hustlers in ways that were not all superficial and stereotypical. From the Jazz scene to performance venues and coffeehouses, some inspiration came from these interactions. Paradoxically, the failure to incorporate Black street literature into the literary history, terrain, and consciousness of African American literature begins not with those 1980s canon-building academic pimps, Henry Louis Gates and Houston A. Baker. Before them, there was the well-intentioned shortsightedness of BAM or its inability to resolve its contradictory relationship to Black popular culture which was not visual, oral, or musical – as well as that old-age problem of representation and uplift.

As this collection demonstrates time and again, the work of Donald Goines and early street literature were very much influenced by Black Power politics. Interestingly enough, Goines and other authors of street literature were never considered as important to the cultural arm of Black Power, BAM. By the time Goines publishes *Whoreson* (1970) and *Dopefiend* (1971), BAM has already constructed a Black

Aesthetic that would make it difficult to incorporate the form of street literature, or this style of street fiction.

Pivotal texts from the movement grappled with uplift, the importance of African ancestry, politics of form, and Black entrepreneurship. According to Larry Neal's essay "The Black Arts Movement":

> The Black Arts Movement is radically opposed to any concept of the artist that alienates him from his community. Black Art is the aesthetic and spiritual sister of the Black Power concept. As such, it envisions an art that speaks directly to the needs and aspirations of Black America. In order to perform this task, the Black Arts Movement proposes a radical reordering of the western cultural aesthetic. It proposes a separate symbolism, mythology, critique, and iconology. The Black Arts and the Black Power concept both relate broadly to the Afro-American's desire for self-determination and nationhood. Both concepts are nationalistic. One is concerned with the relationship between art and politics; the other with the art of politics. (2039)

Neal's attention to an art that speaks to the needs of Black people, that rejects western cultural aesthetics, and the creation and evolution of a separate cultural model seem to be viable ways in which street literature could have been a part of BAM. Yet, for Neal and the majority of the most influential BAM figures, the concerns of Black self-determination and culture mean work dedicated to national aims of uplift and financially supported by Black sponsorship or institutes.

From the beginning, though, street literature produces a hiccup in the rhetoric of Black cultural self-determination. Mainstream publishing houses and presses were not publishing street literature, but neither were those models of cultural self-determination. Because Beck and Goines were published by Holloway House, a non-Black press, as a result of their focus on the ideals of the Black underclass, their novels would not fit within the political missions of, say, Broadside Press, Lotus Press or, later, Third World Press. The Black Aesthetic, for all of its attention to nationhood, failed to see how the street could be useful in constructing an economy for nationhood. That said, there was no room for pimps, thieves, or drug dealers.

In "Prison Writers and the Black Arts Movement," Lee Bernstein does an excellent job of further historicizing the importance of BAM and culture to prison politics and prison reform or abolition movements. In doing so, though, Bernstein unwittingly reveals the uplift elements of Black nationalism and exactly why BAM could promote and get behind prison writers such as Etheridge Knight and Eldridge

Cleaver while ostracizing the work of street literature writers such as Iceberg Slim. Though Neal acknowledges street life and the street writer by dedicating his poem "Brother Pimp" to Iceberg Slim, writing "become a new pimp ... pimp for the revolution" (217), the prevailing idea that pimps could serve as a symbol "of the potential for revolution among the criminals," if they would only "undergo a political transformation" (306), reveals an interesting divide between the street and the Black Arts Movement. Not one anti-street critic recognizes how the opportunity to write and publish from these former hustlers might in some way contribute to a new consciousness or an ideal way to connect with the Black underclass. Chastisement is offered instead.

Neal was not the only writer to feel this way. As Lee Bernstein acknowledges:

> In his introduction to the 1969 anthology, *Black Poetry*, Clarence Major argued that black poetry could be a tool in transforming the pimps into revolutionaries... Majors argued that the new poetry signaled "death cries to the pimp par excellence of the recent capitalistic stages of the world." (306)

Though there still remains a sense of elitism, Majors comes close to seeing how the ex-pimp turned writer could be useful. Ironically, as scholarship on Black Power and BAM have shown, the revolutionary and the pimp were more or less the same, especially when it came to gender and sexual oppression. Echoing the Boggses' earlier concerns about Blacks and the cities, we realize that BAM failed to discuss how artists could use their art to eat, or to feed the people. What labor does the artist do, and does it produce wealth? With Goines, these questions about labor and wealth form the foundation of street literature.

Other writers' attention to a past, static, and mythologized version of Africa as the central foundation for Black cultural nationalism, or the dismissal of popular culture as playing a role in Black revolution, further alienates Goines and authors of street literature from dominant constructions of BAM. As James Smethurst suggested, "after all, even when Amiri Baraka's art and politics were most clearly indebted to Maulana Karenga, the two fundamentally disagreed over the meaning of African American popular culture and its relation to revolutionary black art" (58). In "Black Art: Mute Matter Given Force and Function," Karenga insists that "Black art must expose the enemy, praise the people and support the revolution" (2088). We also hear from Karenga that Black art must be collective and resist the notion of the individual (2089). Furthermore, in a volatile statement that is a foundation for the notion that popular culture does not encourage revolution, Karenga dismisses the Blues by saying, "we say the blues is invalid; for they teach resignation" (2090). Such beliefs indicate why the growing body of street literature was ignored by BAM, despite representing one of the many Black experiences. Karenga's point about the Blues mirrors they ways in which some would assume representation of underclass life must be a glamorization of poverty and violence, a resignation to or acceptance of the situation as opposed to a will or desire to change it.

As I suggest in my reprinted essay here, Amiri Baraka's work on the Black novel serves as a way to validate Goines popular fiction, at once recognizing it for both its politics and pleasure: "Most of the formal literature produced by Negroes in America has never fulfilled these conditions. And aside from Negro music, it is in the 'popular traditions' of the so-called lower class Negro that these conditions are fulfilled as a basis of human life" ("The Myth of a Negro Literature," *Within the Circle* 168). Baraka goes on to assert that the separation between the emotion of lived experience from the cultured calculation of "art for art's sake" is why sports figures like Jack Johnson or Ray Robinson are more political figures than most Negro writers. Notably, aside from all of the canonical Black writers, the writer who Baraka briefly mentions as capturing the emotion of lived experience is Goines's mentor, Iceberg Slim. Again, there are indeed moments when a more nuanced definition of a Black Aesthetic which accounts for class, gender, or sexuality would have extended BAM as a movement.

Hoyt Fuller's "Towards a Black Aesthetic" briefly mentions the radical potentiality of the street but fails to consider that promise as connected to necessary changes in Black literature. Fuller remarks, "the black revolt is as palpable in letters as it is in the streets, and if it has not yet made its impact upon the Literary establishment, then the nature of the revolt itself is the reason" (1853-54). A native of Detroit and a Wayne State graduate, Fuller's words make allusions to political and cultural revolutions; and even as he speaks of the streets, he separates – in ways that Goines cannot – the rebellion on the street and the literary rebellion enacted by BAM through poetry and drama particularly.

He continues, "the rebellion in the streets is the black ghetto's response to the vast distance between the nation's principles and its practices" (1854). Street literature is a textual rebellion based in the Black Aesthetic of rioting; a response to forms, figures, and institutions that reject the Black underclass and to any notions that they are incapable of producing revolutionary written texts based on their street experiences. Revolutionary in this case means the acknowledgement and representation of Black people's politics as well as their pleasures; their impetus for communality, self-determination, and nationhood as well as the way this impetus conflicts with individual identity, aspirations and desires.

Unfortunately, we cannot go back and insert street literature or Goines into BAM since neither was ever fully acknowledged as worthy. However, what we can suggest is that the same impetus for creating a Black Aesthetic existed in early street literature; that the same questions of form and audience preoccupied the authors and publishers of street literature; and that the strategy of moving beyond uplift – of valuing the community and the individual – were a part of its Black Aesthetic. Finally, we can assert that street literature's realistic depictions of race, capitalism, economics and cultural production in America are the reasons why long after BAM and its considerations of a Black Aesthetic ends, street literature and its formulation of one Black Aesthetic persists and continues to flourish. This fact signals perhaps that there was never simply one Black Aesthetic, but many Black Aesthetics parallel and intersecting with one another.

This is why we must begin to query why, when he was locked up in Michigan City Penitentiary, Goines's mother thought to bring her son a typewriter that he, in turn, knew exactly what to do with in prison and thereafter (*Metro Times* 16). Certainly, plural Black Aesthetics are why we should ask how Goines and Beck chose to write extended narratives – not music, not art, and not poetry – as the best way to express their particular experience of Blackness when numerous documents of BAM insisted that poetry and drama were the most effective and best ways to reach the people. The answer to those questions would then reveal how publishers of street fiction, such as Holloway House, paid attention to Black economic models of empowerment and risked going against the grain to believe that the masses of the Black underclass would make time for what has always been conceived of as a specifically bourgeois form: Black people of various classes would seek out and buy Goines's performances of the street in extended form, in the same ways that they would flock to the stage to see an Ed Bullins, or attend the Spoken Word performance of a Gil Scott-Heron. What was it about Goines's upbringing in Detroit, and his experiences elsewhere, that led him to intuit that the novel form would be his tool for being radical, revolutionary, and liberatory? The answers to these questions may begin with the production of cultural capital in Detroit and end narratively with Black Power and BAM in Los Angeles.

As essays in this collection will show, Goines's novels reflect an imprint of Black politics and cultural nationalism publicly and prominently made available to the masses in Detroit and Los Angeles, places where Goines lived. Detroit serves as a relevant site of cultural nationalism, especially as it was influenced by labor movements. A product of Detroit, Goines and his family would have been aware and touched by the strong influences of Motown and its Black musical ideologies; the persistent labor movements initiated and expressed in writing by CLR James as well as James and Grace Lee Boggs during the 1950s; and the cultural nationalism of Dudley Randall, Hoyt Fuller, Robert Hayden or Broadside Press, *Uhuru, Inner City Voice, Correspondence* and *Drum*. The same could be said of Los Angeles's influence on him after he moved to Watts, where Karenga and U.S., the Black Panthers,

Ornette Coleman, the Watts Writers Workshop, Watts Happening Coffeehouse, and the Watts Summer Festival were massive forces in people's daily lives. Sadly, the ways in which critics have decided to divorce early street literature from BAM has shaped the contemporary landscape and debates about Black literature, Black politics and Black nationalism, among other things.

CONCLUSION

During a writing conference, specifically a panel on street fiction, street fiction author Nikki Turner was asked, "If urban fiction represents progress in a sense that we no longer care how we look to others in producing these books, is the term 'embarrassment to the race' obsolete?" Turner replied, "I am not interested in how we look to white people. I am interested in literacy in the community and being able to get people to read books." ("It's Urban, It's Real"). Street literature should make us question the idea of universal representations, literacies, languages, and ideologies. As an art form, street literature serves as a testimony to the inequities of institutional education or mis-education as well as the limitations of bourgeois language and form to convey the experience of poverty (an experience of need, lack, hunger, despair, and, if one is lucky, hope). The form exists because of dominant society's failure to educate the masses, without erasing the masses. In themes and plots, it is about the wretched of the earth and the ever-present colonial rule of the oppressors (Fanon 130).

All of the writers in this collection believe in the popular artistry and intellectual value of Black street literature. *Word Hustle* seeks to begin a legitimate study of the genre and its authors by examining one of its most prolific founders, Donald Goines. The collection represents some of the most frequently used tropes and themes in Black street literature since its inception and within its present day manifestations, though other studies that follow this one may showcase other themes and tropes. In illuminating the layers of Goines's novels, writers engage topics such as Black Power politics, revolutionary violence, domesticity and fatherhood, revisions of the mulatto trope, rape and racialized sexuality, and the prison industrial complex.

The first two essays explore the political and popular importance of Donald Goines's Kenyatta series. Written under the pseudonym of Al C. Clark, Goines produced four novels in the Kenyatta series published between 1974 and 1975. With this series, Goines produced a protagonist who would become emblematic of Black Power, street life, and tropes of Blaxploitation masculinity. Candice Love Jackson's "The Paradox of Empowerment: Colonialism, Community, and Criminality in the Donald Goines's Kenyatta Series" examines the confluence of colonialism, community empowerment and "criminality" in Donald Goines's Kenyatta series. Drawing from the rich historical ideologies concerning violence and self-defense from the Black Panther Party as well as the significance of the "Mau Mau" uprising in continental and Pan-Africanist discourses, Jackson offers a reading of Goines's works as specifically invested in highlighting the importance, failures and paradoxes of Black leadership in regards to poor Black people.

In the second essay on the Kenyatta series, "Revolutionary Hustler: Liberatory Violence in Donald Goines's Kenyatta Series," Terrence Tucker studies the novels in this series for the ways in which they challenge conceptions of canonicity and raises questions about literacy and the cultural traditions from which multiple literacies emerge. His assessment helps to establish thematic precedents and literary considerations for the genre of street literature as it existed during the 1970s, so that we can understand the evolution of the genre as it currently exists today. Both essays perform necessary labor in regard to a series that yields multiple readings and layers of understanding about Black literature as a whole, and street literature more specifically.

Moving from representations of Black Power in the urban city, Greg Thomas's "George Jackson – Ambushing – in *Swamp Man*: Detecting *Soledad Brother* and *Blood in My Eye* in Donald Goines" considers the one non-urban novel Goines wrote, *Swamp Man*. In a move that understands that Black Power was not simply an "East Coast" or "West Coast" phenomenon, Thomas reveals how Goines transplanted Black Power ideologies into his southern protagonist and the novel's themes about racial and sexual violence.

Dennis Chester's "By Certain Codes: Structures of Masculinity in Donald Goines *Daddy Cool*" uncovers the layers of Goines writing concerned with conversations about gender and sexuality. Chester writes that Goines offers a particular representation of masculinity that many critics and readers dismiss as irrelevant to the genre of street literature and Goines's canon. In analyzing Goines's representations of Black men as fathers, brothers, and husbands, Chester examines representational conflicts between Black masculinity within underclass communities and normative middle class representations.

The fifth essay in the collection is a reprint of a journal article that served as the impetus for the collection. L.H. Stallings's "I'm Goin' Pimp Whores!," followed in the tradition of Greg Goode's "From *Dopefiend* to *Kenyatta's Last Hit*: The Angry Black Crime Novels of Donald Goines" to insist upon new consideration of street literature. However, rather than situating Goines's work as popular fiction alone, Stallings offers a reading of *Whoreson*, a novel with less explicit political ideologies than those seen in the Kenyatta series, which highlights the class conflicts within African American literary canon formation. Arguing that Goines writes a neo-slave narrative situated in the urban landscape, Stallings forces readers to reconsider questions of class in popular culture and literary analysis.

Cameron Leader-Picone's essay "Diggin' the Scene with a Gangster Lean: Race as an Institutional Structure in Iceberg Slim and Donald Goines" makes a connection between Goines and his writing mentor, Robert Beck a.k.a. Iceberg Slim. Picone's discussion of the tragic mulatto trope in both authors' works showcases a variation in the representation of the trope stemming from cultural representations of the figure in a different environments (underclass or institutional).

Phyllis Lynne Burns's "'I'll Be There': The Love and Defense Narrative of *Black Girl Lost*" demonstrates that even in the midst of presenting morally ambiguous characters, anger and vengeance, or harsh representations of crime and violence, Goines has also considered the most basic human emotion, love. Far from simply asserting *Black Girl Lost* as a Black love story set "in the 'hood," Burns's work observes how Goines challenges pathologized representations of the ghetto and the very prevalent idea that love cannot and does not exist in its oppressed communities.

Next, Andrew Sargent's "Representing Prison Rape: Race, Masculinity, and Incarceration in Donald Goines's *White Man's Justice, Black Man's Grief*" is published here, confirming the vital utility of Goines for dissecting and interrupting a number of still very pressing discourses of oppression and repression – that is, established discourses of race or racism, sex and gender and rape, as they routinely intersect with those representing race or racism, criminalization and mass incarceration, just to name a few.

The ninth and last essay in the collection, Quincy Norwood's "Beneath the Law: Donald Goines and America's Sliding Scale of Criminality" also looks at Goines's prison novel, *White Man's Justice, Black Man's Grief*. Given the current prison abolition movement, Norwood's essay hones in on elements within the novel that showcase why it has become one of the novels that is currently being taught in universities across the United States. Norwood details how Goines's novel provides a voice for prisoners as a group or social class. Written during a time in which prisoners themselves were actively involved in the abolition of the prison industrial complex, Norwood gleans the importance of the novel's defiance of the racist-classist notions of criminality in the U.S.

While this introduction began with a much needed critique of African American literary studies, it ends with a cautionary tirade: Street literature has existed and survived without any African American literary studies love and understanding for decades. It has prospered, even as the field has given it the cold shoulder, denied it any sort of legitimate criticism or financial-institutional support. Attempts to contain it with dismissal and disparaging comments are futile. But the question remains as to whether this African American field will be a vital part of its evolution or allow it to be appropriated and exploited by those who see its value only in terms of capital rather than its human and artistic value. It is time for the dilemma of class in African American literary studies to be broached in the same rigorous manner that critics have attended to gender (sexism) and sexuality (homophobia) in the late 20th century. For, as Walter Mosley has noted: "Obviously, there can be an art to ghetto lit. I would never dismiss it out of hand… You might read this hip-hop book, and next year read Mosley or even Mark Twain… It's not about the book—it's the idea that reading becomes an important part of your life" ("It's Urban, It's Real"). We hope that *Word Hustle* serves as an intellectual hustle that Donald Goines would be proud of. There are all kinds of hustles, but it's the word hustle that can set a person free.

NOTES

1 This is not to suggest that other writers such as Richard Wright, James Baldwin, or Ralph Ellison were not concerned with the city and the Black poor. But these writers' representation used the city, not the street, to engage the nation and U.S. nationalism. Paule Marshall's *Browngirl, Brownstone* uses the city as well, if it has little interest in representations of the street. Gwendolyn Brooks's collection of poetry, *A Street in Bronzeville*, does indeed consider the street and all its underclass formulas, but its form is poetic and not narrative or the novel.

REFERENCES

Ashford & Simpson (Musical group), Nickolas Ashford, Valerie Simpson, and Quincy Jones. *The Very Best of Ashford & Simpson*. Los Angeles: Rhino, 2002.

Baraka, Amiri. "The Myth of a 'Negro Literature'" in *Within the Circle: An Anthology of African American Literary Criticism from the Harlem Renaissance to the Present*. Ed. Angelyn Mitchell. Durham: Duke University Press, 1994. 165-171.

Beavers, Herman. "African American Women Writers and Popular Fiction: Theorizing Black Womanhood" in *The Cambridge Companion to African American Women's Literature*. Eds. Angelyn Mitchell and Danille K. Taylor. Cambridge, UK: Cambridge University Press, 2009. 262-277.

Bell, Bernard W. *The Contemporary African American Novel: Its Folk Roots and Modern Literary Branches*. Amherst: University of Massachusetts Press, 2004.

Bernstein, Lee. "Prison Writers and the Black Arts Movement" in *New Thoughts on the Black Arts Movement*. Eds. Lisa Gail Collins and Margo Natalie Crawford. New Brunswick, N.J.: Rutgers University Press, 2006. 297-316.

Boggs, James and Grace. "The City is the Black Man's Land." *Monthly Review* (April 1966) Vol 17, No. 11. 35-46.

Crawford, Randy. "Street Life," *Randy Crawford*. Culver City, CA: Westwood One, 1982.

Dubey, Madhu. *Signs and Cities: Black Literary Postmodernism*. Chicago: University of Chicago Press, 2003.

Fuller, Hoyt. "Towards a Black Aesthetic" in *The Norton Anthology of African American Literature*. Eds. Henry Louis Gates and Nellie Y. McKay. New York, NY: Norton, 2004.

Griffin, Farah Jasmine. *"Who Set You Flowin'?": The African-American Migration Narrative*. New York: Oxford University Press, 1995.

Oliver, Terri Hume. *The Oxford Companion to African American Literature*. Eds. William L. Andrews, Frances Smith Foster, and Trudier Harris. New York: Oxford University Press, 1997.

Hakutani, Yoshinobu, and Robert Butler. *The City in African-American Literature*. Madison: Fairleigh Dickinson University Press, 1995.

Karenga, Maulana. "Black Art: Mute Matter Given Force and Function" in *The Norton Anthology of African American Literature*. Eds. Henry Louis Gates and Nellie Y. McKay. New York, NY: Norton, 2004.

Locke, Alaine. "Self-Criticism: The Third Dimension in Culture" in *Within the Circle: An Anthology of African American Literary Criticism from the Harlem Renaissance to the Present*. Ed. Angelyn Mitchell. Durham: Duke University Press, 1994. 21-32.

Matthews, Valerie N. *The Oxford Companion to African American Literature*. Eds. William L. Andrews, Frances Smith Foster, and Trudier Harris. New York: OxfordUniversity Press, 1997.

Mumford, Kevin J. *Interzones: Black/White Sex Districts in Chicago and New York in the Early Twentieth Century*. New York: Columbia University Press, 1997.

Neal, Larry. "The Black Arts Movement" in *The Norton Anthology of African American Literature*. Eds. Henry Louis Gates and Nellie Y. McKay. New York, NY: Norton, 2004.

————. "Brother Pimp" in *Visions of a Liberated Future: Black Arts Movement Writings*. Eds. Larry Neal, Imamu Amiri Baraka, and Michael Schwartz. New York: Thunder's Mouth Press, 1989.

Petry, Ann. *The Street*. Boston: Houghton Mifflin Co, 1946.

Slim, Iceberg. *Pimp*. Los Angeles, CA: Holloway House Pub. Co, 1996.

Smethurst, James Edward. *The Black Arts Movement: Literary Nationalism in the 1960s and 1970s*. Chapel Hill: University of North Carolina Press, 2005.

Venable, Malcolm, Tayannah McQuillar, and Yvette Mingo. "It's Urban, It's Real, But Is This Literature? Controversy Rages Over a New Genre Whose Sales Are Headed Off the Charts." *Black Issues Book Review*. 6. 5 (2004).

CHAPTER ONE

The Paradox of Empowerment
Colonialism, Community, and Criminality in Donald Goines's Kenyatta Series

Candice Love Jackson

After immediate success with *Dopefiend* (1971) and *Whoreson* (1972), and then subsequent novels that included *Black Gangster* (1972) and *White Man's Justice, Black Man's Grief* (1973), Donald Goines became acutely aware of the power his writing afforded him. His new career was a bittersweet redemption for Goines, as it not only kept him in honest work and out of prison, but it also financed his raging heroin addiction. Within three years, Goines published sixteen novels, four of which appeared under the pseudonym Al C. Clark[1]. As Al C. Clark, Goines published four novels: *Crime Partners* (1974), *Death List* (1974), *Kenyatta's Escape* (1974), and *Kenyatta's Last Hit* (1975). Collectively regarded to Goines-philes as the Kenyatta series, the novels center around the singularly-named Kenyatta, a revolutionary resolved to eradicate the Black community of its ills, specifically drugs and bigoted white police officers.

As with his previous offerings, Goines makes a concerted attempt to engage an African American audience largely uninvolved in the socio-political discourse affecting them. The series traces the rise and fall of Kenyatta and his organization from its beginnings in Detroit to its fateful end in Las Vegas, Nevada. Like the revolutionary organizations of the Black Power movement materializing across the country in the sixties and seventies, Kenyatta's organization embraces those of the Black inner city community who are dismissed by the larger society and who gravitate toward Black militant organizations because they foster a sense of hope and self-sufficiency in the community and their members. The Kenyatta series forces readers to examine (and reexamine) the Black revolutionary in America who pursues the greater principle through concerted criminality as well as the long-range effects of that "criminality".

As a revolutionary, Kenyatta's overarching goal is to empower and liberate his community from racial and social oppression. Yet, how Kenyatta seeks this liberation is the ultimate paradox. For Kenyatta's militancy is inextricably linked to his criminality. Elaborate heists fund his growing army of criminals-cum-Black militants, who execute drug dealers and police officers at his command without question. While Goines does not intimate that all revolutionary organizations are, in fact, criminal enterprises, he does recognize and understand how even the noblest of men and well-meaning of organizations succumb to less than "honorable" methods to empower and liberate the Black community.

As the quintessential "badman," Kenyatta operates within a tradition that Jerry Bryant argues

> … was the white man's worst dream: the slave or (after Emancipation) the laborer who refused to knuckle under, who repeatedly ran away, who deliberately slowed down work, surreptitiously or openly throwing sand into the master's machines. He was the out-of-control black man, the surly slacker, the belligerent troublemaker, and occasionally the killer of whites.[2]

Clearly Kenyatta perpetrates trickster/badman actions as he seeks to upend the drug trade and bigotry in the Black community. What Kenyatta refuses to do is to bow to the will of the dominant class; bowing to that will means submitting to social and psychological subjugation and accepting the inferiority of one's Blackness. He consciously hinders the sale of drugs in the Black community in extreme badman fashion: two warnings, then death. This, of course, "deliberately slow[s] down work" for not only the street dealers but also the white power brokers controlling the drug trade from the comforts of their suburban communities.

To characterize Kenyatta as "out of control" might be an understatement; however, it makes readers, this one included, begin to question the connotation of the phrase. Are Kenyatta's actions or reactions in the spirit of revolution that is said to found this country, the U.S., if we consider that the "American Revolution," like contemporary liberation movements elsewhere, was to cast off oppressors—violently, if necessary—to become independent? The American Revolution serves for many in the U.S. as a precedent of righteous warfare, one which led to a sovereignty snatched from foreign powers. Thus, in the Black community, the Black revolutionary movement is akin to that which preceded it centuries ago, only the badman is not dumping tea into the Boston River in the quest for political and economic freedom. In Kenyatta's case, killing the oppressive drug dealer or racist police officer is merely part of a quest for freedom from destruction and death.

Kenyatta, therefore, becomes a folk hero of mythical proportions. In the African American folklore tradition, the badman's criminality as anti-white or anti-oppression garners reverence, not disdain. Often masters in eluding law enforcement and rivals, the badman inspires hope in their impudence. The oral ballad tradition celebrates the badman's exploits with tales of Stackolee and the Signifying Monkey.

> Although black badmen were invariably conceptualized as individuals who ... were accused of breaking the law and became heroic because of their crimes, their acts of lawlessness were conceptualized within a tradition of folk heroic creation that African Americans recognized and accepted as normative expressions of their heroic ideals. (Roberts 173)

Of the badmen within the Goines canon, Kenyatta stands as the most heroic, in spite of his criminality, as a result of his nobility, his unending quest to save his community. Kenyatta is stronger than his compatriots, physically and mentally, respected by his underlings and even the officers who pursue him.

In addition, the traditional badman possesses a supernatural quality that helps elevate him to his heroic status. The conjurer and trickster emerges as archetypal tropes, as the conjurer's actions

> ... served as a model of behavior for dealing with subversive actions directed primarily against other members of the black community, whereas the tricksters had offered a model of subversive and manipulative behavior for dealing with the powers of the masters—an external threat to the well-being of the black community. (Roberts 200)

Kenyatta is both conjurer and trickster. His ability to galvanize Blacks, particularly young Blacks, into believing his program as well as the violence that accompanies it, distinguishes him from other Goines characters. Kenyatta recognizes the hold the drug trade has on the Black community as part of a systemic genocide. His attempts toward community empowerment and liberation force Kenyatta to use the tools of oppression against the oppressors—Black and white—whose actions negatively affect the Black community.

A revolutionary premise allows Goines to interrogate the marginalization of Black liberation movements in America as well as throughout the Diaspora, referencing several revolutions in Africa and Latin America against imperialist, colonial powers. Kenyatta's organization is an amalgam of several Black militant organizations, but particularly the Black Panther Party for Self-Defense. Led by Huey Newton and Bobby Seale from 1966 to the mid-1970s, the Black Panther Party galvanized thousands of Black youths across the country in an effort to liberate Blacks from psychological and social oppressions. Newton and Seale were students of socio-political history, and understood the importance and relevance of the recent independence movements of African nations, Ghana and Kenya particularly. Goines would also have been aware of the struggles against oppression at home and the resistance toward colonial powers in Africa. Goines names his protagonist in homage to Jomo Kenyatta, Kenya's revolutionary leader, and closely designs Kenyatta's program after that of the Black Panther Party's 10-point program.[3] Thus, Goines's Kenyatta synthesizes the plight of the African on both sides of the Atlantic. By linking the campaign for independence from colonial rule in Africa to the Black militancy movement in America, Goines elucidates the colonization of American Blacks and offers that liberation was not only possible but inevitable. The Black Panther Party, Jomo Kenyatta's Kenya African Union (KAU) and the "Mau Mau" coalesce to allow Goines to offer readers seemingly disparate yet comparable movements against oppression.

The Black Panther Party for Self-Defense, though, originated with the assassination of Malcolm X, or El Hajj Malik Shabazz, in 1965. Malcolm founded the Muslim Mosque, Inc. and the Organization for Afro-American Unity (OAAU) to lead Blacks toward psychological and spiritual liberation; and despite shedding his underworld past as Detroit Red during his spiritual reformation, he remains a folk hero to urban Black America. His fiery spirit and threats of impending racial insurrections greatly contrasted to that of Martin Luther King's nonviolent approach to civil rights in the South. Malcolm's longstanding presence as a revolutionary activist cemented him as the voice and heartbeat of urban Black America, his death leaving a void and the future of Black nationalism in limbo.

Mourning Malcolm, however, opened the doors for the Black Power Movement (1965-1975). The Black Panther Party's core mission was community empowerment and uplift through socially-directed programs such as breakfasts for children, free clothing and shoes, legal assistance, medical care, and screening for sickle cell anemia (Deburg 160). However, its most lasting legacies are the images of Newton, Seale, and scores of heavily armed Blacks, men and women, and the systematic destruction of the Panthers by both local and federal law enforcement. The Panthers wielded the gun as both a political tool against white America as well as a recruitment tool for Black youths. Newton and Seale adopted Mao Tse-Tung's philosophy that "to get rid of the gun, it is necessary to take up the gun." More often than not, unfortunately, the Panthers were the target of gun violence rather than its instigators. A bridging the gap between Malcolm's OAAU and the Black Panthers was found in Eldridge Cleaver's statement: "Malcolm prophesized the coming of the gun to the Black liberation struggle. Huey P. Newton picked up the gun and pulled the trigger."[4] The metaphor Cleaver constructs could be easily applicable to Donald Goines's Kenyatta, who not only picks up the gun and pulls the trigger but also shoots first—and often.

The Party's struggles against white American imperialism recognized that "the political machine in America has consistently required Black people to support it through paying taxes and fighting in wars, but that same machine consistently refuses to serve the interests of the Black community" (BPP "10-Point Program"). American Blacks, then, were not citizens with full representation and not unlike the colonials of the Revolution who fought against foreign rule. Thus, the Black Panther Party waged a philosophical and literal revolutionary war against what it considered an imperialist white America. The Party's program, further, explicitly outlines the Black Panther Party's demands to include decent housing, an educational system inclusive of African American history to foster self and race pride, exemption from military service until America achieves racial equality, and the immediate release of Blacks held in correctional facilities because they have not received a fair trial by a jury of their peers. Goines directly incorporates two of those points, which state that "black people will not be free until [they] are able to determine [their] destiny" and calls for "an immediate end to police brutality and murder of black people" (BPP "10-Point Program"). Kenyatta's operation, in its violence, stems from a yearning for economic, psychological, and physical freedom from the white ruling class in America.

His orchestration of the murders of racist police officers, as well, is a reaction to the Black Panthers' call for the end of the abuse of police powers. In *Dick Gregory's Political Primer*, Gregory argues:

> Huey P. Newton insisted, along with the United States Constitution, that oppressed black people have the right of self-defense, or the right to … fight firearms with firearms. When firearms and physical brutality

are used against the black community by agents of the ruling system, either official or self-appointed guardians of white supremacy, the Black Panther Party advocated the right and duty of protection of life, family, and property. (175)

The Black community, as the Black Panther Party suggests and Goines's Kenyatta illustrates, has become a colony of white America and as such, is ruled by a police state. The Black Panthers use of firearms in defense of their person and community becomes transformed in the Kenyatta series as a proactive use of weaponry against the ruling class. According to Eldridge Cleaver, at his initial meeting with the Black Panthers, Huey Newton stated that their message was:

about black people arming themselves in a political fashion to exert organized force in the political arena to see to it that their desires and needs are met. Otherwise there will be a political consequence. And the only culture worth talking about is a revolutionary culture. So it doesn't matter what heading you put on it, we're going to talk about political power growing out of the barrel of a gun. (Cleaver 31)

The revolutionary war Kenyatta wages against white America, then, is the logical next-step to achieving complete freedom from not only the subjugation of white America but also from its tools.

Yet, there were also myriad examples in Detroit from which Goines could glean examples. Still reeling from the "race riot" of 1943, stemming from desegregation of defense manufacturing plants and resulting tensions between white and Black migrants, Detroit soon transitioned into a car manufacturing capital. This further solidified the city as one of the primary sites for migrating Blacks in the 1950s and 1960s as they escaped the economic and physical oppressions of the South. The urban environment was less "Meccan" than imagined and embattled Blacks struggled against housing and labor discriminations, drug abuse, and extreme poverty. With the dawning of the Civil Rights Movement, Detroit's large Black population of displaced southerners made the city a prime location for revolutionary action.

Coleman A. Young (1918-1997), who would later become the city's first Black mayor, was a staunch, determined militant whose career in Detroit politics began in various liberation and socialist movements. The thirty-two year old Young was undaunted by his appearance before the House of Un-American Activities Committee (HUAC) in 1952. He chastised committee members about hearings to find communists when Blacks, "*American citizens,*" were being denied their civil and voting rights in the South; and he refused to provide names of those who were "known or suspected communists." He soon parlayed his position as a labor and civil rights activist into a long-standing political career, serving as both a State Senator (1964-1974) and mayor (1974-1993). Young's first mayoral campaign promised to purge the Detroit Police Department of racist officers and highlighted the fact that the predominately Black city was being "serve[d] and protect[ed]" by a predominately white police force. Goines clearly draws upon the legend and work of Coleman A. Young to construct Kenyatta's character.

At the same time, the grassroots liberation movement led by Detroit's James (1919-1993) and Grace Lee Boggs certainly was also within Goines's purview. Boggs, a labor activist, married Grace Lee, a Chinese American socialist and feminist activist, in 1958. Their forty-year marriage/partnership established Detroit as a center for liberation politics, tackling everything from labor and Civil Rights, both Black and Asian American, to environmental and women's issues. The Boggses' activism, and that of a changing world, would not have been lost on a seventeen-year-old Korean War veteran in 1954. By the time Goines began writing, he knew Detroit, drugs, and the world well.

Goines recognizes the plethora of similarities between the global revolutions of Africa and Latin America and that of the revolutionary movements in America. Goines takes his time in introducing Kenyatta to readers; however, when he does emerge in the first novel, *Crime Partners*, his revolutionary philosophies precede him in the description of his offices. The walls of Kenyatta's offices are adorned with portraits of "Cho and Ho-Chi-Min, and other men of color who were dedicated leaders in various revolutions" (*Crime Partners* 49).[5] Very pointedly, Goines does not include the pictures or even mention the work of Martin Luther King or the Civil Rights Movement in his description of Kenyatta's offices. Kenyatta's mission is so far removed from the non-violence of King that Goines's choice to exclude any reference to King and the South is an appropriate one. Even Malcolm X, whose "By Any Means Necessary" mantra sounded more revolutionary than aboveground action revealed, is also conspicuously absent from the text, as is any reference to Ghana's non-violent quest for independence. Goines's choices directly links the armed revolutionary movements of Africa, Latin America, and Asia with that of America's Black Panther Party, because of the commonality of liberating the oppressed from colonization by a self-appointed ruling class, which meant, Europeans or white Americans.

Kenyatta also trains his army with military precision. "Every man in his organization had been trained to use judo, the deadly art of death. How to kill with the bare hand was something he taught every man and woman who joined his outfit" (*Crime Partners* 66). The image of such training conjures images of Black Panther Party members—men and women—armed with rifles as they asserted their second amendment right to bear arms. When the members of the Black Panther

Party marched into the state capitol of California, it was an act of rebellion against the United States government. The threat to kill whites, even in self-defense, directly resulted from both American revolutionary history as well as the contemporary violence the "Mau Mau" perpetrated against the British. Kenyatta's arming and training his members in the martial arts synthesizes the actual violence of the "Mau Mau" with the preparatory threat of the Black Panther Party.

Although Goines would have been clearly aware of Ghana's efforts toward independence, the passivity of the campaign correlates to the non-violence of the Civil Rights Movement. The first colonized African nation to achieve independence in 1957, Ghana's storied history reveals various colonizers. Since the days of the Atlantic Slave Trade, Ghana had been under both the Portuguese (1471-1642) and the Dutch (1642-1872); however, the British assumed control in 1872. Though the British colonials started to give Black Africans some political power by allowing electoral representation in parliament, Ghana remained a colony. In 1952, Kwame Nkrumah returned from abroad to Ghana and became its prime minister, leading the charge for complete independence from British rule. As a result of his efforts, Ghana achieved independence in 1957 and Nkrumah served as its first president from 1960 to 1966. So peaceful was its initial transition that Ghana became a haven for American Blacks, most notably, W.E. B. DuBois, whose body remains interred at his home there, now a tourist attraction.

Such passivity was lost in the quest for Kenya's independence, as it was storied with violence and death. In Kenya, Jomo Kenyatta, a member of the Kikuyu tribe, returned to Kenya to liberate his people from British rule. Some members of the Kikuyu violently opposed British colonial policies; the British termed the militants "Mau Mau." Warfare erupted in 1952 in which nearly 11,500 Kikuyu, 145 Europeans, and 2000 other Africans were killed; and thousands of Kikuyu were interred in detention centers. The British authorities arrested Jomo Kenyatta, who was noted as the leader of the Kenya African Union, under suspicion of also being the leader of the "Mau Mau." After a lengthy trial, he was subsequently imprisoned from 1953 to 1961. When Kenya did achieve independence in 1963, Kenyans elected Jomo Kenyatta as its first president.

As the Ghanaians had before their independence in 1957 and the Kenyans before theirs in 1963, Blacks in America were likewise living under colonial rule. If Blacks in Africa could achieve independence from their subjugators, African Americans could achieve, at least, the sovereignty of their communities and, consequently, their lives. Goines's Kenyatta is thus the quintessential anti-hero, in one view, for his fight is one that addresses—violently so—a racially oppressive society that treats African Americans as colonial subjects rather than as citizens. Drawing on these contemporary socio-political histories, Goines constructs a formidable, flawed, and unforgettable character in Kenyatta who neither represents the romanticized nor the unsympathetic image of the Black militant, forcing readers to reexamine this community of Black Africans and their existence as modern-day serfs to the white power matrix in America.

Kenyatta appears well into *Crime Partners* after Goines delineates the myriad of plights plaguing Black America. Goines coaxes readers to become as frustrated as prospective members of Kenyatta's organization, so that they "join" Kenyatta in practice and in philosophy. The novel begins then with the tragic death of Tina, a young girl who dies at the hands of her drug-addicted stepfather; he beats her to death when she accidentally causes him to spill his heroin. Billy and Jackie, petty thieves who arrive at the house to rob the stepfather, find Tina's lifeless body and quickly surmise the chain of events. Billy avenges her death through teary eyes, killing both parents almost immediately. Even as they commit murder, Billy and Jackie represent the antithesis of hardened criminals, possessing a humanity that directly contradicts their criminality. If readers know that both men have killed before and have done so with impunity, Billy and Jackie represent the type of recruit Kenyatta seeks—men who are willing to kill for honor and purpose.

Goines also introduces an interracial police partnership in Edward Benson, a veteran Black detective and his white partner, John Ryan. Benson and Ryan take the case more seriously than others might have. Both "want them killers, and [they] want them as soon as possible" (*Crime Partners, 39*). Goines's work consistently blurs the lines between the underworld and the mainstream. Benson and Ryan as well as Billy and Jackie both have visceral, comparable reactions to the sight of Tina's body, only differing in their method of retribution. The series is undoubtedly about Kenyatta, but Goines commences the novel in this manner so that readers understand the heart of Kenyatta's militancy. Tina's death highlights not only the problem of the drug trade by focusing on the death of an innocent, but also serves as a segue to Benson's plight as a Black police officer and the second most important hindrance to full liberation of the Black community—racism or bigotry in law enforcement.[6]

Goines, unmistakably attuned to the prevailing concerns of race in America, purposely addresses the "integration" of urban police departments. The inclusion of Benson and Ryan recognizes this "social progress" but also the constant threat of systematic racism from police officers who are unwilling to accept "integration." While investigating the murders of Tina and her parents, Benson walks behind the house to gather evidence and encounters Jim, a racist, rookie officer who assumes that the suited Black man is a criminal. Though Benson identifies himself as a detective, Jim continues to express racial antipathy, pressing the barrel of his gun into Benson's back. The arrival of Ryan and Kelly, Jim's partner, saves Benson from a certain accidental death. Benson reports both Jim and Kelly, who understands Jim's mistake much more than his partner:

> He had warned Jim, his partner, that his race hatred would get him in trouble. Nowadays you couldn't tell what a black man might be so you didn't treat them all as if they were dirt. But he couldn't get it through Jim's thick head, so he'd have to learn the hard way that those days of abusing every black person you came in contact with were over. (*Crime Partners* 32-33)

Benson could have overlooked the incident, but he feels morally and ethically responsible to rid the police force of such officers and promises Jim that he will "do everything in my power to see if I can't get you out of that uniform" (*Crime Partners* 35).

Goines presents the matter of racism in law enforcement with exact precision, as readers do not miss the pointed similarities between Benson and Kenyatta. The latter makes a passionate plea to Billy and Jackie: "This city will be rid of dope pushers, and race-hating cops. You can bet on it" (*Crime Partners* 58). Racism in Benson's precinct represents a systematic issue within the criminal justice system. As the encounter with Jim suggests, younger officers are particularly virulent, resenting Benson's status as a detective and the respect he receives from some of the other veteran officers. Even as Benson and Ryan work with other officers and agencies outside their precinct in a joint pursuit of Kenyatta, Benson endures racism and begins to question his method of attempting to right the wrongs of racism in America. In *Kenyatta's Escape*, a shoot-out at Kenyatta's country farm becomes a bloodbath; over twenty of Kenyatta's people are killed along with several police officers. Though Benson kills a few of Kenyatta's followers himself and even saves his partner's life, he receives several odious glances from his fellow officers who associate him with Kenyatta's organization simply on the basis of race. Throughout the series, Benson's position as a Black officer is continually tested, especially since he is chasing another Black man. Subsequent novels explore Benson's internal conflict about his complicity in a system that abuses Blacks, people who look exactly like him.

Goines develops Benson's character throughout the series as a man inexplicably caught between two worlds despite never achieving full acceptance in either. As part of the criminal justice system, Benson represents the dominant and oppressive ruling class, or white America. Yet, even within that class, he is rendered a pariah to some on the basis of race. By *Kenyatta's Last Hit*, Benson no longer camouflages his frustration with both Kenyatta as a criminal and the police pursuit of Kenyatta. Though Benson understands from a law enforcement perspective why Kenyatta must be apprehended, he also addresses the lack of concern for "'super-patriot' white groups" who have similar arsenals at their disposal (*Last Hit* 40). Goines makes painfully clear the bias within the system favoring white criminality. Yet Benson realizes the futility of his frustration and acquiesces to his position as a member of law enforcement:

> Benson was a professional, a black who many years before had given up his right to deal with the problem of race outside the law. It was his commitment... At that time Benson had believed in the system. Had seen, or thought he saw, the routes through which he could make a difference. He knew that those routes were closed to him, then all he had to do was to hand in his badge and make that journey to the twilight arena on the fringe. It was there that some of his brothers believed that out of the anarchy and chaos would come order and equality. (*Last Hit* 41)

Benson sees Kenyatta's underlined purpose, but he cannot condone his methods. His character attempts to demonstrate the complexity of certain Blacks within the very system that oppresses them.

Kenyatta is "a tall black man... completely bald and his head had been greased until it had a shine to it.... The most remarkable things about him was the jet black eyes that stared out at you without blinking, giving him a hawkish look that went well with the long, keen nose he had" (*Crime Partners* 50). Throughout the series, his charismatic, imposing presence inspires fear in his enemies and his friends as well as complements the audacity of his mission along with his passion. Jackie, an associate who has not yet joined Kenyatta's organization, acknowledges the power of Kenyatta's fervor:

> The thought of him having over forty people believing in him was crazy in itself. That many people following in his path would give a madman quite a bit of power.... [Kenyatta's] eyes were lit up with an unholy glow that burned too brightly. There was madness there, yet the fire that burned there was also the mark of the strong man, a leader, the kind of man the people could follow with complete trust. (*Crime Partners* 57-58)

When Billy jokingly offers to join Kenyatta's organization, Kenyatta explains that he would not accept *them*. He explains, "My boys have got to be dedicated. You brothers are dedicated, but not to gettin' rid of these white pigs that ride around our neighborhoods acting like white gods" (*Crime Partners* 53). As Billy and Jackie contemplate Kenyatta's statement, so do readers who also find themselves questioning their complacency toward the condition of their community. Kenyatta invites them to participate in the execution of a police officer known for abusing his authority in the Black community. The officer, of course, is Jim, the very officer who accosts Benson at the murder scene. (This is the only such execution that Goines offers readers, although Kenyatta intimates to Billy and Jackie that there were others.) Kenyatta's fervor and his ability to galvanize young Blacks, even to his occasional chagrin, places him squarely within the tradition of revolutionary leaders within the African Diaspora who recognize that political movements, especially revolutionary ones, depend on the loyalties and passions of youth.

Kenyatta cements the controlled organization of these youth by creating an atmosphere of equality and the appearance of community and communal ownership. Yet, this itself presents a paradox. Kenyatta continues to reflect clear colonial attitudes. He firmly believes that the ghetto is his to save, and he invades communities to right its ills by force. Kenyatta's army executes plans and people at *his* will because he believes his is the only answer. He does not help the people in these communities to help themselves, considering them too ill-equipped to effect lasting, tangible change. He will do it for them, taking slight pleasure in their ignorance about his existence or his grand accomplishment. As Goines returned from Korea, he was able to process the experience and see American politics in a way mere civilians were unable. Kenyatta and his organization is very well a microcosm of American/colonial politics with regard to perceived lesser civilizations/communities. Thus, another paradox that the series presents is that Kenyatta in part reflects a very American mentality regarding the Black community in America as well as Black and brown communities around the world.

In *Death List*, the second novel of the series, Kenyatta begins to execute the mission outlined in *Crime Partners*. He refocuses his energies on the drug trade for the remaining three novels of the series. The names of major drug suppliers operating in the Black community comprise the list, many of whom are white. Not only does Kenyatta want to eliminate the street-level dealer and mid-level distributor, but he also wants to find the white men responsible for the initial importation of heroin and cocaine into the Black community of this country. A list of this importance has an asking price of ten thousand dollars, and to pay its asking price, Kenyatta plans the heist of a food stamp office in which at least three, albeit white, civilians are killed. The contradictions are palpable. Kenyatta's organization maintains its lofty goals by operating as a criminal enterprise, which essentially means that he has assembled a group of people otherwise forgotten by American society whose participation in Kenyatta's organization empowers them to be fully engaged and invested in what they consider a positive direction of their community. Comparable here are Kenyatta's directives to drug dealers and the "Mau Mau's" threatening to kill those who refuse to take their various oaths, a refusal which was deemed as an affront to their rebellion against British rule in

Kenya. Black street-level and mid-level suppliers who refuse to cease operation in the Black community are given two warnings. Those found in non-compliance are executed. The white men of the infamous list, by contrast, are summarily assassinated without discussion; and these murders attract the attention of media and police officials. By the close of *Death List*, Kenyatta teeters between the position of a staunch social rebel and an outright egomaniac as he sacrifices his followers while escaping capture during the raid at the farm.[7]

In the third novel, *Kenyatta's Escape*, Goines outlines the personal flaws in the public persona of the Black militant. Kenyatta's flaws as a revolutionary become clear, as he abandons the members of his organization upon notice of an impending police raid. Rationalizing his escape as important in the continuation of the work, Kenyatta takes the organization's savings of thirty thousand dollars and a select few of them hijack a plane to take them "where a Black man can be a man" (*Escape* 14). Kenyatta names Algiers, the capital of Algeria, as such a place; and Goines deliberately chooses another site of liberation. (Not coincidentally, Eldridge Cleaver, avoiding charges stemming from a shoot-out between the Panthers and Oakland Police, fled to Cuba, Algeria, and finally France.) Unlike Kenya and Ghana, Algeria, located in northern Africa, was a former French colony that achieved independence in 1962. Algeria became integral in the development of the Organization of Petroleum Exporting Countries (OPEC), the Organization of African Unity (OAU), and the Arab League. These consistent references to the myriad liberation movements in Africa and Latin America evince that Goines purposefully uses these texts to address the issues of Black militancy throughout the African Diaspora.

By the close of *Kenyatta's Escape*, Kenyatta arrives in the Watts community of Los Angeles determined to rebuild his organization and continue his mission. In the last novel of the series, *Kenyatta's Last Hit*, the quest to execute the largest drug supplier to the Black community continues. Kenyatta rebuilds his organization, renewing his quest to end the importation of heroin into the Black community. For Kenyatta, that means finding the sole man responsible and bringing him to justice. And Kenyatta's justice means murder. Kenyatta learns that man is Clement Jenkins of Las Vegas, Nevada, considered by the people of Las Vegas to be a legitimate businessman and industrialist whose involvement in the drug trade is mere sport. As such, Jenkins represents the colonial power who has invaded a country, or in this case, a community of Blacks, for no other reason than means and opportunity or exploitation. Jenkins's heroin business subjugates Blacks no differently than if it were martial law. Jenkins explains to his assistant that Blacks "dislike themselves so much, through training, that they'll submit to the most ludicrous deals. In other words, Oscar, they are the easiest race of people in the world to give the shaft to" (*Last Hit* 170). The "training" of which Jenkins speaks is merely a continued state of oppression perpetuated by white America upon Blacks. They "submit" to political, psychological, and social subjugation because of this training, and Black revolutionaries like Kenyatta are seeking to reverse that training by empowering Blacks to see themselves as more than "jungle bunnies" as Jenkins dares call Kenyatta.

By this point, Kenyatta, as well as some readers, would have overestimated his immortality and underestimated Jenkins's power. While Kenyatta considers Jenkins "a weak white man," "who smelled of death" (*Last Hit* 210), Jenkins also expresses a similar sentiment about Kenyatta, referring to Kenyatta as an "asshole nigger" (*Last Hit* 211). For a man used to intimidating people—Black and white—with his sheer physicality, Kenyatta is not psychologically prepared for Jenkins's supercilious and disdainful challenges to his person or intellect. The revelation that he has grossly miscalculated the situation and his own abilities shocks not only Kenyatta but also his men. For the first time, Kenyatta and his army are ill-prepared, and Jenkins's army decimates Kenyatta's.

Kenyatta finally meets his end in the very moment for which he has lived. Though Kenyatta wounds Jenkins in the gun battle, his need to see "the white man crawl, the white millionaire who dealt in death," leads him to ignore the other guards who take the opportunity to kill him (*Last Hit* 215). Thus, the drug trade continues as well as the colonization of the Black community within the American polity. This colonization is firmly rooted in the systematic (and, it is rumored, government-sanctioned) use of drugs to create a controlled environment of addiction, despondency, and poverty.

While the works of Donald Goines and his contemporaries, Robert Beck (Iceberg Slim) and Joe Nazel, are enjoying more cultural popularity and scholarly attention, what remains constant is the need to justify their place in the African American literary tradition. Goines's Kenyatta series juxtaposes the social and political actualities of the late 1960s and early 1970s, not in hindsight but at its height. The conversation Goines has with his readers respects their intelligence, even if it acknowledges their potential naiveté. Goines judges neither Kenyatta nor his readers. He presents his infamous character as human, flawed and as complicated as possible so that readers are able to make their own connections to the realities of their communities and the world. Kenyatta must meet his arch-enemy and fall short of his ultimate goal because the powers he has been raging against are systemic, not localized to a particular officer or white drug kingpin, as Kenyatta had seemed to believe.

Though Kenyatta's death is a tremendous disappointment to readers, his demise solidifies the cyclical nature of oppression. The Kenyatta series remains a crowning achievement in the Goines canon because the series aptly explores the paradoxes inherent in the Black nationalist/revolutionary movements of the era. As a character, Kenyatta encompasses so much of the immediate social and cultural concerns of the African Diaspora and is a perfect amalgam of various examples of burgeoning Black leadership figures. Kenyatta embodies the frustration and hopes of the Black community and urban Black revolutionaries. His arguable naiveté of the world beyond the insular, colonized Black community may mirror that of Goines's readers, so that at his end, readers see his mortality as akin to theirs. While Goines does not seek to deter readers from becoming part of revolutionary movements or social activism, he does urge readers to understand that revolutions succeed and fail; to reevaluate any deification of Black leaders; and to navigate new articulations of Black consciousness cautiously and soberly.

NOTES

1 Goines created the name Al C. Clark from that of his associate, Albert Clark, or "Crummie," as Goines refers to him in his will in which he bequeathed to him the royalties from *Never Die Alone* (1974). He chose the pseudonym at the behest of Holloway House editors who feared he was flooding the market with the Goines name.

2 Jerry Bryant, *Born in a Mighty Bad Land: The Violent Man in African-American Folklore and Fiction* (Bloomington: UP Indiana, 2003), p. 2.

3 Black Panther Party "10-Point Program."

4 Eldridge Cleaver, *Post-Prison Writings & Speeches*. Ed. Robert Scheer (New York: Ramparts, 1969), p. 38.

5 Several typographical errors mar the text. The names Cho and Ho-Chi-Min reference Ernesto "Che" Guevara (1928-1967), the Argentine Marxist revolutionary, and Vietnamese revolutionary, Ho Chi Minh, respectively. Che joined Fidel Castro in 1956 as a commander in Fidel Castro's 26th of July Movement and was integral in overthrowing then Cuban dictator and U.S. ally, Fulgencio Batista. His role in the Castro-led Cuban Revolution earned his pop culture status as well as established his legacy as a guerilla warrior and revolutionary. Ho Chi Minh led the Democratic Republic of Vietnam (North Vietnam) before the unification with South Vietnam following the Vietnam War. He led the Vietnamese independence struggle from 1941 until his death in 1969. Saigon, South Vietnam, was renamed Ho Chi Minh City in his honor.

6 In *White Man's Justice, Black Man's Grief*, Goines addresses systematic racism in the criminal justice system, focusing primarily on the bail-bond system.

7 Club members pay dues and there is a sense of community ownership, but in reality the money and property all belong to Kenyatta.

REFERENCES

Allen, Jr. Eddie. *Low Road: The Life and Legacy of Donald Goines.* New York: St. Martin's, 2004.

Barnett, Donald and Karari Njama. *Mau Mau from Within: Autobiography and Analysis of Kenya's Peasant Revolt.* New York: Monthly Review, 1966.

Bennett, George. *Kenya: A Political History, The Colonial Period.* London, Oxford UP, 1963.

Bryant, Jerry. *Born in a Mighty Bad Land: The Violent Man in African-American Folklore and Fiction.* Bloomington: UP Indiana, 2003.

Cleaver, Eldridge. *Soul on Ice.* New York: Ramparts, 1970.

Deburg, William L. Van. *New Day in Babylon: The Black Power Movement and American Culture, 1965-1974.* Chicago: University of Chicago, 1992.

Goines, Donald. *Dopefiend.* Los Angeles: Holloway House, 1971.

———. *Whoreson.* Los Angeles: Holloway House, 1972.

———. *Black Gangster.* Los Angeles: Holloway House, 1972.

———. *White Man's Justice, Black Man's Grief.* Los Angeles: Holloway House, 1973.

———. *Crime Partners.* (As Al C. Clark) Los Angeles: Holloway House, 1974.

———. *Death List.* (As Al C. Clark) Los Angeles: Holloway House, 1974.

———. *Kenyatta's Escape.* (As Al C. Clark) Los Angeles: Holloway House, 1974.

———. *Kenyatta's Last Hit.* (As Al C. Clark) Los Angeles: Holloway House, 1975.

Goode, Greg. "From *Dopefiend* to *Kenyatta's Last Hit*: The Angry Black Crime Novels of Donald Goines." *MELUS* 2 (Summer 1984): 41-48.

Gregory, Dick. *Dick Gregory's Political Primer.* New York: Harper & Row, 1972.

Kenyatta, Jomo. *Harambee! The Prime Minister of Kenya's Speeches 1963-1964.* New York: Oxford UP, 1964.

Levine, Lawrence. *Black Culture and Black Consciousness: Afro-American Folk Thought from Slavery to Freedom.* New York: Oxford UP, 2007.

Roberts, John. *From Trickster to Badman: The Black Folk Hero in Slavery and Freedom.* Philadelphia: UP Pennsylvania, 1989.

Rosenberg Jr. Carl and John Nottingham. *The Myth of "Mau Mau": Nationalism in Kenya.* New York: Pall Mall, 1966.

Wood, Susan. *Kenya: The Tensions of Progress.* New York: Oxford UP, 1960.

CHAPTER TWO

Revolutionary Hustler

Liberatory Violence in Donald Goines's Kenyatta Series

Terrence T. Tucker

Contemporary Black popular fiction has run the gamut from breezy tales of the lives of the African-American elites to Black erotica to violent gritty stories of ghetto life. While the criticism of these works has often been ferocious, as demonstrated by Nick Chiles's *New York Times Op-ed* piece, "Their Eyes Were Reading Smut" (2006), this is not new. And neither, in fact, are the results, which has been a distinct spike in African-American readers across class lines. While the debate rages over the quality and morality of contemporary popular African-American fiction, specifically "street lit" and Black erotica, works that embrace Black revolutionary violence against white supremacist oppression regardless of skin color have all but disappeared from the Black literary landscape. Dismissed— along with similarly-themed films of the Blaxploitation era—as a sign of the militant, Black Power-dominated 1970s, these works have a literary history that dates as far back as Martin Delany's *Blake* (1861) and Sutton Griggs's *Imperio in Imperium* (1899).

In truth, since the nineteenth century there has been a distinct contrast between what has been popular among African-American audiences and what has been anointed by whites and Black elites as definitive or representative texts of the African-American literary canon. Not surprisingly, those less popular have frequently contained conscious, collective uses of violence as a strategy for freedom. So, Delany's *Blake* is often ignored in favor of Frederick Douglass's autobiographies and the poetry of Paul Laurence Dunbar and the short stories of Charles Chesnutt were more celebrated than Sutton Griggs's *Imperium in Imperio*, even though the latter author is said to have had a larger Black readership. The clearest examples, however, comes during the late 1960s and 1970s, as Black and white critics lauded the novels of Toni Morrison, Alice Walker, and Ishmael Reed, many in Black America read the novels of Iceberg Slim and Donald Goines. Much of this work as a whole emerged from the desire to create a distinct Black worldview and rejected the approval of whites in response to the Black Power and Black Arts Movements. What additionally fueled Black urban fiction was the rise of the Blaxploitation era. In the writings of Donald Goines, we see all the elements of Blaxploitation films—cool, unshakable heroes, sexy women, stylish cars, violent retribution, and great music— at work and at play in his fiction.

Picking up where Sam Greenlee leaves off in *The Spook Who Sat by the Door* (1969), Goines's Kenyatta series turns its gaze toward liberating African-Americans from oppressive forces both outside and within urban Black America. Having established himself as the literary successor to Iceberg Slim, Goines's use of the pseudonym Al C. Clark maintains his "street credibility" while producing literature that critiques the world his other novels explore. The Kenyatta novels achieve what other more celebrated Black fiction has not, specifically the display of an active, conscious resistance to attacks on its community, whether they appear in the form of the police state or Black "self-destruction."

Beginning with 1974's *Crime Partners* and culminating in 1975's posthumously published *Kenyatta's Last Hit*, Goines constructed a character—named after Kenyan revolutionary Jomo Kenyatta—whose fearlessness was virtually unmatched and whose willingness to achieve freedom could be admired across the often disparate parts of African America. The Kenyatta series stands, according to Greg Goode's analysis in "From *Dopefiend* to *Kenyatta's Last Hit*" (1984), as the "most interesting and ambitious project of the later Goines." The author may boast in Kenyatta "probably the only such [Black revolutionary series] hero in fiction" (45). In fact, Kenyatta's recognition of drug pushers and pimps as equally destructive to African Americans as the police may be more cogent now than it was at the original time of the novels' publication. For if there is a critique to be levied in mainstream discourse over late 20th and early 21st centuries of popular African-American literature, it must be that portraits of the oppressive elements in lower- and under-class African American life-worlds are too often accepted as an intractable part of their existence. The only response possible, these works seem to concede, is to operate within the world into which they were born as opposed to transcending it. Here we see the manifestation of a "nihilistic threat" against which Cornel West has notably warned. Yet despite the militant spirit infusing Goines's novels, the interracial detective team that often finds itself on the trail of Kenyatta, featuring Black detective Edward Benson and his white partner Ryan, predates "interracial buddy" cop movies of the 1980s and could arguably suggest to some that "peace" between the races might succeed. At any rate, as Eddie B. Allen argues in *Low Road: The Life and Legacy of Donald Goines*, "the Kenyatta series symbolized Donnie's desire for victory." (164). This essay thus argues that Goines's Kenyatta series expands the literary strain of Black nationalism that dates back to the 19th century. Additionally, these novels use Goines's exploration of Black urban life, Black liberation struggle, and ideologies of "interracial co-existence" to form a potent mix of action, critique, resistance, and hope—whose absence from the contemporary canonical Black literary scene reflects a similar, and disturbing, absence of radical Black thought across contemporary Black America in general.

The use of violence by African Americans continues to be the most controversial act of Black resistance in the mainstream U.S. discourse on race. If expressions of Black rage continue to be feared by white America, then Black violence stands as their worst fear of Black retaliation for racism realized. The 1831 Nat Turner-led revolt, alongside other insurrections ("successful" or not), sent literal shivers down the spines of whites in the 19th century. Debates about a post-slavery America often considered whether ex-slaves would seek vengeance on their former masters. The Red Summer of 1919 is notable because of the willingness of Blacks to fight back, captured in Claude McKay's famous poem "If We Must Die." Civil Rights leaders positioned themselves between white America and violent Black militancy, as King does in "Letter from a Birmingham Jail" and as Malcolm X does in "The Ballot or the Bullet." What the latter two works reveal are the ways in which tactics of violence and non-violence complement each other. As Lance Hill points out in his book *The Deacons for Defense*, "Black violence, in the form of riots and militant armed self-defense, fundamentally change the meaning of nonviolence and the role of King and moderate leaders; it provided moderates with a negotiating power that they had never enjoyed before. It was the threat of Black violence, not redemptive suffering and moral suasion, that was now making the political establishment take notice of nonviolent protest" (262). The world that Goines presents in the Kenyatta series had begun the shift to a post-Civil Rights America, when the problems of overcrowding and neglect demystified the idea that the urban North was a refuge from the rural South. Still, rhetorical claims of equality and colorblindness made revealing the reconfiguration of white supremacy a more difficult task. Essentially, calls for violence were most often heard when nonviolent tactics prove insufficient or when it became apparent that "integration" was anathema to Black collective uplift.

Nevertheless, the echoes of violence in Stokely Carmichael's calls for "Black Power" and the presence of the Black Panther Party are frequently seen as destroying the multiracial coalitions of the Civil Rights Movement. In his *Negroes with Guns* (1965), Robert F. Williams questions the discouragement of Black violence, even in self-defense: "Why do the white liberals ask us to be non-violent? We are not the aggressors; we have been victimized for over 300 years! Yet nobody spends money to go into the South and ask the racists to be martyrs or pacifists" (75). The promotion of nonviolence as the sole strategy, particularly in an urban North often teeming with violence, reveals typical anxieties concerning Black liberatory violence. Hill aptly argues that the myth of nonviolence was "a myth that assuaged white guilt by suggesting that racism was not intractable and deeply embedded in American life, that racial segregation and discrimination were handily overcome by orderly, polite protest and a generous American conscience, and that the pluralistic system for resolving conflicts between competing interests had prevailed" (259). The opposition to the Black Panther Party, despite their standing as an organization of self-defense, demonstrates how even the mere possibility of Black violence was seen as the preeminent threat to white supremacist hegemony. Williams, himself a significant influence on Black Panther leader Huey Newton, notes, however: "The principle of self-defense is an American tradition that began at Lexington and Concord" (72). Thus, the rejection of the use of violence in this case can only be seen as racially as opposed to morally motivated.

The calls in African-American fiction for violent rebellion, as we see in the Kenyatta series, are even rarer, although their history goes as far back as David Walker's *Appeal* (1829), Frederick Douglass' *The Heroic Slave* (1853), and Delany's *Blake* (1861). Even though the Black Arts Movement featured artists who employed more aggressive tones and characters, Sam Greenlee's novel *The Spook Who Sat by the Door* (1969), in which a Black former CIA agent trains Blacks to engage in guerilla warfare, often goes unnoticed, as does the 1973 film adaptation which appeared at the height of the Blaxploitation era. We see a similar separation between the Kenyatta series and the number of films that appeared throughout the 1970s. While those films, including *Superfly* (1972), *Black Caesar* (1973), and *Foxy Brown* (1974), reversed film stereotypes like "Mammy" and "Step'n Fetchit" with defiant, independent, and sexual representations, they rarely possessed the radical, conscious manifestations of rage we see in the Kenyatta series. Additionally, the Kenyatta series differs from films like *Coffy* (1973) and *Three the Hard Way* (1974) in its embrace of proactive, collective action. Joe Bob Briggs points out in "Who Dat Man?: Shaft and the Blaxploitation Genre" (2003) that Blaxploitation films eventually became "a sort of cynical white-man's version of what the black audience really wants: a sexually potent black man, constantly oppressed by white guys who he has to beat up and kill, fighting for gangster respect and material wealth." He adds, "Charles Bronson in the *Death Wish* series and Clint Eastwood in the *Dirty Harry* series were white versions of the same myth, but they were always given higher motives for their vigilante violence. They never used women or did anything for money, for example, whereas the black antiheroes were sometimes celebrated for being pimps, armed robbers," etc. (27).

Kenyatta's purpose and actions reject the motivations Blaxploitation heroes seemingly embrace, particularly in his opposition to the very figures upon whom the films focus their attention: pimps, hustlers, and criminals. Although Goines's novels are certainly impacted by the Blaxploitation era in their constructions of Blackness as synonymous with coolness—stylistically and linguistically—the novels frequently present violence through the lens of revolutionary struggle. In particular, Goines's novels fundamentally understand that it is not merely the Black presence in literature, or on screen, that becomes significant, but a substantive presentation of African America that defies stereotypes and embraces a complexity bathed in realism. Kenyatta, then, is presented as a folk hero who reflects the anxieties and desires of those around him.

Thus, the revolutionary spirit and violence that flow throughout Goines's novels are not merely a series made possible by a specific moment of the Black Arts Movement or the Blaxploitation era. Instead, the series stands as part of an African-American tradition that considers the use of violence as a significant element in resisting white supremacy and oppression. The connections, then, between Goines and other contemporary Black urban fiction and some Hip-Hop narratives are incomplete, in large part, because of what the Kenyatta series represents. Various authors and artists may seize upon the tales of Black urban life as demonstrations of the "real," yet fail to recognize the significance of Kenyatta's presence in the very areas they depict. The representation of Kenyatta as folk hero and legend speak to the historical, in African America's tradition of militant ideology and organization, but also to the hopes and anxieties of the Black urban world, which sought to rid itself of white supremacy and the nihilistic threat.

The first of the Kenyatta novels, *Crime Partners* (1974) which was made into a film in 2000, follows two ex-cons, Billy Good and Jackie Walker, as they attempt to make a life for themselves outside prison walls. As they clearly struggle to stay "straight," we come to realize that they are robbing others for money and drugs.

It is only when they go to Kenyatta to buy guns that they become involved in his organization's plan to kill racist police officers. But the novel does not begin with a romanticized version of Black nationalist plots or stories of gratuitous sex and/or violence. Instead, it tells the tragic story of the death of a young girl at the hands of her mother's enraged and drugged-up common law husband. *Crime Partners* follows Goines's willingness to present a world that seems devoid of hope and in which death might offer an escape: "Little Tina had received her last beating. There would be no more sleepless nights for the child because she was too hungry to sleep.... There would be no more fears of uncontrolled beatings, beatings that came for nothing. Yes, Little Tina was beyond that—beyond a mother's love that sometimes seemed more like hate" (16). While many works of "street lit" reflect on the high costs of drug use and violence with regret, what ultimately separates Goines's body of work from many others is the presence of the Kenyatta series and those books' attempt to turn the violence that exists in Black ghettoes into strategy for liberating African Americans from two significant by-products of white supremacist capitalist hegemony: racist police officers and drug pushers, including those wealthy whites who seem to be pulling the strings.

Perhaps more importantly, Goines builds his series around the creation of a singular Black hero, Kenyatta, who attempts to sit in the tradition of Black folk heroes like Nat Turner and Stagolee. Although Kenyatta has supplied Billy and Jackie with guns they use to rob drug addicts, Jackie complains that "when we hit on him to loan us two good men so that we could take off that big caper, what did the guy do? He went nut city on us" (41). Kenyatta, then, is presented as a character interested in crime, per se, but who possesses an overarching desire to eliminate drugs in the inner city and to kill white police officers who are known racists and engage in police brutality. Our first glimpse of Kenyatta in *Crime Partners* reveals an idealized Black masculinity: "He was completely bald, and his head had been greased until it had a shine to it. The only hair he possessed was his beard and mustache.... The most remarkable thing about him was his jet black eyes that stared out without blinking, giving him a hawkish look that went well with the long, keen nose that he had" (43). Throughout the series, Kenyatta – and his eyes – seems capable of virtual second sight. He can often sense the emotions of those around him. Combined with a "voice so heavy that it sounded as if he was talking from inside a barrel" (43), Kenyatta comes across as the ideal revolutionary leader, who commands organizations with ease and instills hope and loyalty in all those around him. Jerry H. Bryant argues in *Victims and Heroes* (1997) that Kenyatta is an "outsized version of the Black Power nationalist," who "is brutal and unforgiving, totally ruthless and utterly without fear" (268).

Initially in *Crime Partners*, however, the title characters follow his next order, to kill Little David, a lieutenant working for top drug lord King Fisher, merely because they need money. Before working with Kenyatta again, Jackie reveals that his motives differ significantly from Kenyatta's: "Working with Kenyatta didn't put any money in their pockets, that was for sure. That dedication shit was for the birds. Fuck killing all the dope men in the city. He could care less about who sold dope. It would be good to knock them off for their bread, though" (94). Throughout the series, then, the depiction and influence of Kenyatta evolves. Billy and Jackie's use of violence is negated by their use of violence for Kenyatta's purposes. Indeed, the plot to rob a food stamp office is delayed, and virtually abandoned, by scenes of Black collective uplift and sharing.

Taking the men out to his farm headquarters after they kill Little David, Kenyatta shows Billy and Jackie a tranquil scene of Black utopia. When Billy hints to Jackie's lover, Carol, that Kenyatta might keep everything for himself, she replies: "You don't have to believe it if you don't want to, Billy, but everything on this place belongs to everybody in the organization. Anyone who wants to can move out here and live, rent free. Where else can a black person stay, rent free, food free, and everything else free?" (124). The farm offers a life outside the city, one that is free of the violence fueled by the pursuit of money and drugs as well as the violence enacted by racist police officers. Billy and Jackie come to see the contrast between the violence that begins the novel and the liberatory violence Kenyatta uses in the pursuit of transforming the Black urban landscape into a utopia similar to the farm. As opposed to a city besieged by white supremacy in the form of drugs and police brutality, Kenyatta offers a feeling the crime partners eventually come to share: "There was a feeling of warmth between them. It seemed to spread until everybody on the farm felt it. A feeling of brotherhood, black love, love for each other" (130). The eventual murder of Billy and Jackie, orchestrated by King Fisher, darkly ends the novel, but maintains the consistency of their characters, especially given doubts about whether or not both men would be able to completely shake off their criminal past and drug addictions. What *Crime Partners* does is continue the Kenyatta saga through its virtual announcement of a sequel: "The Big Man could sleep nights again. Maybe" (159). With the death of Billy and Jackie, Goines centralizes Kenyatta as a character as well as his use of violence as a key form of resistance.

By the end of the four-part series, which ends in Kenyatta's death at the hand of Clement Jenkins, a classic figuration of "The [White] Man" in Blaxploitation films, Kenyatta has been elevated from part of the ghetto world Billy and Jackie navigated to militant Black superhero. In the Kenyatta series, the emotion Goines lays bare is rage—Black rage. Although there is certainly rage to be found in all of Goines's work, the Kenyatta series represents a concerted effort to transform that rage into a constructive response to white supremacist capitalist hegemony. By undertaking this effort, Goines attempts to embody in fiction what bell hooks points out in *Killing Rage* (1995): "Confronting my rage, witnessing the way it moved me to grow and change, I understood intimately that it had the potential not only to destroy but also to construct" (16). Goines extends this expression of rage across four books and from the urban ghettoes of Detroit, Los Angeles and Las Vegas. While the rage in his other novels is often turned inward, through drug use, prostitution, and murder, the rage in the Kenyatta series is turned outward into a militant organization's attempt to rid Black ghettoes of drugs and police brutality. This comes as no small feat given the historic apprehension that emerges when African-Americans willingly express rage and, more specifically, target their rage in the direction of white supremacy. Hooks points out that we are not encouraged "to see black rage as something other than a sickness, to see it as a potentially healthy, potentially healing response to oppression and exploitation" (12).

Frequently, those who express Black rage at white supremacy, particularly in post-Civil Rights America, are demonized as divisive, self-aggrandizing, hustlers who "play the race card." Indeed, the title character of another Goines novel, *Black Gangster* (1972), forms a militant organization as a way to hide illegal activities. However, beginning with *Crime Partners*, Goines clearly establishes Kenyatta and his organization as principled. Billy and Jackie signal this in their initial argument about Kenyatta. Jackie's lover Carol is already a member of Kenyatta's organization when *Crime Partners* opens. Her loyalty to him reflects the feelings members of his organization continually manifest throughout the series: "[Carol] believed in what the man was doing in trying to clean up the ghettos of dope pushers and pimps. No other organization was really doing anything and she could see the results of Kenyatta's work. He had cleaned the streets of whores, since the pimps had moved their girls" (98). Goines continually encourages readers to empathize with Kenyatta's actions by revealing the continuing presence of white supremacist hegemony and the failure of integration to effectively counter it.

For example, the police officer who is targeted and killed at the outset of *Crime Partners*, Jim, has almost killed a Black police officer and spouts racial slurs immediately before his death. Here, Goines makes an important distinction within the police force. The depiction of the African-American detective Edward Benson, one half of the interracial team that pursues Kenyatta throughout the series, is relatively sympathetic and, more importantly, reveals the complex negotiations African-Americans engage in historically and predominantly white settings. Officer Jim's assumption that one "black face was like another as far as he was concerned" (30) almost results in the death of Benson at the very crime scene he is there to investigate. Instead of simply constructing a character that, because of his pursuit of Kenyatta, could easily be considered a totally unsympathetic "Uncle Tom," Goines explores the cost of integration—and thus the appeal of militant violence—and the complex post-Civil Rights negotiations of Blacks in traditionally white, racially charged worlds. Benson's conflicted feelings about his job as a police officer and his life as a Black man are one of the most significant themes underlying the series.

In the midst of drug pushers, gun fights, and urban despair sits a man struggling with his role at the center of the historic tension between the militant rage of the African-American community and the local representative of the police-state. Although many examples of "street lit" possess elements of the first of these three social features, they rarely interrogate the latter two, particularly through the lens of post-Civil Rights assumptions of a colorblind America. Benson's rage at Officer Jim and other racist police officers he encounters mirrors Kenyatta's and makes his use of violence more appealing, particularly given the helplessness Benson often feels when he is slighted by fellow police officers. Therefore, while Benson's white partner Ryan points out in *Crime Partners*, "Ed had been hurt tonight, even though he would never admit it. A fellow officer had disrespected him to a point where he was moody and dangerous," he comes to a different conclusion: "Brooding wouldn't solve it" (32). Kenyatta's use of liberatory violence, then, becomes a more effective strategy for challenging white supremacist hegemony because of the inability of Benson to constructively express his rage, the result of his non-violent, integrationist style. Moreover, as opposed to acts of random violence, Kenyatta's militant organization only targets white officers because, as Kenyatta states, "I don't want to hit no black ones if I can help it, because there's not enough black ones on the force now for us to go along killin' the few that they do have" (58). Kenyatta's restrained use of violence is clearly being used by Goines as a way to make his use of insurrectionary violence more palatable.

Throughout the series Goines seeks to contrast the moral use of Kenyatta's violence against those (i.e., police, drug dealers) whose violence destroys Black lives and communities. So, when Kenyatta and his organization return in *Death List*, prepared to avenge the death of Billy and Jackie, Kenyatta refuses to lose sight of political aims in taking on the drug lord King Fisher: "Ain't but one person responsible for his mess, and that's that nigger Kingfisher.... That nigger is to blame for over half the dope that comes into the ghetto, Ali. Over half the fuckin' poison that finds its way into those dumb-ass addicts' veins" (21). Kenyatta not only contrasts integrationist philosophy embodied in Benson's presence on the police force, but also certain visions of members of his own organization. In *Death List*, Kenyatta frequently clashes with Ali, his second in command who bristles at Kenyatta's plan to kill the top dope pushers in the city, all of whom are white. Wishing that he were the leader of the organization, Ali reveals: "While it was a good idea *preaching* about knocking off the dope pushers, it would pay even better if they just made the pushers *pay them protection*" (22, emphasis added). Ali resembles the protagonist in Goines's *Black Gangster*, in using nationalist rhetoric in order pacify the masses while benefiting from the material gains of the drug dealers. Kenyatta's desire to completely rid the street of drugs by going beyond the by-products, or dealers on the street, to the source of white supremacist capitalist hegemony reduces Ali's materialist vision to greed and fear. When Ali bristles at the task of getting close to the drug lords, Kenyatta offers an apt reply: "'That's the goddamn problem with black men,' Kenyatta stated coldly. 'You big-ass bad brothers are always ready to step in and knock off another black man who's dealing, but when it comes to stepping on peckerwoods' toes, you start shittin' your pants'" (23). Kenyatta's plan, therefore, directs his rage towards the destruction of a key tenement of white supremacy— the value of white life over Black life—and, in addition to rejecting capitalism's materialist distraction, eschews the Black-on-Black violence that often results from a nihilistic threat whose violence is only enacted upon the closest at hand.

In *Death List*, Kenyatta and his use of liberatory violence are contrasted, perhaps most notably, by a figure whose purposes are distinctly apolitical and virtually sociopathic. A member of Kenyatta's own organization known as "The Creeper" is Kenyatta's most fear-inducing assassin and appears only in this one installment of the series. Yet he is the literal and metaphorical opposite of Kenyatta. Whereas Kenyatta draws men and women to him, "The Creeper" repulses others. Goines's description of Kenyatta frequently centers on beauty and sensuality; however, his initial description of "The Creeper," who is covered in blood when he reaches Kenyatta's hideout, resembles a hauntingly grotesque character: "Beneath the rounded dome of a closely shaved skull, large black eyes peered from either side of a jutting, beak-like nose. The mouth below was sunken, the lips puckered, and the chin had a sharp upward hook" (71). Kenyatta's single-minded political aims are contrasted by an aggressively apolitical style in "The Creeper," yet "The Creeper" is similarly single-minded in his commitment to Kenyatta. For it is Kenyatta who once saved him from being killed by the police and Kenyatta who refuses to look away from him as everyone else does. Kenyatta uses "The Creeper" to gather information and perform specific "hits." When Kenyatta asks him to find the Kingfisher's second-in-command, a man named Sam, "The Creeper" not only finds Sam, but kills Sam and his entire family. Kenyatta himself admits regret at "The Creeper's" actions and notes that, had he known his intent, "he would have given the man direct orders to leave the kids alone. They weren't old enough to hurt them, they couldn't identify him because of their age. So the man had killed them out of pleasure" (120). "The Creeper's" lust for killing starkly contrasts, and potentially undermines, the use of liberatory violence by Kenyatta's militant organization. "The Creeper's" inclusion of those outside the organization's targets of drug pushers, traitors, and police officers could hypothetically threaten to supersede Kenyatta's use of violence for Black collective uplift.

Not surprisingly, "The Creeper" dies in *Death List* carrying out another assignment for Kenyatta, the killing of the organization's weapons provider, Angelo, who refuses to sell guns to them and eventually betrays them to the police. Angelo's fears emerge from Kenyatta's willingness to use his weapons to kill people outside the ghetto (i.e., white people). As he waits in his hotel for his flight, he confesses: "He hadn't the slightest notion that the nigger would really follow up his big ideas. He couldn't imagine them spades really reaching the men he had put down on the list. Especially those three men whose names he had used just because they had been in the newspapers lately and everybody took them to be top Mafia men" (124). Here again, Goines reveals that central tenet of white supremacist hegemony, specifically the privileging of white life over Black life. Angelo's willingness to make a profit ends when his belief in the (Black) organization's ability to effectively carry out the killings of those on the death list, which is to say, when white lives are threatened. Despite acknowledging that the men he sees in the paper are most likely agents of organized crime, he refuses to believe that they would be involved in drugs.

While Kenyatta's organization succeeds in killing the white drug lords as well as King Fisher, the police's discovery of their club and farm forces Kenyatta, his woman Betty, and a small band of his closest friends and lieutenants to escape. Taking over a plane by force, Goines ends the novel with a prescient reminder of the revolutionary spirit of the series. Holding a gun to the pilots' head, Kenyatta's close friend Zeke informs them that whatever their destination "'you can bet it will be a black country. Yes indeed,' Zeke said, speaking more to himself than the white pilots" (163). The celebratory tone of Zeke's final statement suggests the idealized Black nationalism of Greenlee's *Spook*. However, the Kenyatta series, like that novel, questions the protagonist's motives and loyalty. His escape at the end of *Death List*, while exciting, is tempered by the fact that he leaves Ali and many of his followers at the farm to face a massive police force without informing them of the oncoming danger. Like the streets Goines depicts, the image of Kenyatta can often seem unforgiving. As Bryant notes, "[Goines] neither romanticizes nor softens Kenyatta's ruthlessness. For all his good aims, Kenyatta's indifference to other lives is still ruthlessness, and he has the impervious hardness of a diamond" (269). In constructing an urban hero who exceeds Richard Wright's Bigger Thomas and fits into the tradition of the "badman/bad nigger," Goines problematizes the tendency to see Kenyatta as overly romanticized in the final two novels of the series, *Kenyatta's Escape* and *Kenyatta's Last Hit*.

In these final two novels Goines casts Kenyatta in a tradition that goes back to slavery and whose postbellum presence acted as a contrast to the racial terror of the late nineteenth century. Lawrence Levine notes in *Black Culture, Black Consciousness* (1977): "From the late nineteenth century black lore was filled with tales, toasts, and songs of hard, merciless toughs and killers confronting and generally vanquishing their adversaries without hesitation and without remorse" (408). Whether codified in Black folk tradition, Blues songs, or actual people such as boxer Jack Johnson, the figure of the "badman/bad nigger" operated outside the law and challenged white supremacist assumptions at every turn. Railroad Bill, for example, "shot and killed a policeman during an argument and escaped on a freight train. For the next three years freight trains were to be his means of sustenance. He robbed trains throughout southwest Alabama, stealing canned foods and selling it to the poor Negroes who lived in shacks along the rails" (Levine, 410). The most famous of these figures is, of course, Stagolee, whose murder of Billy Lyons in St. Louis in 1895 reached across the early twentieth century to the twenty first and from labor camps to rap music. Feared by law enforcement, judges, and juries, Stagolee emerged as a figure whose bold audacity, violence, and unparalleled machismo were appropriated throughout African-American culture.

Cecil Brown notes in *Stagolee Shot Billy* (2003) that the "Stagolee paradigm has produced political figures such as Adam Clayton Powell, Malcolm X, Muhammad Ali, H. 'Rap' Brown, Robert Williams, and Bobby Seale. Seale not only named his son Stagolee but used the narrative toast version as a recurring device to get young black men into the Black Panther Party" (14). A literary equivalent of Stagolee, and by extension the "badman/bad nigger," is Bigger Thomas from Richard Wright's *Native Son* (1940). Bigger is significant because he recast the figure of the "badman/bad nigger" to an urban context, one that Kenyatta eventually extends. In his essay "How Bigger Was Born," Wright lays out stories of the various Biggers he met throughout his life who comprised the central figure of his novel. Those Biggers who appear in both the rural South of Wright's youth and the urban North resemble the "bad niggers" in their defiance of white authority as well as conventional Black community expectations. The Bigger of the novel, however, remains caught within the environment that produces him. He is unable to articulate his rage except through violence, which, in Wright's naturalist narrative, condemns him to die by violence. It also, at times, undercuts the political aspect of his acts of violence. Wright does this purposely because, as H. Nigel Thomas argues in *From Folklore to Fiction* (1988), "to characterize Bigger as sympathetic to any art forms, even a criminal's art, would have risked diminishing the total monster that Wright wished him to become by the time of his capture" (75). Goines's portrait of Kenyatta moves beyond Wright's depiction of the urban "bad nigger" of literature by making Kenyatta wholly aware of the forces that surround him and influence his community. He is not only able to articulate his rage at such forces in his individual resistance, but he is also able to voice that rage in a way that would allow others to constructively articulate theirs. Goines centralizes the theme of Black collective uplift and makes his use of violence a mechanism to achieve that uplift.

In part of the evolving construction of Kenyatta, Goines provides moments in the final two novels when Kenyatta seems to mirror the image of the "overly sexual," apolitically violent "badman" that the conventional Black community is said to often fear. In Jerry Bryant's *Born in a Mighty Bad Land* (1997), he informs us that chroniclers of the "badman/bad nigger" in novel form, in contrast to folk portraits that view him as someone whose violence is as much a threat to Black America as it is to white America, produce "a man who has mastered the violent methods of the conventional "bad nigger" but who has graduated to bourgeois self-control and renounced violence for the rewards that middle-class conformity gives him" (7). Goines seems to be an exception here, and not merely because his lived experience would lead him to promote an unromantic depiction of violence and ghetto life. Although Kenyatta certainly maintains self-control, he never succumbs to the economic benefits of a (white) middle-class, bourgeois life. Moreover, the violence that surrounds him and of which he is a part never seems quite within his control. His lack of control becomes apparent in *Kenyatta's Escape* when the violence he had been able to contain for the first two novels threatens to spin out of control.

True to its title, the violence that appears in *Kenyatta's Escape* appears less for the political purposes of the first two novels than for the more pragmatic goal of maintaining freedom. Yet Goines builds on the popularity of the previous tales. The various destinations of Kenyatta and members of his organization suggest Kenyatta's nationalist aspirations. Moreover, the involvement of the FBI, which teams with Benson and Ryan, displays national anxieties about Kenyatta's defiance of the nation-state's use of violent oppression and its indifference to, if not encouragement of, drug trafficking in the Black ghettoes. Perhaps as significant is the split focus on the organization: Kenyatta and his most trusted lieutenants are headed for Los Angeles, while survivors of the gun battle at the farm are fleeing to Chicago. As a result, we are witnesses to an important interrogation of Kenyatta, through the doubts of his followers, that places his status as an unquestioned folk hero in flux. Still, those doubts reveal the series's establishment of Kenyatta as a folk hero as opposed to a predetermined image to be celebrated. We are even privy to the interior emotions of Kenyatta, not just the symbolic construction of him by others.

The third novel acts as a transition, but also seeks to deepen the connection to and between characters, providing specific adventures to widen the legend and mythology of Kenyatta. The violence in *Crime Partners* and *Death List* established Kenyatta as a "badman/bad nigger" figure, arguably, but *Kenyatta's Escape* explicitly continues the rationale behind his actions. In the novels, as Bryant points out, "violence is their basic motif, meant at least in part as an attraction to their no doubt largely black male readership. But there is an element of the morality tale in them, too, so that exploitation lies in tension with moral disapproval" (269). Kenyatta was almost brought to tears in *Death List* when thinking about the deaths of Billy and Jackie. When the plane which had been on its way to Algiers is forced to land in Nevada because of a gun battle initiated by a white security officer and a glory-hungry detective, Kenyatta must face the death of his friend Zeke and the severe wounding of his friend Red. His sense of loss at the death of Zeke is palpable: "He stared at one corpse especially. It was his friend Zeke. He and Zeke had done a lot of things together, and it hurt deeply to see his lifelong friend stretched out cold on the floor of the airplane" (53). What's more, Kenyatta's guilt when he discovers that members of his group died in a farm firefight while others remain at large speaks to other emotional connections in the midst of graphic violence. Leaving his members without a warning could raise questions about his loyalty, if not political strategizing, but *Kenyatta's Escape* will reveal that his commitment to his organization and its members is unyielding.

As Kenyatta and his group listen to news reports of the farm shoot out, Kenyatta begins to blame himself for the result: "A gun battle was the last thing he had thought would jump off. His well laid plans to call back and get his people out of jail were useless now. His head seemed to swell up on him as he thought about it. An exquisite pain exploded inside of him, and he knew he would never be able to get rid of the feeling of guilt whenever he thought about the farmhouse" (162). Curiously, Kenyatta underestimates the dedication of his members to him and to the use of violence as a strategy. His expectation that the members would surrender themselves, and that he would only have to place a call to free them, reveals a now obvious miscalculation. He is only proven partially correct when we realize that the police not only fired the first shot at the farm, but also killed unarmed members who were trying to surrender.

None of this matters to the four members who escape the farm and head to Chicago or even some of the men with Kenyatta in Los Angeles. Despite reaching Chicago and the prearranged safe house manned by an organization member named Tiny, the group consisting of Victor, Dickie, Peggy, and Irene wonders whether or not Kenyatta knew the police were coming when he left. In considering Kenyatta's motives, the novel questions Kenyatta as a re-envisioned folk hero as well as his particular strategy of liberatory violence. If Kenyatta is only concerned with his own survival now, then, as Dickie considers, "it meant that Kenyatta had intentionally tossed the rest of his people to the dogs while he made his escape" (157). The questions the group poses to Tiny and one another have significant ramifications. In the novel it could result in a group plan to kill Kenyatta. However, an indictment of Kenyatta as a traitor would also negate his use of violence for liberation because of his betrayal of the collective.

The inclusion of this group discussion moves the novel beyond Kenyatta's singular pursuit of justice to a collective desire for justice most explicitly. We behold the impact of Kenyatta's rhetoric on his followers. While members like Ali sought to undermine him for their individual gain, other members were genuinely and heavily invested in his program of Black collective uplift and revolutionary violence. Even in his disagreements with Tiny, who is unable to imagine that Kenyatta could have intentionally left members behind at the mercy of the police, Dickie struggles because of his own loyalty to Kenyatta: "A year ago, it would never have entered [Dickie's] mind to doubt anything Kenyatta did. But now it was different. If by chance he found out that Kenyatta was guilty, justice would have to be served" (161). The reader's knowledge of Kenyatta's feelings of guilt as well as his attempts to get the injured Red medical attention is important and instructive here. However, even with doubts removed, the questioning of Kenyatta is significant inasmuch as it negotiates his portrait as a folk hero and "badman/bad nigger." The novels become a mechanism by which such a mythic image is forged via the use of revolutionary violence.

Hence, *Kenyatta's Escape* goes further than its predecessors in expanding the story beyond Detroit to Chicago, Nevada, and Los Angeles. The absence of the plot-driven violence of *Crime Partners* and *Death List* also allows for more commentary to unfold on Black violence as a response to white violence. The disruption of white supremacist ideas of "acceptable" expressions of Black rage leaves white America scrambling for answers. The media relies on stereotypical ideas of Blackness, referring to the escapees as "mad dogs" (77). The presence of the official, violent enforcers of white supremacist hegemony, and the employment of the national domestic representatives (i.e., the FBI), should plainly echo of the same statewide response to the Black Panther Party.

Dismissing Kenyatta as insane, the police instead focus on his supporters. Called back on Kenyatta's trail by the FBI, Benson and Ryan find themselves in the car with two federal officers named Evans and Gary. As they leave the downed plane filled with dead bodies, Evans considers Ann, Zeke's lover, and her possible motive for joining Kenyatta's group: "It just beats the shit out of me, really. Here's this young, attractive girl who has been to college, so she's not a ghetto child who had never seen what the other side of life looks like. Her people saved and planned to send their daughter to college. Then she has the bad luck to run into some creep like this fuckin' Kenyatta and blows the whole ball of wax" (149). Benson bristles not at Evans's contemplative monologue, but at Gary's belief that Ann "must not have been too fuckin' smart" (149). Both officers assume that college should automatically confer not only education but ideology. Specifically, the officers see college for African-Americans as part of the cultivation of loyalty to white supremacy and a rejection of Black resistance struggle. Underlying this dynamic of loyalty and rejection is the promise of admission into the Black bourgeoisie, a group supposedly privileged because of their imitation of white, bourgeois culture and ideals. Part of this expectation involves an individual separation from community. Certainly the use of violence, as a result, becomes unconceivable. The officers fail to understand, however, that Kenyatta's members use violence as part of their project of collective uplift.

The final novel of the series, *Kenyatta's Last Hit*, is as significant for what it indicates about Goines's intentions as it is for the continuation of Kenyatta's crusade and the introduction of Oscar Manning and his boss, drug kingpin Clement Jenkins. Both are classic figurations of "The [White] Man" in Blaxploitation films, singular white males who seem to be the source of the oppression suffered by urban Black America. The description of Jenkins, who is a heroin addict, is familiar to any basic student of Black films of the 1970s: "Clement Jenkins was one of those men to whom wealth was immaterial. It was making the money that counted, the continual process of gaining more and more, stockpiling it until there was nothing left to do but count it" (168). *Kenyatta's Last Hit* also introduces Elliot Stone, a former college football star who seems to be the only figure that Kenyatta considers to be his equal. As Kenyatta's main contact in Watts, Stone gathers the information on the drug dealers and traffickers that eventually leads them to Manning and Jenkins. At one point, the novel points out: "With Stone's intelligence and youth, Kenyatta had envisioned the younger man as a son, someone who would carry on his fight after he was gone" (25). The possibility of Stone's ascendancy represents a shift in Black resistance to the oppressive forces of white supremacy. While Kenyatta represents the overtly militant, unyielding presence of Black rage, Stone demonstrates a response to white supremacy's reconfiguration in post-Civil Rights/post-Black Power America.

Recognizing the intersection of race and class, Stone's work at the Office of Economic Opportunity (OEO) in South Central allows him to help "[Stone's] black brothers and sisters to achieve some kind of reasonable start in the community. As a former football star and student, the job had come easily to the well-mannered, soft-spoken black youth" (10). Despite the obvious contrast with Kenyatta, Stone uses the OEO to discover the web of pushers, middle men, and drug lords that Kenyatta and he need to identify in order to clean up the streets. Stone provides the perfect face for a country in the midst of a conservative revival: "In the old days, men like

H. Rap Brown and Eldridge Cleaver frightened off the soft, white businessmen from the Valley and Beverly Hills.... It had worked for a number of years, but now the clean-cut, well-educated men like Elliot Stone were making their climb. And it was making life easier for the nervous white men who dealt with them" (11).

Stone's masking mirrors Kenyatta's own in the novel, an act in which Kenyatta has rarely, if ever engaged. In order to get close to Jenkins, Kenyatta poses as a drug dealer. After the heroin is received from a contact overseas, the novel narrates an important moment of foreshadowing: "The arrival of the powder signaled a new era in the black man's methods. As he drove from the airport with the parcel resting on his lap, Kenyatta felt a twinge of disgust. His hatred of the stuff was something that had driven him through the years, motivating him to strengthen his army, to blast away at the pushers and junkies in the ghettos who were quickly destroying the hope of the black people" (103). While Kenyatta's "new methods" are successful, in that they bring him face to face with Jenkins, they initiate a descent towards death that all of Goines's characters eventually experience.

The death of Kenyatta leaves both the legacy of Kenyatta and liberatory violence open for a myriad of interpretations. Published after his death, the novel could appear to forecast Goines's own death and perhaps his inability to kick his drug habit. Eddie Allen remarks: "The fact that Kenyatta meets his death disappointed me on two levels: first because he is a metaphor for Mr. Goines's desire to overcome his addiction to drugs; second, because it suggests that good can never defeat the larger societal evils that afflict our black communities, even in fiction" (175). What Allen and other critics miss is what the presence of Stone suggests about the evolution of Goines's use of violence. While Bryant argues that "Kenyatta's methods doom him to failure" (268), Goines provides a response to the limitations of violence that appear in the final novel. Bryant's critique dismisses violence as a successful strategy – practically and morally – for Black resistance struggle. This dismissal falls squarely within the tradition of anxiety surrounding Black violence against whites, which dates back to slave insurrections, especially as it constructs any and all Black violence as morally corrupt. Yet what we see in Goines is not an abandonment of liberatory violence, but a complement to that violence that effectively combats more subtle forms of white supremacy. Goines's novels build on the work of Sutton Griggs and Sam Greenlee in examining the viability of violence alongside – and sometimes in opposition to – other modes of African-American resistance. Kenyatta's death, in other words, is not an indictment of the use of violence generally, but a recognition that violence utilized apart from other modes of resistance cannot be sustained in certain historical contexts. For example, Kenyatta's notion of Black life after the death of drug kingpins is tenuous and abstract and rarely undergirds the violence that appears in the novels. Thus, the survival of Stone is crucial here because he represents a new vision in resisting white supremacist capitalist hegemony and because he carries the revolutionary spirit that informed Kenyatta's crusade.

Goines uses his final novel to interrogate the reliance on violence as the only revolutionary mode of resistance. Although Greg Goode claims that "the fact that Goines killed [Kenyatta] off might have indicated that Goines thought that even organized violence means would ultimately fail" (47), Kenyatta's survival and success would have been overly romantic and inconsistent with Goines's other narratives. The Kenyatta novels remain a treatise on resisting nihilism and directly confronting oppressive forces through collective effort. Finally, the death of Kenyatta does not diminish his standing as a folk hero or a figure, like other "bad men," whose invocation can inspire instead of dishearten or discourage us.

The Kenyatta series does not merely expand our interpretation of Goines's work. It reveals how Black rage and Black resistance can give way to an apolitical commercialism. Contemporary African-American literature – both popular and critically anointed – has been preoccupied with questions of "authenticity." On the one hand, some authors examine the internal, isolating world of the Black elite, particularly as their characters wrestle with questions of "post-raciality" and "post-Blackness." On the other hand, different writers construct urban tales committed to a representation of the "real" by means of its depiction of an underclass Black life filled with drugs, violence, and nihilism.

The Kenyatta series fills an important gap in contemporary African-American literature because it includes both a Black rage aimed at resisting the destructive forces impinging on Black urban life and the hope that Kenyatta and his peers will organize to reverse the self-destruction they witness in urban Black America. The novels are consistent with Goines's treatment of his heroes who are immersed in violence and are unable to free themselves from the forces of white supremacy. The series is not separate from the moment in which they are produced and, as a result, possess an obvious mix of the Blaxploitation plots of the era that threaten to negate the nationalist, socio-political tradition that we see in Black resistance struggle from David Walker to Huey Newton. Goines's intent is nonetheless clear. He transforms the nihilistic violence in which the heroes of his other books often find themselves into a liberatory act of resistance. The absence from critical consideration of fiction like the Kenyatta series, or even of a folk figure like Kenyatta in contemporary African-American literature, is a void that speaks volumes about the continued discomfort with Black violence and Black rage in post-Civil Rights America; and it eliminates an important perspective that could bridge the divide in our discourse about the continuing distinctions being made between popular African-American fiction and critically-acclaimed works anointed to join the official, elite African-American literary canon.

REFERENCES

Briggs, Joe Bob. *Cineaste* 28 (Spring 2003): 24-30.

Brown, Cecil. *Stagolee Shot Billy.* Cambridge: Harvard University Press, 2003.

Bryant, Jerry H. *Victims and Heroes: Racial Violence in the African-American Novel.* Amherst: University of Massachusetts Press, 1997.

————. *Born in a Mighty Bad Land: The Violent Man in African-American Folklore and Fiction.* Bloomington: Indiana University Press, 2003.

Goines, Donald. *Crime Partners.* Los Angeles: Holloway House, 1974.

————. *Death List.* Lost Angeles: Holloway House, 1974.

————. *Kenyatta's Escape.* Los Angeles: Holloway House, 1974.

————. *Kenyatta's Last Hit.* Los Angeles: Holloway House, 1974.

Goode, Greg. "From *Dopefiend* to *Kenyatta's Last Hit*: The Angry Black Crime Novels of Donald Goines" *MELUS* 11 (Autumn, 1984): 41-48.

hooks, bell. *Killing Rage: Ending Racism.* New York: Henry Holt, 1995.

Levine, Lawrence. *Black Culture and Black Consciousness: Afro-American Folk Thought from Slavery to Freedom.* New York: Oxford University Press, 1977.

Thomas, H. Nigel *From Folklore to Fiction: A Study of Folk Heroes and Rituals in the Black American Novel.* New York: Greenwood Press, 1988.

CHAPTER THREE

George Jackson—Ambushing—in *Swamp Man*

Detecting *Soledad Brother* and *Blood in My Eye* in Donald Goines

Greg Thomas

The central character of Donald Goines's *White Man's Justice, Black Man's Grief* (1973) is "Chester Hines." This naming is an act of signifying and itself signifies a practice of reading that should lead interpreters beyond the stock references to Robert Beck or "Iceberg Slim" in discussions of this school of writing. Chester Himes is clearly important to Goines as a fellow, formerly imprisoned Black author of fiction. Both were born in the U.S. Midwest. Both began their literary careers while incarcerated with crucial support from their mothers. The eventual "expatriate" Himes's *Cast the First Stone* (1952) would follow *If He Hollers Let Him Go* (1945) and is in many ways recast by *White Man's Justice, Black Man's Grief*, especially given its narrative concern with taboo sex, politics and prison cells.[1] The many biographical connections between Himes and Goines can be traced early in *The Quality of Hurt: The Autobiography of Chester Himes, Volume I* (1971) and later in *My Life of Absurdity: The Autobiography of Chester Himes, Volume II* (1976). But Eddie B. Allen, Jr. suggests in *Low Road: The Life and Legacy of Donald Goines*

(2004) that this naming of "Chester Hi*nes*" is likely "an uncanny coincidence" (Allen 2004, 152). What critical assumptions produce such a conclusion, here or elsewhere?

The symbolic naming of other characters in Goines makes a mockery of it. For example, David Walker and Robert Williams are introduced in the eighth chapter of *White Man's Justice, Black Man's Grief* as well. Walker of the novel is imprisoned for the alleged "rape" of a white woman which was not committed when he was passed out cold in the backseat of a car; David Walker of Black history and literature is remembered, arguably resurrected, as the great political author of *An Appeal to Coloured Citizens of the World, But in Particular, and Very Expressly, to Those of the United States of America* (1829). Williams of the novel is captured on the same bogus charge; Robert *F.* Williams of Black history and literature is remembered as the world-famous politico and author of *Negroes with Guns* (1962) and polemics like "U.S.A.: Potential of a Minority Revolution" (1964). This is not yet to mention Goines's four-part Kenyatta series which includes *Crime Partners* (1974), *Death List* (1974), *Kenyatta's Escape* (1974) and *Kenyatta's Last Hit* (1975), whose revolutionary hero is clearly the namesake of Jomo Kenyatta, "Father of Kenyan Independence." There is a literacy and a literary activism in Goines's writing and its practice of naming that is lost on interpreters who see such meaning-making as "accidental" or "coincidental" in popular fiction in general, perhaps, and Black popular fiction in particular. This may be nowhere more evident than in *Swamp Man* (1974), the novel whose central character is none other than "George Jackson."

The conventional study of literature as *bourgeois* literature is what explains the lack of recognition and appreciation for Goines's extensive body of work in U.S. academia and the West at large. Eminently, Richard Wright reflected on "The Forms of Things Unknown" – or "folk utterances, spirituals, blues, work songs, and folklore" – in "The Literature of the Negro in the United States" or *White Man, Listen!* (1957). But those who have found this essay useful have tended to ignore how this author of *Native Son* (1940) felt these forms of the Black folk masses would have to disappear, logically and desirably, in his promised land of "integration." Neither Wright nor conventional Black literary criticism would envision how Malcolm X's "grassroots," which created these "folk utterances, spirituals, blues, work songs, and folklore," could come to create novels, themselves, transforming the historically Western and bourgeois novel in accordance with their own artistic values and political interests, as does Goines in no less than sixteen novels from *Dopefiend, The Story of a Black Junkie* (1971) and *Whoreson* (1971) to *Inner City Hoodlum* (1975).

Ostensibly, an isolated exception to the typical intellectual neglect of Goines was found in Greg Goode's article in *MELUS*, "The Angry Black Crime Novels of Donald Goines" (1984), where he observed: "With respect to standards of literature, the books of Donald Goines are not considered subliterary, for they are not even considered" (Goode 1984, 42). Very little has changed in two and a half decades. What's more, Goode could not identify or challenge those unidentified, unquestioned "standards" which continue to place the likes of Goines beyond the pale of consideration, if he makes minor and more "sociological" than literary concessions to Goines as "a successful Black author of mass market fiction written by and about Blacks." After all, Goines is continually "devoured by legions of Black Americans everywhere, from the inner city to American military bases abroad" (41). He was a "most prolific, popular writer of a [once] quickly growing publisher," Holloway House (48), which still bills him (convincingly) as "America's #1 Best Selling Black Author."

It is a healthy respect for Himes's self-described "domestic fiction" and the whole *policier* or "crime fiction" genre that could generate a series of French blurbs which would for years appear inside the paperback cover of almost all of Goines's novels. They reflect a different set of "standards," to be sure:

> *"A flashing talent straight from the streets of the lost."*
>
> L' EXPRESS

> *"After Chester Himes, the 'Série Noire' could not overlook Donald Goines, the most interesting black crime writer in many years. Goines writes with guts 'n blood."*
>
> LA RÉPUBLIQUE DU CENTRE

> *"What is great about Goines is that you feel you've become more intelligent once you have read his stories of pain and grief..."*
>
> LA LIBERTÉ DE L'EST

> *"[Donald Goines] dives into the hellish world of the ghetto dear to Chester Himes, minus the humor. Policemen shoot before asking questions. Fear and hatred can be read on all faces."*
>
> LA CROIX

To date, Éditions Gallimard has translated and published at least ten of Goines's novels in France: *Ne Mourez Jamais Seul* (1993) and *Enfant de Putain* (1994) in its esteemed "La Noire" collection, along with *L'Accro* (1995), which is even distributed as a "Folio Policier" therein; and then its classic "Série Noire" includes *Vendeurs de Mort* (1994), *Truands and Co.* (1994), *La Cavale de Kenyatta* (1996), *Daddy Cool* (1997), *Justine Blanche, Misère Noire* (2001), *Street Players* (2003) as well as *Le Dernier Coup de Kenyatta* (2005). (The former set is translated by

Alexandre Ferragut. The latter set is translated by Daniel Lemoine.) All the same, Goode's "standards of literature" proceed to categorize Goines – in the only essay of note on his texts until L.H. Stallings's "'I'm Goin Pimp Whores!': The Goines Factor and the Theory of a Hip-Hop Neo-Slave Narrative" (2003) – as "offensive to many because of the obscenity, sex, and violence, all well before their time in graphic explicitness." (42). Goines's violation of middle-class protocol, social and literary, is an offense applauded by legions outside criticism and academia; and this is clearly the root cause of Goode's negative evaluation, or non-evaluation, in elite institutional circles.

Tellingly, when Goode addresses the Kenyatta series with its bold Black revolutionary aims, their "violence" for him places them in "literary limbo" along with their stylings (46). An outlaw association with Black radical tradition compounds an outlaw association with those whom Frantz Fanon named "*Les Damnés de la Terre*" or "The Wretched of the Earth" (1961). Small wonder then that *Swamp Man* is projected by Goode as Goines's "worst book" (45), instead of an exception of a different sort. For *Swamp Man* is in truth one of Goines's most important and Maroon-identified books by far. It is his urgent yet lasting intervention into white and Black history at a pivotal moment in time. It is a testament, or Goines's radical rewriting of the "life and legacy" of George L. Jackson, "Comrade George," "The Dragon," Field Marshal of the Black Panther Party as well as revolutionary author of *Soledad Brother* (1970) and *Blood in My Eye* (1972), after his tragic murder by agents of the counter-revolutionary state of the United States of America.

Life of a Revolutionary: George L. Jackson
(September 23, 1941 – August 21, 1971)

The author of my hunger, the architect of the circumstantial pressures which are the sole causes of my ills will find no peace, in this existence or the next, the one following that; never, never. I'll dog his trail to infinity…. What I … feel is the urge to resist, resist, and never stop resisting or even think of stopping my resistance until victory falls to me.

GEORGE JACKSON, *Soledad Brother* (1970)

Once, a British documentary entitled *Death of a Revolutionary* aired sometime in 1971 to "record the mood surrounding the funeral" of George Lester Jackson, "among his own people," for whom it was "a political event – to be commemorated with music, poetry and speeches." The film's narrator provides an introduction for his audience as sounds of Nina Simone ("I Wish I Knew How It Would Feel to Be Free") play and images of Black Panther Party members unfold at St. Augustine's Episcopal Church in Oakland, California:

George Jackson went to prison a rebellious nineteen year old Black. Eleven years inside, most of the time locked alone in a cell for twenty-three and a half hours a day, turned him into a revolutionary. In a series of letters from prison, Jackson recorded his developing insight into the conditions of his country and people. Their publication made him famous. They became a vital text for Black revolutionaries in America.

On screen, Bobby Seale reads messages sent from around the world from "people and organizations" as well as "brothers and sisters" incarcerated in U.S. prisons. Elaine Brown is seen and heard singing throughout. Huey P. Newton provides the eulogy and an interview. The film's introduction can and should be revised in certain, key respects:

> George Jackson went to prison a rebellious [Black teenager], to be sure. In the course of eleven years inside, most of the time locked in a cell of solitary confinement for twenty-three and a half hours a day, he and his comrades studied and transformed themselves into revolutionaries. In a series of letters from prison published as *Soledad Brother: The Prison Letters of George Jackson*, he recorded his developing insight into the conditions of his people and all oppressed people. [*Blood in My Eye* would appear after his assassination – to the serious dismay of the FBI]. Their publication made him famous. They became vital for Black and other revolutionaries in the Americas and across the globe.

Before the close of *Death of a Revolutionary*, appropriately, Georgia Jackson will be pictured making this declaration about her son at a press conference: "George Lester Jackson's spirit did *not* expire on August 21, 1971."

On September 23, 1941, he was born in Chicago to Georgia and Robert Lester Jackson, who would move their family to Los Angeles, California, when their first-born son was fourteen. A series of conflicts with the state would land him in juvenile detention centers (e.g., "Youth Correctional Facility" in Paso Robles). This "law and order" he would soon enough define as "fascism," of the "colonial" sort. He would define the Black condition as one of "neo-slavery." Autobiographical reflections on his early years read like tales of a young Maroon running away from containment or enslavement in the twentieth-century cities of North America. At the age of eighteen, he was convicted for allegedly "stealing" seventy dollars from a gas station; and, for this "crime," he received a "one year to life" sentence. The now pervasive practice of "plea bargaining" made an early and awful appearance here. While imprisoned at San Quentin and Soledad Prisons, all places his writings refer to as *"concentration camps,"* George L. Jackson came to embody what he would so famously espouse, a transformation of "the Black criminal mentality into a Black revolutionary mentality," toward a Pan-African, Black and international, Communist revolution (Jackson 1970, 16; 3-16).

It was in this "Dachau" that he was "pleased" to "meet" Marx and Lenin as well as Mao and Fanon, whom he said "redeemed" him (16).[2] A phenomenal and visionary dialectician, he would study, teach, reach and mobilize effectively enough to be hailed by many as the architect of the modern anti-prison movement. Favorable comparisons to Malcolm X are plenty in commentary on his significance, given his own revolutionary radicalization and his systematic radicalization of others while behind prison walls. While at Soledad, he would co-found a chapter of the Black Panther Party, the international Black Power organization for which he would become Field Marshal. This political position would align with the major intellectual position of his second book, *Blood in My Eye*, a militant treatise on the very real possibility and necessity of guerilla warfare in the cities of what he called "the Black Colony" of U.S. settler-imperialist rule.

An undeniable tour-de-force, his first book was *Soledad Brother* because he, John Clutchette and Fleeta Drumgo were known as the "Soledad Brothers," collectively. In 1970, they were accused of killing a white prison guard (John V. Mills) in retaliation for a murder committed by another white prison guard (O.G. Miller) whose killing of three Black prisoners (W. L. Nolen, Alvin "Jug" Miller and Cleveland Edwards) was labeled "justifiable homicide" by the white racist state, as is usual. Since Jackson had already been given a "life" sentence, this charge would spell certain death – the gas chamber –beyond the long-term deprivations of solitary confinement.

There would be a spectacular protest of all of this by his younger brother, Jonathan. A brilliant thinker at seventeen years of age, he is quoted at length by the elder Jackson in the opening essay of *Blood in My Eye*; and, on August 7, 1970, the younger Jackson would aim to wed theory and practice by storming a Marin County courthouse with a machine gun in hand to demand the freedom of the "Soledad Brothers." He freed the San Quentin prisoners at trial (James McClain, William Christmas and Ruchell Magee) and took the judge, assistant district attorney and three white female jurors hostage. Jonathan, McClain and Christmas as well as the judge were killed, however. As the police put a premium on the death of Black men (and, ideally, radical political activism) over the life of one white judge and the welfare of the white assistant district attorney and "three female noncombatants" (Jackson 1972, 101). "He was free for a while," the caged Jackson would both mourn and boast of Jonathan in the final letter of *Soledad Brother* (Jackson 1970, 329). For him, "life" or freedom comes only to those who dare to rebel, revolt and win. Earlier, it was written:

> I have a young courageous brother whom I love more than I love myself, but I have given him up to the revolution. I accept the possibility of his

eventual death as I accept the possibility of my own.... I accept this as a necessary part of our life. I don't want to raise any more black slaves. We have a determined enemy who will accept us only on a master-slave basis. When I revolt, slavery dies with me. I refuse to pass it down again. (250)

From then on, George Jackson would call his movement the "August 7th Movement" in honor of this fallen soldier who is memorialized in each of his passionate, powerhouse books.

Etched into the near-hieroglyphic credits of Ethiopian filmmaker Haile Gerima's *Child of Resistance* (1972) is perhaps the most prominent of all George Jackson's words: "They'll never count me among the broken men" (Jackson 1970, 27). Those who could never break him would shoot him at San Quentin, fatally, claiming he was in the midst of an escape from prison aided by an automatic pistol smuggled in by his lawyer, Stephen Bingham, who would be acquitted of this charge (after fleeing the country, for thirteen years, out of fear) in 1986. A former political prisoner himself, Dhoruba Bin Wahad would point out in *Still Black, Still Strong: Survivors of the War against Black Revolutionaries* (1993): "Documents that surfaced under the Freedom of Information Act subsequently showed that George Jackson was a target of the Counterintelligence Program aimed at the Black Panther Party" (Bin Wahad et. al, 1993, 79). This lethal "COINTELPRO" strategy of "neutralization" as "liquidation" led to a number of other operations, many of which have been recycled to the present day, such as "Operation PRISAC," a program whose primary focus was systematic repression or suppression of prison activists in the wake of George Jackson.

At the outset, *Death of a Revolutionary* addressed the confusion stemming from the absurd explanations circulated by "authorities" in the establishment media: "But Panthers insist he was murdered by prison guards. Many in the Black community cannot accept that such a man would have died in a pointless escape attempt," adds the film's narrator. With more clarity, Bobby Seale refers to it as a case of capital punishment resisted by their "Field Marshal [who was] acting as a General to defend himself, a human being protecting his human dignity." When interviewed, Huey Newton reads through the official alibi (to "cover their murder") as he did in his eulogy which would reappear in the posthumous publication of *Blood in My Eye* (Newton in Jackson 1972, 193-97). Poignantly, and radically, Georgia Jackson elaborates:

It should be understood that my son was not a mad dog killer; that he has been portrayed to be a mad dog killer. His love was for all people, except for those that sought to oppress others. Against this group he leveled the constancy of his intellect, the might of his articulation, the power and passion of his manhood. To the former group, he dedicated his writings, gave all of the funds from his published and unpublished works and his boundless warmth and love. Now that they have murdered the body of George Lester Jackson, which they are attempting to conceal, with the Hitlerian technique of the Big Lie, they will attempt to eliminate the rest of the family through phony indictments and charges. We expect charges to be brought against us. But we have no fear. George Lester Jackson's spirit did *not* expire on August 21, 1971.

In the end, despite its title, *Death of a Revolutionary* echoes this sentiment with a direct quotation full of promise. It is taken from *Soledad Brother* (which is dedicated to Jonathan Peter Jackson, his mother "Georgia Bea," and Angela Y. Davis), as it intersects with *Blood in My Eye* (which is dedicated to "the Black Communist youth" and "their fathers"). Simultaneously, Elaine Brown is singing and sending "The Meeting (The Black Panther Party National Anthem)" throughout the church in the background: "They won't defeat my revenge.... I'm part of a righteous people who anger slowly, but rage undammed. We'll gather at his door in such a number that the rumbling of our feet will make the earth tremble. I'm going to charge them for this, twenty eight years without gratification. I'm going to charge them reparations in blood" (Jackson 1970, 222).[3]

George Jackson in *Swamp Man* (1974): Against Neo-Slavery – Sadism and Fascism

> The sun had just come up when George Jackson pushed back some tall brown willow weeds he was hiding behind.... Even with the appearance of the sun over the tree tops it was still dark in the Mississippi swamp.
>
> DONALD GOINES, *Swamp Man* (1974)

> The only form of attack employed by the guerrilla forces is the ambush, the surprise attack.... We fight to live. And we're learning to fight; it'll be a war, to the knife if necessary.... It's as predictable as nightfall.... We can only be repressed if we stop thinking and stop fighting.
>
> GEORGE L. JACKSON, *Blood in My Eye* (1972)

Only a couple of years later Goines would resurrect the legend, reanimating him in a text and context of guerilla resistance, a narrative imagination of those fabled "reparations in blood." "*George Jackson was a Swamp Man*," reads the back cover synopsis of Goines's novel: *"Slipping through the swamps like a ghost."* Dedicated to the author's own mother, Myrtle, it opens with the man – or "man-child" – in a new setting.[4] This is not the urban locale of every other Goines offering; it is neither Detroit, Watts or Los Angeles nor Las Vegas of the Kenyatta series. It is certainly not the space of any California state prison. The rural context and moniker invoke the space and spirit of *maroonage*, as in the Great Dismal Swamp of Nat Turner or Monifa A. Love's *Freedom in the Dismal* (1998), where the voices of Nat Turner and *Soledad Brother* resurface together. *Swamp Man's* first lines could suggest a successful escape made, a double-escape even—his escaping from San Quentin prison and his escaping assassination's death as well; for here in Goines the sun rises and signifies a new day in a new place for "George Jackson," who turns out to be the "man-child" as a young boy in Mississippi: "A tall husky boy of fourteen, George already had the build of a man. It was evident that he would be an exceptionally powerful man when he was full grown" (Goines 1974, 9). But it is not a childhood biography that Goines rewrites. His fictive reanimation or resurrection of George Jackson in *Swamp Man* will reframe the meaning of his life and struggle; it will contest and rewrite the vilifying narratives of the white racist state's prison propaganda; and it will rearticulate *Blood in My Eye* and *Soledad Brother's* immortal resistance to neo-slavery and fascism in favor of guerilla resistance and Black revolution in North America and beyond.[5]

This George Jackson will plot an ambush to avenge the rape and torture of his sister – in the local, southern context of a larger regime of racial terror. Henrietta is scheduled to return home from Lincoln College, which she attended on scholarship: "It was a way to get out of the swamps – away from the white trash she had always despised" (12). They call her "Miss Nigger" and resent her Black self-respect as well as her memory of their murder of her father. George's "long-awaited reunion" with Henrietta will never quite be (21). The "Jones brothers" plan to beat him to the arrival of her Greyhound bus with the knowledge and complicity of apparently all the white townspeople. They trap her in the forest on her way to her family's swamped abode. Deprived of his rifle by their paternal grandfather, who thought he would be safer without it, her brother is too late to do anything but witness the sadistic violence against her that may be the most graphic, gruesome scene ever depicted by Donald Goines: "He refused to open his eyes. The guilt lay on him heavily, each scream was printed in his memory" (46). Eye-witnessing is tied to writing and plotting as well as remembering, politically, eyes literally open or closed.

Recalled in this scene of racist rape and sexual torture is the graphic scene of lynching, a related form of torture frequently sexualized with a pretext of racist accusations of rape. George and Henrietta's father had been lynched by this same party of white men, "before the shocked eyes of [his] little boy and girl" (54), when he refused to "loan" out (or hand over) his gun to them (51).[6] His sense of his own entitlement to self-defense and self-determination was a threat to be posed anew in the person of his son George. *Swamp Man* includes a character that is known as "Little Bro, a huge Negro who was a hard worker but a slow thinker. The huge man's mind had been snapped when, at the age of fourteen, he had been beaten up by a bunch of white men in the woods. He had interrupted them while they were raping two young black girls from the plantation" (76). The social and sexual violence of "white-supremacy" is chronic, systematic, and endemic; and the psychological consequences are treated as sometimes unbearably tragic. Surviving physically, Henrietta snaps and retreats into a childlike state much like "Little Bro" – a sort of traumatized "woman-child" to his "man-child" as a matter of fact.

Their grandfather's heart would give way at the sight of her recovering in the forest. He dies trying to help her. At his burial in the swamps, George Jackson takes stock and makes a vow that will leave him ambushing: "Tears began to roll down George's cheeks. He stood beside the grave and cried. Between tears he promised himself that one day there would be an accounting. The Jones brothers would pay for the crimes they had committed against his family, and they would pay with their only possessions, their lives" (75).[7] This class of white men has no other possessions. "They may be oppressed themselves, but in return they are allowed to oppress millions of others," thanks to the psycho-social as well as political-economic structures of racism (Jackson 1972, 183).

"This was the sixties," thought the protagonist in a moment of youthful naïveté shared by Henrietta, before Goines charts the condition of "neo-slavery" charted first and classically by *Soledad Brother* (Goines 1974, 17). Both sister and brother betray a hope that some mythical social "progress" out of the past will protect them from white racist terror in the present. Yet the Jones brothers knew to expect Henrietta because "Old Man Williams, who ran the post office, had been reading [George's] mail again" (17), placing him and Henrietta under surveillance. "The thought that nothing could really happen to his sister was no more than a foolish dream" (44). An "old man Jefferson" warns Henrietta at the bus station, "Gal, get back on the bus!" (25). He cannot convince her: "'You little fool!' he yelled angrily. 'If 'n you'd only listened, but you can't listen 'cause you done went and got too smart!'" "'Them honkies got somethin' in mind, 'bout you. I say they been talkin' 'bout it ever since last night'" (30). For him, her formal mis-education and misguided belief in mere liberalism rob her of every possibility of self-defense. Just seconds before she is assaulted, she thinks: "She had worried over nothing, all because an old man had seen a ghost behind every tree. In this day and age, things just didn't happen like they used to" (38). In the midst of her mauling, as she constantly calculates resistance, a belief in the white legal system (of "justice") persists: "After that, Henrietta made

78

up her mind to stop trying to fight them off and to save her strength so that one day she would be able to testify against the four brothers" (47).[8] George had thought that if "this had been in the time of slavery, they would have been patrollers, the men who ran down runaway slaves" (15). This is before he decides to become such a "runaway slave" or "Maroon." For Goines moves *Swamp Man* from the "sixties" of "civil rights" reformism and U.S. "Americanism" to the "sixties" of George Jackson's *Blood in My Eye* and *Soledad Brother*, ideologically, revolting against slavery or "neo-slavery" along with fascism and the sadism it entails.

Jackson's world-famous letters from prison reappear as letters from Henrietta to her brother George. *Soledad Brother* includes letters from George to his mother, his father and his brother Jonathan, most notably, besides his lawyers and Angela Davis, his "revolutionary love" interest and comrade. He is also concerned about his sisters Delora, Frances and Penelope ("Penny"). In *Swamp Man*, George is written by Henrietta in an interesting set of reversals and reiterations:

> Every other Friday he would go into town, and sure enough there would be a letter for him. Sometimes she even mailed a few dollars so he could buy the stamps to answer her letters. Sometimes she sent small lessons for him to do, even though she knew he went to the small school on Master Wilson's plantation. She was always trying to teach him things herself. (14)

The pride they take in each other as siblings evokes George and Jonathan Jackson's exchanges. It is fruitful to consider the flexibility of these fictional and non-fictional positions in detail: Goines renders Henrietta in the place of George L. Jackson, the older brother and teacher; plus, Henrietta's brother George in the position of Jonathan Jackson, the younger brother to be taught, or mentored; and George L. Jackson is pictured as an adolescent in the position of Jonathan Jackson, the younger brother who learns from an older sibling (here, Henrietta), transforms and then becomes a teacher himself – en route to militant guerilla actions driven by another variety of "revolutionary love."[9]

Confirming a whole network of kinship (literary and familial), there is also the father and grandfather of *Swamp Man* whose positions are similarly reversed and reiterated. In *Soledad Brother* the father is addressed as "Robert" or "Lester" and he is notoriously difficult to reach in terms of politics of resistance: "I would venture that there are no healthy brothers of his generation at all…. I would have him understand that although he had saved his body he had done so at a terrible cost to his mind" (Jackson 1970, 241). His fearful conservatism is embodied by the grandfather in Goines's *Swamp Man*, not the father who is a rebel to be lynched: George is ashamed of the grandfather who would not give him his gun, on the day his sister was set to return, because of the way he cringes whenever whites come around (Goines 1974, 20). A measure of redemption and understanding awaits him at any rate, for this was the case with Robert Lester Jackson and, far more so, Georgia Bea Jackson. The grandfather in *Swamp Man* reflects: "When he watched his only son die, he had held back for the children's sake, or he would have died beside his son that night. But someone had to live to take care of the small children. Now his job was finished. He believed George could survive without him" (64).

George only has a first name in *Swamp Man*. This is "because his father refused to give his freeborn son a slave name" (Goines 1974, 20). George's father in the novel embodies the spirit of self-respect, self-defense and self-determination of George's great-grandfather (more fully than his grandfather, "Ben"). It is this father who teaches George the byways of the swamps "that were only known by a handful of men" (10). It is he who helps rear George as a Maroon-in-the-making: "the boy had the same wild streak this his father had had" (21). George Jackson's own grandfather played this role in *Soledad Brother*:

> My grandfather, George "Papa" Davis, stands out of those early years more than any other figure in my total environment. He was separated from his wife by the system. He was living and working in Chicago – sending his wage back to the people downstate. He was an extremely aggressive man, and since aggression on the part of the slave means crime, he was in jail now and then. I loved him. He tried to redirect my great energy into the proper form of protest. He invented long simple allegories that always pictured the white politicians as the animals (jackasses, toads, goats, vermin in general). He scorned the police with special enmity. He and my mother went to great pains to impress on me that it was the worst form of niggerism to hook and jab, cut and stab at other Blacks.
>
> Papa took me to this his little place on Lake [sic] and fed me, walked me through the wildest of the nation's jungles, pointing up the foibles of black response to crisis existence. I loved him. He died alone in southern Illinois the fifth year that I was in San Quentin, on a pension that after rent allowed for a diet of little more than sardines and crackers. (Jackson 1970, 9)

He traces his *maroonage* back to this grandfather who died in the relative South, where his mother sent him for summers to get out "from harm's way" and where George himself dreams of cultivating a fine revolutionary force: "I learned how to shoot rifles, shotguns, pistols.... I learned how to identify some of the food plants that grow wild in most areas of the U.S.... Almost everyone in Harrisburg is a relative of mine. A loyal, righteous people; I could raise a small army from their numbers" (8). By and by, *Swamp Man*'s George will form an aggressive one-man army or rural force of vengeance in the absence of greater revolutionary numbers or circumstances, while he and Goines portray his enemies as animals in a deadly swamp country that only an ancestor's Maroon intelligence has taught him to navigate.

The author of *Blood in My Eye* had maintained with so much relevance for *Swamp Man*: "The lynch-murder of a friend – it makes me angry, not afraid. I'm the next man to be lynched! My forefather trembled when his brother was lynched, but my brother's immolation means war to the death, war to the utmost, war to the knife" (Jackson 1972, 34). What happens in *Swamp Man* to young George's father, sister and grandfather is what compels him to war, even if he has to wage it all by himself.[10] *Soledad Brother* defined neo-slavery as an "economic condition, a small knot of men exercising the property rights of their established economic order, organizing and controlling the life style of the slave.... [A]n economic condition which manifests itself in the total loss or absence of self-determination" (Jackson 1970, 252). "The forms of slavery merely *changed* at the signing of the Emancipation Proclamation from chattel slavery to economic slavery" (68). It initially defined fascism as a "police state wherein the political ascendancy is tied into and protects the interests of the upper class--characterized by militarism, racism and imperialism" (18). For praxis, *Blood in My Eye* would attack the problem of fascism more than any other text in Black radical tradition. It presents itself as a guerilla warfare manual to abolish fascism as well as neo-slavery locally as well as globally.[11] With an innovative focus on cities or urban sites of battle, it is partitioned into sections which speak volumes: "The Amerikan Mind," "Amerikan Justice," "Toward the United Front," "After the Revolution Has Failed: On Withdrawal," "Fascism," "Classes at War," "The Oppressive Contract" and, of course, "Blood in My Eye," where it is written: "We will organize a violence of our own, hidden and more aggressive. We fight from a position of weakness, but there are tactical devices that if employed without restraint will afford us a very real advantage" (Jackson 1972, 44).

Avenging the gruesome rape and lynching of his "shattered little family" (Goines 1974, 73), for a justice never codified in the history of North America, so long as it has been occupied by the United States of America, George Jackson in *Swamp Man* ambushes the Jones brothers one by one. These white men systematize their sexual violence against Henrietta and other Black women until it is brought to a no less violent end. Thus, Goines writes: "Two long, helpless years and the young boy developed into a young man. The day finally came when George wasn't a boy any longer but an avenging black man. He had gotten the size his youth had promised.... He had succeeded in keeping himself and Henrietta alive, surviving for only one purpose" (95).

First, returning to his cabin on a given night, George ambushes Jamie Jones and his friend, Willie, a handyman, in the gruesome-rapist act; he knifes Willie in the back, slits his throat and proceeds: "Jamie realized something was wrong when he felt himself being lifted up bodily from the young girl.... He raised his knife and stabbed upward into Jamie's gut" (98). He commanders Jamie and Willie's pistols to maximize his future chances. Capitalizing on white men's underestimation of Black men and his swamp sense, he keeps seeking "just the right spot to lay his ambush" (127). George uses the swamps for protection, a former "hiding place" for his father and grandfather (122), and historical Maroons. Before the other Jones brothers, the sheriff and his deputies figure out his big plan, he begins to stalk their party of hunters. Second, in spite of his lack of a long-range rifle, he is able to shoot "Sonny Boy" Jones dead, out of a slow moving boat, when they least expect it (154). Third, after he sneaks up behind Jake Jones on dry land and speaks a rare sentence aloud ("Now that's what I call a right pretty sight"), George shoots a begging Jake in the stomach with Jamie's pistol and brings Jake to his knees (178-79). Fourth, after sending a shotgun blast to Zeke Jones's stomach earlier, leaving him to suffer for several scenes or chapters as he is carried around by white men stricken with paralyzing fear, George finally kills the begging and suffering Zeke by "butchering" his genitalia (181).

This was "revolutionary love," also. He had used anger to help him "carry his burden" until this day of reckoning (73). The grown George Jackson gets an anti-rapist vengeance in *Swamp Man* by organizing a hidden, aggressive violence of his own; fighting resourcefully from a recognized position of weakness; and employing tactical devices without restraint to turn his disadvantage into a decisive advantage instead.

Relatedly, Jayne Cortez's poem "Rape" would reappear in a collection no less concerned with blood, and justice, *Coagulations* (1984), after its original publication in *Firespitter* (1982). The first stanzas speak to and on behalf of Inez Garcia in California. The second part is for Joanne Little of North Carolina. "Rape" speaks of and on behalf of "sister" Joanne, who had slain (in the year *Swamp Man* was published - 1974) the guard who entered her jail cell for the purpose of sexual violence: "This being wartime for Joanne / she did what a defense department will do in times of war." He forced oral sex at the point of an ice pick. When his guard is let down, reportedly after his rapist orgasm, she takes his ice pick and she takes his life: "Joanne came down with an ice pick / in the swat freak mother fucker's chest / yes in the fat neck of that racist policeman." The sadist and his system of pleasure get attacked in turn. The rapist is cast as disgusting in every way while a new form of pleasure is derived from resistance, one that slays the sadist and his sadism as an act of war. The Black Arts Movement poet has the survivor do a dance of celebration to be gleefully joined in: "from coast to coast / house to house / we celebrated day of the dead rapist punk / and just what the fuck else were we supposed to do" (Cortez 1984, 64). There is no question mark to punctuate this sentence repeated twice. JoAnne Little was vindicated of the charge of "first degree murder" thanks to many voices of support organized behind her, for justice. How many such stories have a much worse outcome, however? Henrietta does not survive in this same fashion outlined in "Rape" or Cortez's *Coagulations*. But who does in *Swamp Man*, or any Goines narrative? Indeed, Cortez had already written for the Jacksons themselves in "Libations," a poem from *Scarifications* (1973): "I witnessed / the lynchings of Jonathan and George / and heard bulldozers coming / for our ghetto tears" (Cortez 1973, 30).

Far from incidental to the war "to the knife" he wages in Goines's *Swamp Man*, George's castration of Zeke was the culmination of his guerilla strategy of justice which includes a dose of graphic "sexual poetic justice" as well. His slaying of Jamie and Willie puts an end to a sexual assault in progress. He castrates Jamie and mutilates this part of the white male that was the most offensive weapon in his rape or rapes of Henrietta, not to mention other Black women and girls. Jamie screams again and again, "like a wounded animal" (99), just as George heard Henrietta scream in the initial violation to be avenged. The tables are turned, politics of pleasure and pain rearranged: "It hadn't really been George's intention to get pleasure out of killing Jamie slowly" (99): "The taste of revenge was sweet" (103), nonetheless. On Willie and Jamie's corpses were "two faces that wouldn't bother him during the nights any more" (100). He feeds their bodies to "man-eating reptiles" (102), which was one of the most dreadful fates that could meet a man (12). Ironies abound. Not only does George go on to slay one Jones brother with another brother's gun, his aim is to slay them all with "no witnesses" (152). He witnesses for Henrietta and his family, mournfully. He knew and knows this witnessing to be vital, for the survivors and for the bereaved. George "laughed wildly" when he realizes Zeke hadn't been slain immediately, or without prolonged pain (179). If "Sonny Boy" never gets to see his slaying coming, Jake will scream and scream, too, more than he begs for mercy. For George: "The man's screams were music to his ears" (180). Jake is even *fed* his mutilated offending organ in the end (180). The white man will never get to "cut the black bastards nuts off," as he swore, to punish George for his own brother's death (167). Crucially, each of the Jones brothers is placed by Goines back into the position into which they had forced Henrietta; each of the men is left with a crippling sexual assault or victimization and a loss of life as they knew it – this time, again, for justice. Strategically, George has to slay each of the slain for justice as well as collective self-defense. If any remained alive, "it would mean that Henrietta would have to live the rest of her life back in the swamps because he would never be able to come out" (158). To put an end to the radical injustice of the systematic and ritualized sexual violence of the Jones brothers, and to avenge it in the ambush, a certain "sexual poetic justice" is required; and it has white men castrated instead of the Black male who is guerilla in *Swamp Man*.[12]

The title of George L. Jackson's *Blood in My Eye* comes from an experience writ large as an epigraph following its dedication page. It was written by one of his parents on the anniversary of his brother Jonathan's death:

> My dear only surviving son,
>
> I went to Mount Vernon August 7th, 1971, to visit the grave site of my heart your keepers murdered in cold disregard for life.
> His grave was supposed to be behind your grandfather's and grandmother's. But I couldn't find it. There was no marker. Just mowed grass. The story of our past. I sent the keeper a blank check for a headstone – and two extra sites – blood in my eye!!! (Jackson 1972, vii)

Even a resting place may be something else denied by this world. So in *Swamp Man*, George wanted at least to die in peace (Goines 1974, 158). The narrative carries him to a gravesite as well, where he visits his father and promises "to one day kill the bastard who had killed him for the rifle" (160). George is not afraid to die. "He had the eyes of a dead man, not yet dead" (86). In *Soledad Brother*, George Jackson boasts: "I might be the most resilient dead man in the universe" (Jackson 1970, 234). A "desperate man," George in *Swamp Man* is afraid that he will die without vengeance, without justice and without his sister Henrietta's safety secured.[13] Provocatively, Goines likens George to "the mother she never had" (Goines 1974, 99), across or beyond, even against gender now. Further, when George was burying his grandfather in the novel: "The thought occurred to him as he dug that he would never be lucky enough to be buried beside his father and grandfather. There was no one to bury him. The feeling was powerful, he knew he'd never rest beside them" (74). Henrietta will die in quicksand, "quietly, finally at rest" (137). Death is far from unusual for the major characters in Goines, yet Henrietta's final death is unusual in *Swamp Man* insofar as it is the novel's only death lacking in brutality. George is shot upon completing his mission – not once, but twice. When the brother of a Seminole named Jericho Canaan who was deputized by the sheriff to help track down George was killed, by accident, the surviving Seminole sibling "mopped the blood out of his brother's eyes" (117), in the identical language written to George Lester Jackson about his brother Jonathan.[14] The shelf life of *Soledad Brother* and *Blood in My Eye* is neverending in Goines's literary embrace of guerilla *maroonage*.

The link between sadism, neo-slavery and fascism should not go ignored. Classically, Aimé Cesairé would identify fascism in Italy and Nazism in Germany as colonialism's boomeranging back to Europe in *Discourse on Colonialism* (1955). Frantz Fanon would identify fascism or Nazism and sadistic torture as an essential element of French and all colonialism himself throughout *Toward the African Revolution* (1964). A Harlem-based "Black woman Communist of West Indian descent," Claudia Jones would identify the U.S. empire as a drive toward fascism in essays such as "An End to the Neglect of the Problems of Negro Women!" (1949). Like a good Black Panther, George L. Jackson's makes a series of these identifications over and again, ever mindful of the centrality of neo-slavery to life and death under capitalism and colonialism: "Born to premature death, a menial, subsistence-wage worker, odd-job man, the cleaner, the caught, the man under hatches, without bail – that's me the colonial victim." He is a theorist and practitioner of resistance to repression for good reason: "In every sense of the term, in every sense that's real, I'm a slave to, and of property" (Jackson 1972, 7). He condemns "the fascist industrialist state" (47) and fascism as "corporativism" (132), capitalism re-formed in crisis. His revolutionary responsibility is to "rip away its mask" (138): "Fascism and its historical significance is the point of my whole philosophy on politics and its extension, war. My opinion is that we are at the historical climax (the flash point) of the totalitarian period" (130). The terror and torture of this totalitarianism or repression is epitomized by official, "chattel slavery" on the plantation as well as neo-slavery on and off of official plantations. The U.S. is described for "the Black Colony" as "the greatest slave state in history" (10), "the greatest imperialist of all time" (16), and "the prototype of the international fascist counterrevolution" (134). "And of course [its] prisons attract sadists," he continues after his first definition of fascism in *Soledad Brother* (Jackson 1970, 18). He elaborates in *Blood in My Eye*, "I simply have never managed to develop a technique against nine armed men who are fascinated with damaging my private parts!!" (Jackson 1972, 99), linking sadism, neo-slavery and fascism systematically.

The revolt of George Jackson in Goines's *Swamp Man* (for "reparations in blood") is a revolt against sadism which subtly and sharply alludes to the Marquis de Sade, whose original "Sadism" was adapted by Italian filmmaker Pier Paolo Pasolini to make a different critique of fascism (without a critique of slavery) in *Salò or The 120 Days of Sodom* (1975). The Jones brothers of *Swamp Man* enact a routine and rather public, white-supremacist sadism in the form of the rape and torture of Black women (and, in all probability, the castration of Black men, etc.). Pasolini's *Salò* takes Sade's *The 120 Days of Sodom* (1785) from an earlier, eighteenth century French location and sets it in the mid-twentieth century near the end of official fascist rule in Italy. The point of this controversial, once-censored film is to critique the abuse of power by making shocking sexual abuse or violence an extended metaphor for political violence and its abuse of the people it reduces to subjects of their ruling-class desire for power, itself – a power which is very sexual and more than sexual at the same time.

Sade wrote *The 120 Days of Sodom* while himself in prison. It is located in a medieval castle, surrounded by forests, where four wealthy, powerful men lock themselves up with some accomplices and a number of male and female, adult and child victims of their every sexual whim. (Many of them will be murdered.) In *Swamp Man*, Goines speaks to this scenario of Sade's work *and* Sade's no less scandal-filled life. Henrietta is trapped and raped not in a castle, but outside in the forest; not by four "aristocrats," even, but by four "white trash" men who are now enabled in the Americas as sadists by their colonial race and racism. They organize this socio-sexual torture in an effort to "break" (Goines 1974, 66) and *zombify* Henrietta and other Black women and girls whom they desire to possess as permanent historical "slaves," regardless of the century of reference. A key component of this *Sadistic* strategy is Jake's use of "Spanish Fly" (36; 50-64). Outside his text, *The 120 Days of Sodom*, Sade was imprisoned for an orgy of violence he organized involving four female prostitutes. It would end in the forcible use of "cantharsis," or "Spanish Fly." Assumed to be an "aphrodisiac," it led to a court case and arrest for Sade under the charge of poisoning. For "cantharsis" is known to cause an excessive, excruciating irritation of a woman's urethra when ingested orally – a condition which was infamously exploited by "libertines" of eighteenth and nineteenth century Europe who valued "liberty" when it was their own, while conceding no "libertine" freedom whatsoever to women, prostitutes, "plebeians" or "commoners."

The young George Jackson in *Swamp Man* needs his grandfather to explain to him the effects of this sexual cruelty and the exploitation it is designed to facilitate, since it casts the illusion that the victim and eventual survivor of torture actually enjoys the torture: "It was too big for him to figure out himself" (Goines 1974, 62).[15] Goines comprehends and underscores the racial politics of sadism, its totalitarian assault on Black (male and) female embodiment, whereas Pasolini's *Salò* does not. Cinematically, it uses Black women and Black servants much like Sade would use "Spanish Fly," or "cantharsis," to advance its own European agenda with no regard for Black independence of body or mind. The George Jackson of *Soledad Brother* and *Blood in My Eye* enables Goines and *Swamp Man* to revolt against sadism, fascism and neo-slavery, in one fell swoop, beyond Italy, France or Europe, of course, under U.S. settler-colonial imperialism.

CONCLUSION

There is a tragic, unjust irony in the climax of Donald Goines's *Swamp Man*, even though it is politically and historically correct or accurate. George is shot fatally by Jericho, the deputized Seminole who lost his brother in the white sheriff-led hunt for George. This is a betrayal of the maroonage shared by Blacks or Africans and indigenous peoples of the Americas. The problem of the faithful (if ambivalent) servant is a running problem in the writings of George Lester Jackson, whether they are Black or non-Black "running dogs" of the colonizer (Jackson 1972, 5). Yet and still, Goines's concluding line is rich with significance as George falls back into a river, a welcoming river: "The Black waters of the swamp had finally gotten their man" (184). Since the river is traditionally the place of African spirits and the swamps historically the place of Maroons, George is falling back into the welcoming of an ancestral abode, or simply moving from one metaphysical plane to another, where and while all manner of political struggles continue. Before the shot was fired, this motion will invoke George Lester Jackson in no uncertain terms: "The tall black youth moved with the swiftness of a panther" (183). This is how *Swamp Man* brilliantly rewrites the scene of this Black Panther Party Field Marshal's passing on – as a murder by agents of the fascist slave state and society; in the midst of his unimpeachable practice of self-respect and self-defense toward self-determination and freedom; and as an ambiguous, physical death that is spiritually transcended by a revolutionary force which may be reanimated or resurrected at anytime, anywhere.

Three decades later, Freedom Archives would produce "The Murder of George Jackson" for *Prisons on Fire: George Jackson, Attica & Black Liberation* (2001), an audio documentary on the thirtieth anniversary of his unnatural death. On it Jonathan Jackson, Jr. recites: "Prison guards at San Quentin ruthlessly murdered George Jackson." Mother of George and Jonathan, Georgia Jackson offers more on what happened on August 21, 1971: "They set up his murder just like they do everybody else that speaks out against them; and they'll probably do me the same way because I am going to speak every chance I get…. People don't *love* this country so much; they're *afraid* of what their own country will do to them." As Lee Bernstein puts it in "The Age of Jackson: George Jackson and the Culture of American Prisons in the 1970s" (2007): "There were memorial services, work stoppages and silent protests at prisons around the country, but the most dramatic response to Jackson's death occurred at Attica State Prison" (Bernstein 2007, 319). The inspiration he provides for that uprising is detailed on *Prisons on Fire*; and it is an inspiration that continues to register today in alternative traditions of music and political activism, for example. All this confirms what his mother would maintain when asked by a reporter how she felt about losing a second son "under such violent circumstances" (and in such a short span of time): "I have sons throughout the world wherever people are fighting for freedom."[16]

Soon after his assassination, Donald Goines decided to usher him back into this existence via *Swamp Man* and, hence, to launch an intense discourse not only on his life and murder, but also what the revolutionary would term our hunger, our ills, our lack of peace; sadism and fascism as well as neo-slavery; our options for guerilla warfare – or the ambush; and a world to be "liberated from trash, pollution, racism, poverty, nation-states, nation state wars and armies, from pomp, bigotry, parochialism, a thousand different brands of untruth, and licentious usurious economics" (Jackson 1970, 266). This novel is Goines's major, incisive and timely contribution to "Comrade George" discourse, which is almost totally lacking in academia, most especially, even four decades later.

It would take a bizarre form of reasoning to suggest with Eddie Allen in *Low Road* (with its moralist, "low-rating," bourgeois title) that Goines's naming of *Swamp Man*'s "George Jackson" could just be an "uncanny coincidence." A body of criticism worthy of Goines is still in the waiting. Greg Goode could project *Swamp Man* as his "worst novel" because "anger" is viewed as a virtual "crime" in "From *Dopefiend* to *Kenyatta's Last Hit*: The Angry Black Crime Novels of Donald Goines" and elsewhere in the established order of power, knowledge and politics. After *Swamp Man*, Goines wrote the four-part Kenyatta series as if he were effectively led to his "Black Liberation Army" of fiction by George Jackson, *Soledad Brother* and *Blood in My Eye*. Contrary to Goode, the "fact that Kenyatta had to do battle in the streets against police and gangsters, and the fact that Goines killed him off" (Goode 1984, 47), this does not mean that Goines had "mixed motives" (46) concerning Kenyatta's motives or this violence of resistance. It indicates what the namesake of his ambushing Maroon protagonist in *Swamp Man* had written from Soledad Prison: "We attempted to transform the black criminal mentality into a black revolutionary mentality. As a result, each of us has been subjected to years of the most vicious reactionary violence by the state. Our mortality rate is almost what you would expect to find in a history of Dachau" (16). The lesson learned and taught beyond *bourgeois* "standards of literature" (whether white or Negro, of course) is that only through Black resistance, resistance and more resistance will Black revolution come despite the white-supremacist state and society of the United States of America and its global Western regime of repression and exploitation.

NOTES

1. *Cast the First Stone* was republished in its original, unedited and uncensored form years later as *Yesterday Will Make You Cry* (1998). Himes is born in Missouri and grows up in Cleveland, Ohio; Goines is born and raised in Detroit, Michigan. Both Black men knew "middle-class" upbringings as children but did not live "middle-class" lives or promote "middle-class" world-views as adults or artists, interestingly enough.
2. Dachau was "the first concentration camp for political prisoners" (not simply "Jews") in Nazi Germany and, further, a model for other concentrations opened after it.
3. The politics of *Death of a Revolutionary* are distinctly different from those of KRON 4's *Day of the Gun* (2002), a documentary program televised for local consumption in the San Francisco Bay Area.
4. "Dedicated to my mother, Myrtle Goines, who had confidence in my writing ability."
5. Huey Newton makes a Maoist distinction between deaths with heavy meaning or significance and those without any meaning at all when he eulogizes George Jackson. See his account of the "revolutionary death" versus the "reactionary death" in this appendix to *Blood in My Eye* (Newton in Jackson 1972, 196).
6. The setting of Henrietta's rape "under the trees of the forest" (80) can be read as a critical narrative connection made between the racist historical practice of lynching (with "Black bodies swinging in the southern breeze" – from trees, as Billie Holiday put it in song) and this racist historical practice of rape.
7. In the following decade, August Wilson would revisit these concerns of *Swamp Man* in *Ma Rainey's Black Bottom* (1981), as the trumpeter Levee remembers witnessing the rape of his mother by "a gang of white mens" when he was an eight year old boy—in Mississippi, too, no less:

   > My daddy came back and acted like he done accepted the facts of what happened. But he got the names of them mens from mama. He found out who they was and then we announced that we was moving out of that county. Said good-bye to everybody … all the neighbors. My daddy went and smiled in the face of one of the crackers who had been with my mama. Smiled in his face and sold him our land. We moved over with relations in Caldwell. He got us settled in and then took off one day. I ain't never seen him since. He sneaked back, hiding up in the woods, laying to get them eight or nine men."
   >
   > (*Pauses*)
   >
   > He got four of them before they got him. They track him down in the woods. Caught up with him and hung him and set him afire.
   >
   > (*Pauses*)
   >
   > My daddy wasn't spooked up by the white man. (Wilson 1985, 70)

8. Henrietta worked with the elderly at a "Martin Luther King convalescent center" (25), while away at a college evidently named for Abraham Lincoln, a president of slavery as well as neo-slavery in the social and political economic logic of George Jackson.

9. A commitment to "revolutionary love" prevails in the latter pages of *Soledad Brother*, powerfully. See Elaine Brown's "Love Beyond the Wall: The Resurrection of George Jackson" (2003), for more on this theme.

10. Even in his solitude, George's modus operandi in *Swamp Man* communicates the logic of the Deacons for Defense and Justice, for example, who were based in his Mississippi and Louisiana.

11. This is the "poor man [or woman's] war" (Jackson 1972, 83) – of the "mobile have not" (85), according to *Blood in My Eye*.

12. See the second chapter of *Hip-Hop Revolution in the Flesh* (Thomas 2009), for more on this concept of "sexual poetic justice."

13. George Jackson speaks of "the desperate men, and women, people" in *Soledad Brother* (321-22).

14. Jericho is not the only character in *Swamp Man* with "bloodshot eyes."

15. "He was so naïve that he really believed his sister was enjoying it," Goines writes (63), before George's grandfather is scripted to intervene.

16. This is why her son came to call her "a perfect revolutionary's mama" in the concluding letter of *Soledad Brother* (Jackson 1970, 329).

REFERENCES

Allen, Eddie B., Jr. 2004. *Low Road: The Life and Legacy of Donald Goines*. New York: St. Martin's Press, 2004.

Bernstein, Lee. "The Age of Jackson: George Jackson and the Culture of American Prisons in the 1970s." *The Journal of American Culture* 30:3 (September 2007): 310-323.

Bin Wahad, Dhoruba, Mumia Abu-Jamal and Assata Shakur. *Still Black, Still Strong: Survivors of the War against Black Revolutionaries*. Eds. Jim Fletcher, Tanaquil Jones and Sylvère Lotringer. New York: Semiotext(e), 1993.

Brown, Elaine. "Love Beyond the Wall: The Resurrection of George Jackson." *PROUD FLESH* 2 (2003): www.ProudFleshJournal.com.

Césaire, Aimé. *Discourse on Colonialism*. New York: Monthly Review, [1955] 1972.

Cortez, Jayne. *Firespitter*. New York: Bola Press, 1982.

————. *Coagulations: New and Selected Poems*. New York: Thunder's Mouth Press, 1984.

————. *Scarifications*. New York: Bola Press 1973.

Death of a Revolutionary. "World in Action" (Documentary Series): London, UK: 1971.

Fanon, Frantz. *Toward the African Revolution: Political Essays*. New York: Grove Press, [1964] 1988.

Freedom Archives. *Prisons on Fire: George Jackson, Attica & Black Liberation*. San Francisco, CA: AK Press/Alternative Tentacles, 2001.

Goines, Donald. *White Man's Justice, Black Man's Grief.* Los Angeles, CA: Holloway House Publishing Company, 1973.

————. *Swamp Man.* Los Angeles, CA: Holloway House Publishing Company, 1974.

Goode, Greg. "From *Dopefiend* to *Kenyatta's Last Hit*: The Angry Black Crime Novels of Donald Goines." *MELUS* 11: 3 (Autumn 1984): 41-48.

Himes, Chester. *Yesterday Will Make You Cry.* New York: W.W. Norton & Co, 1998.

————. *My Life of Absurdity: The Autobiography of Chester Himes, Volume II.* New York: Thunder's Mouth Press, 1976.

————. *The Quality of Hurt: The Autobiography of Chester Himes, Volume I.* New York: Thunder's Mouth Press, 1971.

————. *Cast the First Stone.* New York: Coward McCann, 1952.

————. *If He Hollers Let Him Go.* Garden City, NY: Doubleday, 1945.

Jackson, George. *Soledad Brother: The Prison Letters of George Jackson.* Chicago: Lawrence Hill Books, [1970] 1994.

————. Jones, Claudia. "An End to the Neglect of the Problems of Negro Women!" *Political Affairs* 28 (June 1949): 51-67.

Love, Monifa A. *Freedom in the Dismal.* Chicago: Academy Chicago Publishers, 1998.

de Sade, Marquis. *The 120 Days of Sodom.* New York: Grove Press, [1785] 1994.

Stallings, L.H. "'I'm Goin Pimp Whores!': The Goines Factor and the Theory of a Hip-Hop Neo-Slave Narrative." *CR: The New Centennial Review* 3:3 (Fall 2003): 175-203.

Thomas, Greg. *Hip-Hop Revolution in the Flesh: Power, Knowledge, and Pleasure in Lil' Kim's Lyricism.* New York: Palgrave Macmillan 2009.

Wilson, August. *Ma Rainey's Black Bottom.* New York: Plume, 1985.

Wright, Richard. *White Man, Listen!* New York: Doubleday, 1957.

CHAPTER FOUR

By Certain Codes

Structures of Masculinity in Donald Goines's *Daddy Cool*

Dennis Chester

I.

Much critical discussion of African American literature published between 1965 and 1975 focuses on the problematic association of patriarchal images of Black masculinity with the nationalist political agenda of the Black Power Movement. Several contemporary scholars have addressed the troublesome pairing of these issues, analyzed the prevalent gender assumptions of the era, and shown a repeated tendency of many of the period's leading figures to marginalize the role of Black women in the struggle for social and political equality.[1] For a number of literary works produced during the era of the Black Arts Movement,[2] whether essay, poem, fiction, or drama, these criticisms are justifiable and significant. At the same time, the wide influence of this critical approach has overshadowed many important works by Black men of the period who were much more ambivalent at least toward the ideas about masculinity proposed by the movement's most vocal or publicized representatives. While some members of the era's intellectual vanguard did valorize this male-centered perspective,[3] they were only a portion of a larger body of works written by and about Black men from a variety of points of view. Nevertheless, the patriarchal nationalist models of masculine identity forwarded by some Black Arts era cultural theorists have remained for many the primary representations of the time, drawing critical attention away from other representations of Black male experience.

The less doctrinaire voices from the Black Arts Movement, those that expressed uneasiness with the pairing of Black nationalism and Black patriarchy and who looked for other ways of expressing their notions of manhood, have found some scholarly attention. But even then critics have largely drawn these examples from statements produced by the era's intellectual elite. Some recent studies have addressed representations of Black men that did not easily fit into dominant masculine Black Power paradigms.[4] However, even as these critics examine alternate statements about Black masculinity, they still focus on authors who wrote from within established academic and critical circles; writers such as James Baldwin, John Edgar Wideman, and Ernest Gaines were able to find outlets for their dissenting ideas in respected journals and magazines and have, as a result, maintained a presence in contemporary discourse. However, while the notion of Black masculinity contained in their works provided a counterpoint to the masculine image established by writers like Amiri Baraka or Eldridge Cleaver, it was also closely engaged with a Western, academic literary aesthetic. Though these more formalist authors took the Black working classes as their subjects, their methods – and, in many instances, their readership – were of the elite.

Both of these critical approaches to Black Arts era representations of Black men therefore leave important questions unaddressed. What other literary representations of Black masculinity emerged during this turbulent decade? Were there expressions of Black masculinity that were not part of either nationalist or formalist positions? If so, how did Black audiences respond to and interpret these alternate masculine images? And how might these lesser known images shape or reshape our understanding of the Black Arts era? Some of these questions can be answered by turning to other bodies of fiction that have typically found little critical attention. In particular, a number of key themes and issues intersect in some of the period's genres of fiction – particularly, paperback crime and romance novels conventionally thought to be produced for rapid consumption rather than deliberate study. These books are revealing both as historical products and as engagements with their contemporary ideological discourses. As expressions of popular culture, they define points of contestation between dominant and subordinate groups over the interpretation of their lives and the meaning of their experiences.[5] In the words of John Cawelti, one of the central cultural functions of this formulaic literature is to "enable the members of a group to share the same fantasies" (34). Identifying and examining these shared fantasies in this genre of fiction is an important task for scholars wishing to further understand the concerns and ideals of African Americans during the Black Power era.

The body of work created in the brief career of novelist Donald Goines is a revealing example of the kind of meaningful questions raised by these understudied texts. Despite a lack of critical attention, Goines's novels became so popular that he would be credibly billed by his publisher as "America's #1 Selling Black Author." As an outsider author creating fiction for mass distribution, Goines faced considerable obstacles in his efforts to be taken seriously as a writer. However, despite the occasional mechanical problems contained in his book publications, these problems were secondary issues for the many Black people who purchased and continue to purchase and read Goines's novels. For these readers, Goines's picture of African American life resonated with their own. Reconsidering Goines and other figures considered marginal to or unassociated with the discourse on the Black experience brings these important resonances to the foreground.

Situating Goines within the discourse on Black masculine identity during the Black Power era, then, is important because his writing captured the popular Black imagination in a way that many more "serious" works did not and, as a result, engages with and challenges the attitudes and ideologies associated with his contemporaries. Goines's 1974 novel *Daddy Cool* is one specific example of the complex and multifaceted ideas about Black masculinity that emerged from within the Black community of the time. A grim look at crime and vice in the ghetto, *Daddy Cool* is also a family drama and draws on generic narrative structures to tell its tale. Throughout the novel, Goines's use of these genre structures problematizes any unifying understanding of Black masculinity and reinforces Hazel Carby's assertion that "ideologies of masculinity always exist in relationship to other ideologies" (4). *Daddy Cool*'s illustrations of masculine experience help to reveal these ideological relationships as they intersect in the ghetto underworld. Reconsidering Goines and widening the scope of Black Arts era texts under critical consideration to include this genre of fiction greatly enhances our understanding of this transformational era.

II.

"Pulp fiction" crime novels have a history that dates back to the early parts of the 20th century. *The Black Mask* magazine, which began publication in 1920, was one of the first outlets for a new kind of naturalistic prose about criminals and detectives and it opened the door for authors such as Dashiell Hammet and Raymond Chandler to create stories concerned with the same themes. Created under a model with explicit money-making aspirations, these early works of pulp fiction found less respect among critics who saw "literary fiction" as more artistic.[6] By the 1970s, though critical attitudes toward crime fiction had begun to soften, the genre was still rarely discussed in the academy. Like the majority of scholars in the white critical mainstream, most critics who associated with the Black Arts Movement found little to celebrate in these works. Some, in fact, saw specific problems created by pulp fiction's sensationalist nature. In a response to some works of Black literature focused on crime in the ghetto, for example, Black Power activist and poet Amiri Baraka asserted that just "[b]ecause someone can summon up the reality of black life doesn't mean that it's politically true. This fad of talking about whores and junkies and pimps! We who have a revolutionary commitment have to transform reality. If not, we are enemies of the people" (quoted in Towns, 17). For Baraka and others, these works were a fad; and if they simply depicted the more illicit aspects of the Black experience without including a specific effort at revolutionary social change, they were at best politically irresponsible. Therefore, while these critics could applaud a book like Sam Greenlee's pulp novel *The Spook Who Sat by the Door* (1969) because of its explicit revolutionary content, they found little to say about pulp novels like some of those written by Donald Goines that were less overt in their advocacy of social activism.

Despite this critical resistance, crime fiction maintained a significant audience in African American communities. Holloway House, the company that Donald Goines would eventually contract with, had successfully published works like *Pimp* (1967), the autobiography of confessed pimp and hustler, Robert "Iceberg Slim" Beck, and demonstrated the existence of an audience eager to read these gritty depictions of Black life. This was the same audience that, in film, was looking to the flashy styles of Blaxploitation. In short, many Black audiences were said to want entertainment that was accessible, drew on familiar formulaic structures, and that featured stars and protagonists who looked like themselves. Many publishers recognized the economic gains to be made by appealing to such audiences; and, like *Superfly* and *Shaft* did in the realm of action films, *Daddy Cool* and other African American pulp fiction works turned the crime fiction genre to African American subjects and themes.[7]

In *Daddy Cool*, these subjects and themes emerge through an intricate reinterpretation of the crime novel's basic structures – patterns set in place by the earliest crime novels of the mid-19th century. In the broadest sense, most crime fiction novels are comprised of three parts detailing the commission of the crime, the investigation of the crime, and the punishment for the crime. This broad category, however, is commonly subdivided into sub-genres based upon the degree of emphasis that the narrative places on the different components of the three part structure. *Daddy Cool* interweaves two well established crime fiction subgenres – the crime-narrative, which focuses on the commission of the crime, and the detective novel, which focuses on the investigation – in a way that brings unique qualities of Black masculine experiences to the foreground. Moreover, Goines's inclusion and reinterpretation of other crime fiction tropes and figures, specifically that of the femme fatale, bring a new complexity to the novel's representation of Black masculine roles.

Goines's innovative use of crime fiction's generic structures is apparent from the novel's opening moments. The book begins in the middle of things as the main character, Larry "Daddy Cool" Jackson, completes his work. Daddy Cool is a professional assassin for the Detroit underworld and the book starts as he closes in on his latest target:

> Daddy Cool relaxed. If William [his victim] could find anything to laugh about at this stage of the game, it showed that the man was shaking off the fear that had made him so cautious earlier in the day. Now it was just the matter of the right opportunity presenting itself. Then Daddy Cool would take care of his job and be on his way home in a matter of moments.
>
> At the thought of home, a slight frown crossed Larry's face. His wife would be cuddled up in the bed watching television at this time of night. Janet might be anywhere. Without him at home she would surely run wild, staying out to daybreak before coming home, because she knew her mother would be sound asleep by the time she came in. (9-10)

This opening scene, with its emphasis on Daddy Cool's criminal act, establishes the novel within the crime-narrative subgenre of crime fiction. This aspect of *Daddy Cool* provides the book with its most sensationalist qualities; in this opening scene and the ones that follow, Goines depicts the main character's criminal acts with fetishistic detail. In addition to their sensationalism, crime-narratives are further noted for their in-depth portrayal of the criminals' thoughts and interests as they go about their activities, a characteristic that *Daddy Cool* exemplifies. In the passage above, as Daddy Cool prepares to commit murder, his criminal act is far from the center of his thoughts. Instead, what he can't help thinking about is his home – his wife and his daughter.

Larry's daughter Janet is particularly important to the development of the narrative as she serves as the novel's femme fatale, one of crime fiction's recurring figures. In many crime fiction novels, the femme fatale tempts the protagonist into compromising positions with her beauty and allure. She is an object of desire that puts the main character at risk and who convinces him to take dangerous actions.

This is certainly the case in Goines's novel as Larry's concern for his daughter motivates one of the novel's central themes. By placing Daddy Cool's daughter in the femme fatale role, the novel shines a critical light on Larry's definition of himself as man, father, and comrade.

Janet's role as a femme fatale is also an essential component which allows Goines to utilize a second crime novel subgenre, the detective novel. The most popular of the crime fiction sub-genres, detective novels typically pay most attention to the second investigative portion of the crime fiction structure. The detective investigates the crime, using wit and skill to discover the culprit. In *Daddy Cool*, this detective story emerges as a result of Janet's actions: immediately after the opening scene, Janet runs away to live with Ronald, a pimp who has seduced her into a life of prostitution; as Daddy Cool tries to find Janet and bring her back home, he takes on the detective's role.

By bringing the crime-narrative and the detective novel into dialogue, *Daddy Cool* is able to explore themes of Black masculinity in unique and intricate ways. Daddy Cool is both a hit-man and a family man, and by contrasting the different crime fiction sub-genres the novel's opening scene juxtaposes these two facets of his personality. As he contemplates his victim, "Daddy Cool"—the hit-man persona— is as ruthless as his name implies; and the sense of paternal order and the possibilities for familial warmth suggested by "Daddy" are undercut by the detached ambivalence of "Cool." As Daddy Cool's thoughts turn to his family, however, Goines calls his character by the more personal, given-name of Larry and conveys the man's domestic concerns, thus fracturing the protagonist's image around the dense themes of the Black family, violence, and crime.

This nuanced vision of Black masculinity challenges other well-established images of Black men in American popular culture. In 1974, images of Black men in white mainstream culture were shaped by the legacy of public policy from the previous era of Civil Rights. Documents such as the 1965 Moynihan Report (officially titled "The Negro Family: The Case for National Action") had a lasting impact on American perceptions of Black men. Liberal in its intent, the Moynihan Report was commissioned by President Lyndon Johnson and authored by then Assistant Secretary of Labor and future Senator Daniel Patrick Moynihan. The stated purpose of the document was to encourage government agencies to assist Black families with economic achievement. The Report's rationale, however, was that Black families were caught in a "tangle of pathology," and undermined by a system of matriarchy caused by the absence of Black men (Rainwater 75). The negative image of Black men as unlawful, uneducated and unemployable that the report both defined and purportedly hoped to change, was drawn upon by later administrations and became part of the rationale for the "white backlash," a term that former president Richard

Nixon used to describe the turning of white attitudes and opinions away from the kinds of liberal advances brought about by the Civil Rights movement.[8]

Daddy Cool responds to this mainstream public image of Black men absent from their families by depicting Larry as a character primarily concerned with family issues. In so doing, the novel aligns with Black Power era artists and intellectuals who took it as their mission to define Black people in general and Black men specifically in ways that contradicted the white mainstream view. As Stokely Carmichael and Charles Hamilton would state in 1967, Black people would "have to struggle for the right to create our own terms through which to define ourselves and our relationship to the society, and to have these terms recognized" (35). Larry's focus on the family provides a stark contrast to the white mainstream view. Goines's entire novel, in fact, exemplifies Keith Clark's claim that because "Western culture has traditionally withheld 'subject positions' from 'captive' black bodies, literature has served as a vehicle for interrogating the pain of native sons trying to situate themselves within the confining discourses of Anglo-American male subjectivity" (2001, 203). Through Goines's use of generic pulp-fiction structures, *Daddy Cool* illustrates some of the effort and difficulty required to fit into these confining discourses. The crime-narrative's focus on Larry's innermost thoughts, for example, reveals his personal struggles and complicated relationship with mainstream society.

Among these thoughts, Daddy Cool's feelings about his house are particularly revealing of the problems many Black men faced and the strategies they used to claim a space in a discourse that granted them little opportunity to represent themselves:

> The neighborhood was still mixed but was quickly becoming predominantly black. The homes were well taken care of because the blacks in the neighborhood had paid top dollar to purchase the high-priced homes from the fleeing whites.... Daddy Cool had a feeling of pride as he drove slowly up to his expensive ranch-style home. He had it built from the ground up, after first putting his money into a poolroom so that he could give the appearance of being a smart businessman. He had been around too long to fall into the trap that many of the other money hungry blacks fell into: buying high priced homes with no apparent means of support. (20)

The symbolic functions of houses as signs of family, economic stability, and social achievement are well known. For Daddy Cool, the home where he lives with his wife, daughter, and two step-sons is a tangible sign of his success as a provider, a sign of his participation in mainstream ideas of success.

Daddy Cool's purchase of his home, however, also reveals yet another aspect of the crime-narrative, for this subgenre typically highlights individuals who exploit systems of order and power to their own advantage. In contrast to detective novels which normally show the commission of the crime as a disruption of order that is resolved when the detective solves the case, crime-narratives rarely show any concern with the disrupted social order. Instead, crime-narratives often depict characters that feel no regret for their criminal actions, and frequently justify them as the only means of achieving in a system that is inherently unfair. In Daddy Cool's case, he notes that he has attained entry into this middle-class enclave through the use of his criminal activities, most notably by using the poolroom he owns as a cover. Larry has attained the important middle-class marker of the home but has not had to otherwise adhere to the methods of achievement established by the white mainstream, methods which had been traditionally closed to Black men. Of course, even as he has attained this important marker, Larry's thoughts also reveal fissures in the image of Black middle-class status. Larry notes that his purchase of the house is associated with the idea of "white flight," and even though he may have achieved economic success, it is not a success that brings him entry into the white world. Nevertheless, Larry is content with his home as a sign indicating success to his Black community, even if the white world grants it no recognition. By foregrounding the novel's crime-narrative characteristics and the character's disregard for establishment policies, Goines speaks to a Black audience who looked to define themselves despite the objectifying gaze of the white mainstream. Larry's house is a sign of achievement not for the fleeing whites who don't matter to him, but to the Black community that understands Larry's obstacles and shares his views.

This Black community to which Daddy Cool belongs shares some characteristics with the ideas of community promoted by Black Arts era activists. Operating under the gaze of a white mainstream culture, but resistant to its influences, Black Arts scholars such as Addison Gayle would insist that "[w]hat black men demand from America is not validation of their identity as Americans, which would only assimilate them into the present society, but freedom and justice which would lead to the creation of a new society" (9). In other words, Gayle and other Black Arts intellectuals saw the present white-mainstream society as a problem in itself and sought a new society of their own free of the present society's flaws. As Larry's acquisition of his house demonstrates, he knows he is not moving into white society with his purchase; and, like Gayle, he actually has very little interest in assimilating into white society. In a fashion similar to Gayle's statement, Goines's characters are interested in defining a new society shaped by its own rules and values. It is here, however, that this similarity may end; the society envisioned in this Goines novel is one that rejects a white standard, but that falls short of articulating any sort of ideal society based on the "freedom and justice" that Gayle claims above. Instead, through the use of crime fiction formulas, Daddy Cool presents a deeply flawed society whose fundamental principles are contradictory. The nature of these contradictions reflects the precarious position of many Black communities in the early 1970s.

Larry's poolroom and the Black men who gather there are the principle representatives of this new community. Daddy Cool's poolroom, which provided him with the cover to purchase his house, is the source of an alternate social order where Black men of the community are able to find a stable sense of order. Earl, Daddy Cool's simple and hulking bodyguard, characterizes the pool hall's role as a sanctuary from the chaos of the ghetto street. Deformed and misshapen, Earl lives at the pool hall and finds in it a refuge from the cruel, prying eyes of strangers; the pool hall offers Earl a kind of protection from outsiders. Further, the poolroom is the one location where the men of the community can find compassion. After Janet has run away, for example, Larry is only able to reveal his true emotional distress to his companions at the poolroom.

At the same time, the masculine poolroom community does not welcome all men into its embrace. It is a selective community and only those who follow a strict code of behavior are allowed access. Earl runs the pool hall "the way a captain ran a ship," making sure that everyone follows his severely enforced codes of propriety. These codes re-emphasize the fairly traditional patriarchal roles that emerged in the novel's opening; among Larry and those other men he considers part of his circle the paternal role of father is idealized. In place of a state authority, which Daddy Cool and his community treat with disregard, the law of the father is invested with the greatest authority. Those men throughout the book with the greatest achievements, the numbers-runners and drug king-pins, are also and primarily presented as fathers. As stated above, Larry's identity as father allows the novel to provide a counter to images of Black men as absent fathers. Further, Larry's role as patriarch provides him with one of the few legal means he has for resisting the interpolating gaze of the mainstream power-structure.

Within the masculine community of the poolroom, fatherhood establishes one of the order's most basic rules as demonstrated when Daddy Cool takes on his last assignment. In Larry's last case, he is hired to kill three men who have transgressed the order of the poolroom community by raping the daughter of one of Larry's associates. Daddy Cool responds to the case with outrage:

> He knew it was going to be a grim job ahead of him, but it would have to be done. Men lived by certain codes and, when they were violated, a man had to take a stand. There were few things that Daddy Cool hadn't done in his lifetime. But he was proud of one thing: he had never raped anyone, woman or child. (177)

Daddy Cool takes on the job because he recognizes the actions as an affront to the "certain codes" of Black men's society. In particular, it is the assault on the child, undermining the protection of the father, that Larry sees as most abhorrent and deserving of punishment as a transgression of the masculine code. As he prepares for the case, Daddy Cool states that if it had just been a matter of theft, he would not have to kill the culprits. But with the rape of the child, the culprits have gone too far and must be punished fatally. That these men are also Larry's step-sons ultimately endorses the paternal hierarchy: because the boys have usurped the power of the father, arguably, they are appropriately targeted. The violation of the father's law can justify retribution, and the book provides detailed representations of the punishment Daddy Cool deals out to the men who committed the crime.

In dealing out its violent punishment, *Daddy Cool* provides another twist on the crime-narrative genre. Crime-narratives, after focusing on the criminal act, are usually fairly ambivalent about the notion of punishment. Daddy Cool, for example, never pays any price for his repeated acts of murder, and Goines's poolroom community focuses on punishment in only one instance, in this case of rape and when the law of the father has been disrupted. But if the punishment is presented as a "just" one that endorses the father's law and the masculine community, Goines's ideas about punishment in the detective novel components of the story reveal the arbitrary application of these "certain codes."

At the novel's conclusion, Larry's investigation of his daughter's disappearance has led him to new leads. In the poolroom Larry learns of Janet's whereabouts. She has gone to stay with the pimp, Ronald, who has started her working as a prostitute. When Larry finds out where Janet is, however, he also learns that the poolroom community does not condemn Ronald's actions. Instead, this same community which had previously condemned Daddy Cool's step-sons for transgressing the father's law condones Ronald's exploitation of Janet as a part of the hustler's code. In their eyes, Ronald has done no wrong and Daddy Cool has no right to punish the pimp despite what he has done to his daughter. The novel's ultimate tragedy occurs, in fact, as a result of a chain of events set in motion by Ronald's death. This basic contradiction in Daddy Cool's "certain codes" reveals that they are in fact quite uncertain. The law of the father and the hustler's code intersect in a way that creates significant difficulties to building a stable family or communal structure.

III.

Daddy Cool is noteworthy for its exploration of some significant ideas about self-representation that were parallel to those of the Black Arts Movement. Goines was certainly familiar with the popular news stories of his time and was aware of the Black activist community nationally and locally in Detroit.[9] Goines's response to Black nationalism, however, is also affected by a sense of realism or pragmatism concerning the conditions of life in the ghetto. The men of Goines's novel, the hustlers who used their best wits to survive on the street, embody this pragmatism. From Stagolee to Superfly, African American literature and culture has had a long tradition of focusing on Black men as outlaws. The moral impasse that Daddy Cool faces as he tries to save his daughter brings a new light to this tradition and opens up more compelling questions about the nature of Black American literature and the discourse on Black masculinity.

NOTES

1 For detailed discussions, see Paula Giddings, bell hooks, and Michele Wallace.

2 For further definitions of the Black Arts Movement, see Hoyt Fuller, Addison Gayle, and Larry Neal.

3 Examples of patriarchy and misogyny in Black Arts era texts are not unusual occurrences. For example, in *The Liberator*, a radical magazine of the era, William H. Banks argues that the struggle for women's rights should be secondary to the struggle for Black rights, going so far as to name the Women's Movement an "irrelevant revolution."

4 See Rolland Murray and Keith Clark.

5 See Grossberg and Stuart Hall for further definition and discussion of popular culture, its uses, and its interpretations.

6 See Tony Hilfer, Maureen Reddy, and Steven Soitos.

7 For a discussion of the more troubling aspects of the Blaxploitation era in American film, see Ed Guererro.

8 See Jeremy Mayer on the Nixon campaign's use of racial imagery.

9 Goines had previously included explicit mention of Black nationalism in his novel *Black Gangster*.

REFERENCES

Allen, Eddie. *Low Road: The Life and Legacy of Donald Goines*. New York: St Martin's Press, 2004.

Banks, William H. "Women's Lib: A New Cop-Out on the Black Struggle?" *The Liberator* 10.9 (September 1970): 4-5.

Carby, Hazel. *Race Men*. Cambridge: Harvard University Press, 1998.

Carmichael, Stokely and Hamilton, Charles. *Black Power: The Politics of Liberation in America*. New York: Vintage Books, 1967.

Cawelti, John. *Adventure, Mystery, and Romance: Formula Stories as Art and Popular Culture*. Chicago: University of Chicago Press, 1976.

Clark, Keith. *Black Manhood in James Baldwin, Ernest Gaines, and August Wilson*. Chicago: University of Illinois Press, 2002.

———. "Healing the Scars of Masculinity: Reflections on Baseball, Gunshots, and War Wounds in August Wilson's Fences" in *Contemporary Black Men's Fiction and Drama*. Ed. Keith Clark. Chicago: University of Illinois Press, 2001. 200-221.

Fuller, Hoyt. "Towards a Black Aesthetic" in *The Norton Anthology of African American Literature*. Ed. Henry Louis Gates. New York: W.W. Norton Company, 2004. 1853-1859.

Gayle, Addison "The Black Aesthetic" in *The Norton Anthology of African American Literature*. Ed. Henry Louis Gates. New York: W.W. Norton Company, 2004. 1912-1918.

Giddings, Paula. *When and Where I Enter: The Impact of Black Women on Race and Sex in America*. New York: W. Morrow, 1984.

Goines, Donald. *Daddy Cool*. Los Angeles: Holloway House Publishing, 1974.

Grossberg, Lawrence. "On Postmodernism and Articulation: An Interview with Stuart Hall" in *Stuart Hall: Critical Dialogues in Cultural Studies*. Ed. David Morley. New York: Routledge, 1996. 131-150.

Guerrero, Ed. *Framing Blackness: The African American Image in Film*. Philadelphia: Temple UP, 1993.

Hall, Stuart, and Whannell, P. "The Young Audence" in *Cultural Theory and Popular Culture*, 2nd ed. Ed. J. Storey. Hemel Hempstead: Prentice Hall, 1998. 61-67.

Hilfer, Tony. *The Crime Novel: A Deviant Genre*. Austin: University of Texas Press, 1990.

Hooks, Bell. *We Real Cool: Black Men and Masculinity*. New York: Routledge, 2004.

Karenga, Ron. "Black Art: Mute Matter Given Force and Function" in *New Black Voices*. Ed. Abraham Chapman. New York: New American Library, 1972.

Mayer, Jeremy. *Running on Race: Racial Politics in Presidential Campaigns*. New York: Random House, 2002.

Murray, Rolland. *Our Living Manhood: Literature, Black Power, and Masculine Ideology*. Philadelphia: University of Pennsylvania Press, 2007.

Neal, Larry. "The Black Arts Movement." *The Norton Anthology of African American Literature*. Ed. Henry Louis Gates. New York: W.W. Norton Company, 2004. 2039-2050.

Rainwater, Lee and Yancey, William. *The Moynihan Report and the Politics of Controversy*. Cambridge: The M.I.T. Press, 1967.

Reddy, Maureen T. *Traces, Codes, and Clues: Reading Race in Crime Fiction*. New Brunswick, Rutgers University Press, 2003.

Soitos, Stephen F. *The Blues Detective: A Study of African American Detective Fiction*. Amherst: University of Massachusetts Press. 1996.

Towns, Saundra. "Black Autobiography and the Dilemma of Western Artistic Tradition." *Black Books Bulletin* 2:1 (January 1974): 17-23.

Wallace, Michele. *Black Macho and the Myth of Superwoman*. London: Verso, [1978] 1996.

CHAPTER FIVE

'I'm Goin' Pimp Whores!'

The Goines Factor and the Theory of a Hip-Hop Neo-Slave Narrative

L. H. Stallings

My life is like a Donald Goines novel!

NAS[1]

With a discovery of the so-called underclass, terms like nihilistic, dysfunctional, and pathological have become the most common adjectives to describe contemporary black culture…. Unfortunately, too much of this rapidly expanding literature on the underclass provides less an understanding of the complexity of people's lives and cultures than a bad blaxploitation film or an Ernie Barnes painting. Many social scientists are not only quick to generalize about the black urban poor on the basis of a few "representative" examples, but more often than not, they do not let the natives speak.

ROBIN D. G. KELLEY[2]

Why have I never read an intense study of the films of Rudy Ray Moore, the novels of Iceberg Slim or Donald Goines, the music of Tyrone Davis, etc.? Why?

TODD A. BOYD[3]

I was seven years old when I first encountered the work of Donald Goines. An intelligent, curious, Southern Black girl living in 1970s Southern-fried poverty, I lifted the paperback from an aunt. After my first read I was hooked. It was easy to complete *Dopefiend* (1970), *Whoreson* (1971), *Swamp Man* (1974), *White Man's Justice, Black Man's Grief* (1973), and many of his other works by the time I entered middle school. Coincidentally, Hip-Hop provided me a soundtrack for these books. Just as I memorized the lines from all of the Roxanne battles, I learned to memorize passages and phrases from Goines's work before I had encountered Richard Wright, James Baldwin, or Ralph Ellison. I became literate and even more aware of my own class-consciousness amongst middle-class Blacks by reading the Goines canon about poor urban life and hardships. I did all of these things before I learned that I, as a Black female, it has been suggested, should not like or enjoy that kind of work. The blunt, violent, sexual, gritty realism was not supposed to appeal to ladies; but I wasn't a lady, simply a Queen B(itch) in the making. In the end, I am aware that if I had not found Goines I might never really have come to Wright, Baldwin, and Ellison. More importantly, I might have missed Gayl Jones, Toni Morrison, and Toni Cade Bambara. Goines was responsible for my finding and coming to them early. The issues of class so readily highlighted in his texts drew me to the study of literature. Like Hip-Hop culture does for those who live it, the themes and aesthetics of Goines's work demonstrate an in-depth understanding of class and the all-important difference between Negroes, niggers, and Blacks.[4]

Currently, the few existing critical articles on Goines offer a great admiration of, and devotion to, the "pulp fiction" of this writer. The same articles provide a brief biography of the author, examine his work in the context of gangster or popular fiction, and make the connection between Hip-Hop and Goines.[5] As evidenced by Nas, Tupac, Jay Z, and others, it is easy to see the love connection between Hip-Hoppers and Goines. However, it's much more difficult to understand the importance of his work to Black culture as a whole, especially when so many critics would just as soon ignore these texts. Fortunately, Hip-Hop culture has made it difficult to continue doing so. Very few Black cultural critics have the appreciation that would lend itself to a rigorous critical analysis. This analysis here begins with much appreciation and love.

Although most cultural critics ignore this fact, a solid connection exists between Hip-Hop and written narratives. The title of this essay contains a significant and memorable line from Donald Goines's *Whoreson: The Story of a Ghetto Pimp*, a coming-of-age tale about how a boy becomes the pimp he always dreamed he could be. The statement seems as if it could be a line from any number of current rap singles, but this exclamation of identity and purpose derives from a written narrative rather than an oral one. The narrative's very existence becomes a signification on African American popular and literary studies because it exists in the margins of both fields. If Hip-Hop culture and critical communities can move away from the mistakes of "authentic ghettoism," highlighted by the imagined life of Vanilla Ice, for example, to embrace and evolve styles and variations from coast to coast, then perhaps it does contain a place for the written. Similarly, if Black literary and cultural critics can rescue Pauline Hopkins's *Contending Forces* and Frances Harper's *Iola Leroy* from the abyss of Black literary texts, then surely someone should be doing, as Boyd suggests, an intense study of the work of Donald Goines, Iceberg Slim, and other writers who might very well be defined as producers of a Hip-Hop narrative themselves. For those detractors who think that may be too much praise or not an applicable comparison, please remember that it wasn't too long ago that the works of Hopkins and Harper were relegated to "silly women's sentimental romance fiction" not worth the time to analyze. However, contemporary critics continue to find valuable insights in each of those texts. Notably, Nas and other Hip-Hop artists proclaim that the lives of poor urban city dwellers mirror the life-situation portrayed in Goines' texts. Hip-Hop does not inspire or come to a Goines novel, then; Hip-Hop culture reflects back and samples Goines's texts, even though they are written.

This essay attempts to expose the field of African American cultural and literary criticism to its own class elitism as well as re-envision the current criticism of Hip-Hop away from the traditional and limited ideologies that work to narrowly define Hip-Hop culture. In bringing together my two concerns about African American literary criticism and the cultural phenomenon of Hip-Hop, I provide a cultural and literary analysis of Donald Goines as the basis for my theory of both the Hip-Hop narrative and Hip-Hop neo-slave narrative. I hope to build a bridge that will highlight the fluidity and boundlessness of Black culture. To be certain, this essay argues that Hip-Hop culture, despite all major studies to date, does indeed have a written text on paper. However, I will not call it "the novel" or "literature," but a ghetto neo-slave narrative of the highest qualities, those qualities being sustained and defined by the form itself rather than anything outside the tradition. In the end, my examination of Goines will provide evidence for my initial assessments of current Black cultural criticism, and display the importance of developing a late, but critical, investigation of Hip-Hop written narratives.

In *Yo Mama's Disfunktional!: Fighting the Culture Wars in Urban America* (1997), Robin D. G. Kelley discusses the impact of the sociological construct of the "ghetto" on how we view, disseminate, represent, and understand urban Black culture. But even as he argues the complex and rich cultural contributions of the "underclass," his analogy still manages to generalize values of Black, poor inner-city dwellers.

One of the major works to critically consider Black underclass culture, Todd A. Boyd's *Am I Black Enough For You?* (1997), falls prey to Kelly's ill-stated but correct assessment. Boyd's work makes tremendous strides in analyzing why we fail to offer insightful studies on poor Black culture: "Because they do not easily fit with what we consider acceptable, and because they are the work of the lower class that has never transcended the world of folk culture in which they exist" (9). Boyd acknowledges the detrimental impact of politicizing the objects studied. Black underclass culture contains a different set of politics and a variety of contradictions as far as gender, sexuality, and race are concerned. Despite Boyd's clever logic, his entire work becomes devoted to already sweeping notions of urban poor culture. He asserts the importance of Black, male urban culture of the West coast in opposition to the commercialization of Afrocentricity. His textual analysis centers on rap music, 'hood films, and basketball to ascertain the "real" of ghetto mentality and culture. Granted, Boyd cannot cover every piece of Black urban culture; but why does he bring up the work of Donald Goines and Iceberg Slim, as well as the films of Rudy Ray Moore, if not to address them? Just as the cultural products he chooses to examine contain politics contradictory to Black empowerment politics, the cultural art he chooses to avoid contains obstacles to his theoretical task of representing the "real." The films of Rudy Ray Moore contain some of the most folkloric metaphors and allegories in Black popular culture—some urban and Northern, but others rural and Southern. An analysis of Moore's films would destabilize his focus on West coast urban culture as the real. Most significantly for this piece, the work of Donald Goines serves as a major contradiction to what is said to be real about ghetto culture and ghetto mentality.

Exploring the Definition of Hip-Hop and Literary Text

In recent years, the field of Black Studies has exploded with work on Hip-Hop culture. In *Black Noise: Rap Music and Black Culture in Contemporary America* (1994), Tricia Rose states: "hip-hop replicates and re-imagines the experience of urban life and symbolically appropriates urban space through sampling, attitude, dance, style, and sound effects" (22). Geneva Smitherman (1999) insists, "the term hip-hop refers to urban youth culture in America. Hip-hop is manifested in such cultural productions as graffiti art, break-dancing, styles of dress (e.g., baggy pants, sneakers, Malcolm X caps worn backwards), love of b-ball (basketball), and so forth" (268). Cultural critics such as Russell Potter (1995), William Perkins (1995), Nelson George (1999), and Bakari Kitwana (2002) concur with this definition. In examining this accepted definition of Hip-Hop, it is the "and so forth" of the culture that I wish to further explore. When we seek to examine all of the cultural productions in which Hip-Hop may manifest itself, there is routinely an absence of one particular cultural production: the written text.

In today's Hip-Hop hungry and greed-driven atmosphere, it seems timely to address questions of the production, reception, and distribution of the written text, the aesthetics of the folk, and Hip-Hop culture. Once we remove elitist notions, it might appear obvious that written texts arise from Hip-Hop culture and Hip-Hop heads. One need only witness the rise and proliferation of Hip-Hop websites or magazines such as *Vibe*, *The Source*, and *One World* to garner a glimpse of Black middle-class appreciation of Hip-Hop, along with advertisements of a few choice white mainstream product lines.

However, when talking about Hip-Hop culture and a written text we should turn more centrally to texts put out by those conscious of lower-class creators and purveyors, like *F.E.D.S.* (*Finally Every Dimension of the Streets*), *FELON* (*From Every Level of Neighborhoods*), *Murder Dog*, not to mention the now defunct *BLU* magazine or all the regional and local newspapers and files. These magazines, which advertise independent artists and rarely some of the bought advertisement of material culture, provide a reminder that Hip-Hop is a product self-sustained by the Black cultural masses. However, with the bombardment of false or ill-conceived notions of Hip-Hop culture and written texts, and the mainstream "embracing" of select Hip-Hop culture for monetary purposes, it behooves Black Cultural Studies to begin a serious analysis of Hip-Hop narratives.

Forget that everything we know about Hip-Hop is based on this romanticized notion of the folks not being able to read, and pay attention to the producers of the culture. When Nas raps about Goines, it's because he reads. If rappers such as Noreaga, Tupac, Jay-Z, Foxy Brown, Lil' Kim, and Queen Pen can cite references or sample lines from a Slim or Goines text, then surely this is evidence to dispute the misconception that the urban folk don't read. When prison inmates, constituted from a majority of Black and Latino men, reportedly not readers, construct magazines or write books, something is definitely going on with the folk.[6] This work does not seek to fetishize the written word, but to fully investigate Black folk culture, even if it means going to a written text. Every oral art form isn't for the masses. Every written piece isn't simply for the bourgeoisie.

Arguably, we should not entertain ideas in our heads of Pookie, Peaches, Lil Mo, Bo-Bo, and Ray-Ray lounging in a Barnes and Noble, selecting a 'hood reader of the month. But shouldn't we allow for some middle ground? What about the masses partaking of some fried fish, drinking a "40," and arguing about how they can be like Whoreson or Kenyatta? Or what about those sistas over somebody's house, getting their hair "did," discussing the sad real-life predicaments that could lead many poor Black females to be in the same situation as Chink in *Black Girl Lost* (1973), a female dealing drugs for survival? Where is an understanding of the middle ground that reveals Donald Goines as the writer who explores the underclass's struggle to become "Black" rather than niggers or Negroes? Current theory and criticism of Hip-Hop fails the culture itself because it falls prey to the discourse of social scientists and anthropologists who have ethnocentrically defined ghettoisms and the Black oral tradition. In addition, critics appear fearful that if they admit the possibility of such a text, then Hip-Hop loses its Black authenticity.

While concerns of authentic Black culture may explain why Black cultural criticism has failed to embrace notions of a written text from the urban Black underclass, the same cannot be said of Black literary criticism. The failure of Black literary critics to fully comprehend a text from and about the ghetto native becomes very much an issue of politics. In *(Dis)forming the American Canon* (1993), Ronald T. Judy recalls the Yale seminar in (1977) that he deems a significant historical moment in the construction of African American literary theory: Robert Stepto, Jr. organized and directed the seminar. Stepto stated that the goals of the seminar were to yield an under-standing of Afro-American literature in order to reconstruct its mode of instruction:

> This particular project of canon formation that emerged from the Yale seminar established the strategic importance for Afro-American cultural studies to delineate the genealogy of its thought as a means of nullifying the interdiction placed on it in the authorized historiography of American culture. (3)

Judy connects the Yale seminar's effort with that of the poststructuralist work of critics such as Henry Louis Gates, Jr., Houston A. Baker, Kwame Anthony Appiah, and others at the Yale seminar. Thus, poststructuralist work becomes a prevalent factor in the shaping of African American cultural criticism, but it is a mixed blessing. At this point, no one is concerned with how poststructuralism may or may not affect which works will be considered canonical—and why should they be if, as Yale scholars testified, the signifying Black difference for the canon was Black language. If Black language were the only qualification for the shaping of literary canon formation, criticism, and theory, then Goines would not be so easily dismissed from African American cultural theory; but criticism reveals other factors. The manufacturing of a canon is problematic in any context, but especially in Black culture. The conscious beginning of a crucial effort to theorize the cultural texts, products, and experiences of Black Americans takes place in a white, elitist institution. The site of cultural criticism shapes the nature of the criticism.

In *Black Literature and Literary Theory* (1987), Gates poses several important questions for the development of African American literary theory:

> What is the status of the black literary work of art? How do canonical texts in the black traditions relate to canonical texts of the Western traditions? How are we to read black texts? For whom do the critics of

black literature write? How does this split readership affect the work of criticism? (1)

Questions of status and comparative analysis of two separate traditions problematize canon formation, primarily because critics and promoters have to be concerned with how a body of work is going to look and appeal to whites. Canon formation asks what whites will think; is it as good as some Western texts, and are the images and representations too negative, too guttural, too animalistic, or too "ghetto"? *What if a text does not have the split readership?* What becomes of this theory and the question concerning status for someone like Goines, whose work has that signifying Black difference—whose work, for all intended purposes, is a Black writer writing for a mass Black audience?

To circumvent the mistakes of previous literary and cultural studies, any theory concerning Hip-Hop and a written text must focus on the conception of the narrative, as opposed to a novel or literature, avoiding privileging the written over the oral. Amiri Baraka's "The Myth of a 'Negro Literature'" (1966), published under the name of Leroi Jones, makes possible the notion of a Hip-Hop narrative theoretically. The title of Baraka's piece may at first seem to be tied to sociological questions: does the Negro have a history or culture? It moves beyond the simple answer of "yes." As he comments on the imitative writing styles practiced by early African American writers from Phyllis Wheatley to Charles Chestnut, Baraka's essay exemplifies a necessary critical insight: "In most cases the Negroes who found themselves in a position to pursue ... the art of literature have been members of the Negro middle class, a group that has always gone out of its way to prove to America, and to the world at large, that they were not really who they were" (106). Baraka's point signifies on the myth of nothingness or the Negro as *tabula rasa.* In this case, a particular class of Black people strives to create an art that validates them; but they are, at the same time, imitators of the very white culture that creates the Negro, not acknowledgers of their African cultural heritage. Their conceptions of literature and the novel are automatically embedded with class values, middle and bourgeois; and, for this reason, it becomes difficult to conceive of a written text by the underclass folk.

So what would a Hip-Hop narrative look like, let alone a Hip-Hop neo-slave narrative? If we did not have to consider concerns of production, labor, and value, it would be all too easy to suggest that the Hip-Hop narrative is one that reflects the dominant language, dress, values, and cultural creations of the Black urban underclass. Artificially, a Hip-Hop narrative might look something like Syndicated Media Group's new line of "Hip-Hop" texts. Syndicated Media Line (S-line), conceptualized by Marc Gerald and actor Wesley Snipes, publishes short fictional works about the lives of various underclass characters immersed in a world of crime. Gerald, a contributor to the *Village Voice*, has always described himself as a huge fan and critic of Iceberg Slim and Donald Goines. He, like a small number of other U.S. critics and numerous French critics, has voiced consistent critical praise for both writers. Yet he falsely proclaims himself as responsible for "unearthing and re-releasing" Black pulp fiction. As we will see later, the works of both authors have always been known to the Black masses, without critical attention from white as well as Black literary critics. Despite Gerald's adept skill at influencing W. W. Norton to begin an Old School series of Black pulp fiction, featuring two works acquired from Holloway House authors Goines and Slim, S-line texts appear to be poor imitators of original Hip-Hop texts.

If we are only concerned with surface appeal, this line has all the potential to be called Hip-Hop fiction. A CD including rap songs by notable Hip-Hop artists accompanies the book. The actual fiction incorporates the slang and language of the street, rapping, mixing, graffiti art, and current aspects of materialism present in Hip-Hop culture. For example, one of the first works from the line, Ronin Ro's *Streetsweeper* (2000), depicts main character Jerome Usher as a thuggish professional killer. Jerome wines and dines enough women to cast a Nelly and Luke video put together. The character could have easily stepped out of a pricey, commercially successful Hip-Hop video. The storyline of the work centers on Jerome's mistakenly shooting a little girl, in the process of killing his original mark. When Jerome falls in love with the child's mother and decides to start a new life with her, he decides to complete one last hit to help finance the little girl's life-saving surgery. However, even this touching turn of the plot cannot overcome the basic lack of critical depth necessary for a work that its publishers bill as Hip-Hop fiction. In one passage, Ro narrates Jerome – admiring his own crib:

> The place was enormous, befitting his status as a player: high ceilings, clean white walls, white shag carpeting and big bay windows that overlooked the enormity of the New York City skyline.... He had everything a muthafucka could want ... fully stocked bar, sedate leather sofas and chairs, an 80-inch mission armoire and matching bookcase ... 46-inch Sony Flat Panel ... $1500 Blatt Billiard table ... Versace, Armani, Valentino ... Cartiers, Patek Phillipes, Boucherons. (13)

While early critical commentary on these works focused on the materialism and cartoonish violence of the text, this work chooses to focus on why the publisher heralds these books as Hip-Hop texts.[7] As one reviewer of the fiction argued: "For its first forty pages or so, *Street Sweeper* attempts to integrate hip-hop into its narrative in the most irritating and distracting way possible: by having random rappers show up every few pages for wordless cameos. No matter where the protagonist may go, or what he does, there always seems to be a member of Mobb Deep or Mack 10 or Guru waiting to give him mad props for being such a down brother. It's an obnoxious ploy, as is Ro's clumsy employment of hip-hop slang."[8] Again, if these elements comprise the aesthetics and culture of Hip-Hop culture, then the S-line does not incorrectly label itself. However, with the text price ranging from $14 to $16.99, a hefty sum of money from the masses whom the line is supposed to be geared towards, we should analyze the production a little more closely.

Based on the quotations that opened this essay, we should argue that Hip-Hop heads were already reading the texts of Goines and Slim. The two forms become interchangeable. Hence, Gerald's pitch for his new line of fiction becomes a misconception of the very urban lower class he seeks to exploit: "I wanted to create a place where people who'd never really thought of picking up a book for entertainment could turn. My mission was to bring books to people. We want people to be able to read them in two hours, between subway stops. We want to make them democratic.... A lot of people don't know what it means to pick up a book for pleasure" (Gardiner 2000, 2). At almost twenty dollars a pop, can we really accept Gerald's assessment? No; and like the academic critics who ignore written texts of hip-hop culture, Gerald mistakenly interprets literacy and literature through the bourgeois Victorian values of the novel. He never considers the actual written text produced by the folk, the narrative. He doesn't have to take up the colonial role of missionary to bring anything to the folk because they already have what he wishes to offer, if not more. Furthermore, by separating pleasure from utility, Gerald situates his line of books in a Eurocentric conception of culture. Narratives by Black folks encompass an African understanding of art as both practical and pleasurable.

In the end, context acts as the biggest determinant in seeing Syndicated Media's line of books as mere imitators of Hip-Hop texts. Gerald commissioned music journalists and novelists to turn his ideas into books that are about 150 quick pages. No different from record executives, Gerald seeks to mass-produce and automate a culture that came into existence to defy human automation. To conceive of Syndicated Media Group's line of books as Hip-Hop texts is to forget that Hip-Hop culture derives from the conditions and contexts of neo-slavery, and neo-slavery, rather than 150 paid staff journalists, produces Hip-Hop neo-slave narratives.

Neo-Slave Narratives and the Culture of Hip-Hop

Imagine a narrative that contains the wisdom of George Jackson's experience of bondage, the brutal "confession" tone of Nat Turner, the controversial stance of Etheridge Knight, the skill of transgressing gender and sexuality perfected by Iceberg Slim and Red Jordan Arobateau, the creative voice and aesthetics of Ishmael Reed, the timing and rupture of Grandmaster Flash, and the soulful street insight of Tupac. The imagined narrative is the Hip-Hop neo-slave narrative, and we no longer have to imagine such a work because Goines perfected it. Yet, without the proper critical tools, the text becomes problematically defined and limited to something less than it is.[9]

In the past, slave narratives conveyed the experience of the slave in a way mindful of abolitionist and antislavery rhetoric. As Toni Morrison (2002) once said of the original slave narratives, "No society in the history of the world wrote more—or more thoughtfully—about its own enslavement. The milieu, however, dictated the purpose and the style.... [P]opular taste discouraged writers from dwelling too long or too carefully on the sordid details of their experience" (12). Consequently, the neo-slave narrative continued the tradition of exposing Black bondage with notable differences and goals. Scholars have defined neo-slave narratives as: "modern or contemporary fictional works substantially concerned with depicting the experience or effects of New World slavery. Having fictional slave characters as narrators, subjects, or ancestral presences . . ."[10] However, the literary definition of neo-slave narratives seems limited by notions of antebellum chattel slavery and constraints of canon-making.

Other definers of neo-slavery used criteria with a more continuous and materialist frame of slavery. Activist George Jackson admitted in his neo-slave narrative, *Soledad Brother: The Prison Letters of George Jackson* (1990):

> Slavery is an economic condition. Today's neo-slavery must be defined in terms of economics.... Chattel slavery is an economic condition which man-fests itself in the total loss or absence of self-determination. . . . The new slavery, the modern variety of chattel slavery updated to disguise itself, places the victim in a factory ... working for a wage.... [T]oday's neo-slavery does not even allow for the modicum of food and shelter. You are free to starve. (251)

Despite promises and hopes of a better future, Jackson writes his words during the Black Power/Civil Rights era. His work represents a key example of a neo-slave narrative dedicated to the abolition of twentieth-century Black bondage. As white mainstream and academic communities co-opt the literary neo-slave narrative form, new narratives evolve and emerge. The Hip-Hop neo-slave narrative combines the fugitive slave's narrative with the free ex-slave's narrative, linking the autobiographical with the fictionalized. It accomplishes the neo-slave narrative's assessment of economic slavery in addition to the original slave narrative's discussion of chattel slavery.

Hip-Hop culture becomes the evolved neo-slave narrative, the byproduct of neo-slavery. As Rose (1994) determines, "Hip-Hop emerges from the deindustrialization meltdown where social alienation, prophetic imagination, and yearning intersect. Hip-hop is a cultural form that attempts to negotiate the experiences of marginalization, brutally truncated opportunity, and oppression within the cultural imperatives of African-American and Caribbean history, identity, and community." Hip-Hop attempts to "negotiate new economic and technological conditions" (24), and consistently creates neo-slave narratives of breakdancing, graffiti drawing, rapping, and deejaying. Hip-Hop acts as the cultural marker of a decolonization process. Because hip-hop incorporates the body as form, in addition to technology, expressing oppression, concerns of chattel and economic slavery are embedded into any Hip-Hop discourse. But even before the emergence of these Hip-Hop neo-slave narratives, another was present.

The Labor(er) of the Hip-Hop Neo-Slave Narrative

Jackson's definition of neo-slavery exposes a fatal flaw in current literary theories that define neo-slave narratives. While literary scholars appreciate the text, they forgo an analysis of the genre's authors as neo-slaves. Whereas criticism of nineteenth-century antebellum slave narratives consistently diagrams the text, it also pays notable attention to the conditions and bondage of the author, a consideration that has been absent from neo-slave narrative analysis. The only way to allow a full critique of neo-slave narratives is to be guided by the wisdom of Jackson and others. It is Black nationalist rhetoric about "the new slavery" that reveals the complexities embedded within the works of Donald Goines. In examining the labor and production of early Hip-Hop, we've already noted the impact of deindustrialization on the formation of Hip-Hop culture, as a culture created from broken parts: "hip hop transforms stray technological parts intended for cultural and industrial trash heaps into sources of pleasure and power" (Rose 1994, 22). The innovations of the culture stress its resilience and stamina in a space of clutter, overpopulation, and socially oppressive policies. Ironically, the very traditional forms deemed Hip-Hop—breakdancing, graffiti tagging, rapping, and deejaying—are at once the result of a loss of place and space, politically and socially, but at the same time the practice of corporeal freedom.[11]

Donald Goines began his career as a writer in prison. Even before physical incarceration, after a stint in the army, he became a life-long heroin addict. Soon thereafter, he engaged in criminal activity to support the habit that held him in bondage all his life. In the span of 15 years, he was arrested numerous times.

During one period of incarceration at Jackson State Prison in Michigan, Goines began to write Westerns. However, after reading the work of Iceberg Slim, Goines began writing ghetto narratives (see Light 1999). Goines's background, like that of Grandmaster Flash, DJ Kool Herc, and Crazy Legs, provides a context in which we can fully understand the written Hip-Hop text, the Hip-Hop neo-slave narrative. Before enlisting in the army, Goines, a high school dropout, had been socially and economically oppressed. As an adult, he had no access to technological advances, only heroin. Consequently, because of his heroin addiction and his time in prison, he had little or no access to his body, unlike the previously mentioned forefathers of Hip-Hop culture.

In a prison cell devoid of turntables, microphones, records, paints, or buildings, Donald Goines helped create the Hip-Hop narrative. Unlike the original slave narrative, these Hip-Hop neo-slave narratives do not fetishize the written word or privilege literacy. Literacy, or writing words on paper, simply becomes a means to an end to replace those other unavailable outlets in which the oppressed can express their bondage. In the Hip-Hop neo-slave narrative, literacy is not merely about learning how to read and write *belles lettres*, it is about maintaining rather than coming into consciousness despite the absence of body. African American cultural aesthetics, always credited as aural and oral, in this genre survive the limited confines of a steel cage. In the case of Goines, this absence of body becomes further complicated by his heroin addiction. In addition to physical confinement, the chemical addiction controls his body. Like the postindustrial/deindustrialized New Yorker, the bound and oppressed body has to find a form. This is not to echo the theory of the slave writing himself into being, which implies writing himself into consciousness.[12] The authors of Hip-Hop neo-slave narratives are already conscious about the oppressive nature of their existence in the new world. They understand that they are not the Negro because the "Black Belt"[13] has shown and provided the writer with all of those elements since birth. Yet, under the influence of drug addiction or in the penitentiary, even as physical well-being or brute strength of the body may be stressed through weightlifting or sports, the person in bondage has no use-value for his own body. Deprived of body and technology, the physically bound Goines turns to an old form that it previously rejected. Paper and the written text becomes the form, the carrier of the consciousness previously trapped in the devalued body. Ironically, the risk of enslavement persists long after the author has found the form.

Production and Commodification of
Hip-Hop Neo-Slave Narratives

Like many slave narratives and neo-slave narratives, Goines's texts, as well as his image as a writer, remain impacted by editors and publishers. Holloway House geared the early production of Goines's work to a lower-class, supposedly barely literate, segregated Black population. The covers had to be cheap and mass marketable in a way that would turn a quick profit. Every part of the cover had to submit to Black aesthetics and sensibilities. Hence, the all-black cover reflected a cultural awareness of Black Power, and at the same time, the colorfully animated drawing of Black characters provided a vision of Afrocentricity not reproduced on many book covers during the 1970s. The titles of the novels were often in ruggedly bold type font. Every facet of the cover worked to convey the dangers and morbidity of Black underclass tales. Often found in Black-owned businesses, consumers who rarely had money to spend on a newspaper could walk away with a cheap Goines work that reflected their own life and cultural aesthetics.

As Goines grew in popularity, and the cultural phenomenon of Hip-Hop culture crossed over into the mainstream in the mid-1980s, Holloway House changed the covers of Goines's novels to benefit from mainstream appreciation of poor urban Black culture. The publisher replaced the all-black covers with all-white covers, amid titles in neat bold lettering. While the black cover exhibited rough animation, the white cover exudes the sophistication of small photographic clips that mirror the title's underworld theme. The marketing strategies of Holloway House mirror mainstream society's marketing and commodification of Hip-Hop, while colliding with early eighteenth- and nineteenth-century promotion strategies of slave narratives. Holloway House controls the textual product, but they also control the body product—the writer as well as his image.

If Frederick Douglass may have eventually been able to address the way abolitionists wanted to control his words, writing, and image,[14] Donald Goines did not have this option with Holloway House. He died in the midst of his promising career. In ways that mirror Tupac Shakur's career and relationship with Death Row and Suge Knight, Holloway House controls all things related to Donald Goines. In an interview with a *F.E.D.S.* magazine writer, Goines's sister, who read and corrected drafts of her brother's work, reveals the extent of Holloway House's control:

> There's an autobiography out their called "Donald Writes No More." Its fake, its bull. They came to my grandmother's house when he first died. He wasn't even cold yet and they had her answer a bunch of questions,

and then they came with the book under Holloway House. That book's a fake … it's called "poetic license." (Goines Interview, 15)

As Goines's sister explains the way Holloway creates a characterization of her brother, one can't help but be reminded of the way white editors and abolitionists authenticated or inserted their own words through footnotes, prefaces, and introductions to control the image of the slave. Just as abolitionists needed to know and manipulate the audience of the slave narrative for purposes related to an antislavery campaign, so too must Holloway's understanding of contemporary readership relate to its campaign of capitalist profit. Information on Goines and his contract with Holloway House is not publicly available to scholars, people who can contribute little capital to the publisher.

While the exploitation of Black writers by white patronage is nothing new, Goines's son and sister have vocally exposed the depths of Holloway's exploitation. Goines entered into a lifetime contact with Holloway House Publishing Company in ways that cement his status as a fugitive neo-slave author. In discussing how much compensation Goines received for his work, his family notes: "Twelve cents per copy, and at the time the books were selling for $1.45 … and as the price of the books went up, he still only got twelve cents per copy" (15). If Goines sold a million copies at that price, he would receive $120,000 while Holloway House received $1,330,000. Today, the prices of those books range from $4.95 to $6.95. Holloway House could receive any- where from $4 to $5 million, while Goines's family would receive the same $120,000. Unconfirmed statistics suggest that with the rights to Goines's sixteen books, Holloway House has sold at least ten million copies worldwide.[15] Considering that Goines published sixteen novels with the same company, the publishing house has made millions of dollars in the double-digits with book rights as well as any money that would come from other lucrative media deals. Holloway House sold the rights to only one Goines work: W. W. Norton obtained the rights to Goines's *Daddy Cool* for Gerald's "Old School" series. In addition, rumors of Goines's work being made into more and more films have increased with the popularity of Hip-Hop.[16] Holloway's contract with Goines explicitly works within the boundaries of both chattel and economic slavery of the Black body. While Goines may have never toiled in cotton and tobacco fields like his ancestors, the "millions of copies sold" and "#1 America's Best Selling Black Author" banners so visibly imprinted on his book covers suggest the conditions of his bondage, as well as the lasting effects of that bondage on his family.

Even as production and labor analysis of Goines's work situates him in the neo-slavery contexts of other Hip-Hop forms, it is not only that context but also the themes and aesthetics that reveal Goines's books as Hip-Hop neo-slave narratives.

There are a number of fictional neo-slave narratives: Toni Morrison's *Beloved* (1987), Gayl Jones's *Corregidora* (1973), Sherley Anne Williams's *Dessa Rose* (1986), Ishmael Reed's *Flight to Canada* (1976), and Charles Johnson's *Oxherding Tales* (1982) and *Middle Passage* (1990). But none of these works possess the aesthetics that we so readily find in Hip-Hop culture. Goines's neo-slave narratives do just that. While some of the top Black literary figures utilize their neo-slave narratives in a way that shows chattel slavery's impact on Black America today, Goines's work adheres strictly to the previous definition of neo-slavery provided by George Jackson. Jackson defined neo-slavery as specifically an economic bondage.

Narratives by Donald Goines utilize the inner city/ghetto and poor urban culture, be it in the North or the South, as its critical neo-slavery context. In other narratives, setting may be secondary to the main characters and plot's theme; for Goines, the inner-city setting maintains a presence of neo-slavery. Goines's first-written, second-published work, *Whoreson: The Story of a Ghetto Pimp* (1972), from the very beginning emphasizes the space as oppressive:

> From what I have been told it is easy to imagine the cold, bleak day when I was born into this world. It was December 10, 1949 and the snow had been falling continuously in Detroit all that day. The cars moved slowly up and down Hastings Street.... Whenever a car stopped in the middle of the street, a prostitute would get out of it or a whore would dart from one of the darkened doorways to get into the car (7).

It is not the counterculture appeal of whoring, pimpdom, and trickology that makes this work and its passage so notable. From the snow and slush to the hidden corners of dark doorways, every descriptive element in the passage emphasizes a void and hole of oppression. *Whoreson's* fictional realistic setting has much in common with the village of Frantz Fanon's *The Wretched of the Earth* (1961). By setting his novels in the inner-city ghettos (mostly Detroit), Goines creates the perfect modern-day place for colonization and decolonization. Fanon (1961) notes:

> The town belonging to the colonized people, or at least the native people, the Negro village, the medina, the reservation, is a place of ill fame, peopled by men of ill repute... It is a world without spaciousness; men live there on top of each other. (39)

In order for Goines to portray the impact of colonialism rather than chattel slavery on contemporary Blacks, he must go to the inner city. Goines allows the native to speak outside the sociological discourse of ghettoism, choosing instead the frame of neo-slavery, the discourse of colonialism, and the aesthetics of Black culture that are now found in Hip-Hop culture.

A Black readership draws from certain aesthetics. Goines's aesthetics seem to emulate those assigned to Hip-Hop culture, subsequently, which may explain why Hip-Hop artists flock to his work. Rose remarks that Arthur Jafa's theory about stylistic continuities in Hip-Hop culture derives from three concepts: "flow, layering, and ruptures in line. In hip-hop, visual, physical, musical, and lyrical lines are set in motion, broken abruptly with sharp angular breaks, yet they sustain motion and energy through fluidity and flow" (Rose 1994, 38). While it may seem difficult to accomplish such things in a long written narrative, Goines manages to achieve the feat.

He employs the ghetto setting as a way to establish his flow. Jessie, a Black female prostitute, is the focus of early attention. Her Black pimp has run off with a white whore, while she remains behind to give birth to a high-yella baby boy, which, according to the character Big Mama, means that she "done went and got herself pregnant" by a white John (Goines 1972, 10). When the doctor asks Jessie what name she will give him, we can observe that the narrator, Goines, not only reaches into his literary bag of tropes and reaches for the *topos* of (un)naming, he proceeds to layer his narrative with all the realities of ghetto life that he can muster. Jessie replies, "Of course, doc, I've got just the name for the little son of a bitch— Whoreson, Whoreson Jones" (11). Jessie's career as a prostitute begins the narrative flow; her son's name, repeated for emphasis, layers that narrative. Goines then abruptly breaks the underclass flow of the narrative with moral commentary from Big Mama: "You can't do that, Jessie. Give the child a good Christian name" (11). Big Mama's commentary acts as the rupture in the narrative because, as products of the sociologically constructed ghetto, readers assume an absence of "morals." They really have no place in hard times. After a noticeable pause and misgivings from Big Mama and the Doctor, Jessie explains, "I'm naming my son what he is. I'm a whore and he's my son." (11). Goines reestablishes the flow in his narrative with this return to Jessie's naming of her son.

While the caricaturist use of poor urban culture found in S-line, hyped-up Hip-Hop novels has little meaning, Goines, like the "prophets of rage" who follow him, uses the inner-city setting and culture narrative to express how:

> Poor people learn from experience when and how explicitly they can express their discontent. Under social conditions in which sustained frontal attacks on powerful groups are strategically unwise or successfully contained, oppressed people use language, dance, and music to mock those in power, express rage, and produce fantasies of subversion. (Rose 1994, 99)

Jessie, a poor single Black mother whom society oppresses, comments on her neo-slave status through the naming of her son. Similarly, the author employs the female character and the name, Whoreson, to express rage, powerlessness, and to produce a fantasy of subversion that suggests what might seem like an embracing the culture of pimps and whores. However, Goines's use of naming serves as a subversive attack on the society that strangles inner-city dwellers. In this case, naming acts as an aesthetic device of Hip-Hop, but it always follows the trope in African American literature aesthetics.

Kimberly Benston (1984) asserts that "(un) naming is the unspeakable figure of an unnameable African linguistic difference, the visual sign of which is an unadulterated blackness.... Every black act of naming, then, is simultaneously an act of un(naming), an act of linguistic appropriation" (17). For Whoreson, his name is the visual sign of an unadulterated oppression of Blackness, his state of colonization signified in the horror of his name. He is no one, just the son of a whore. Whoreson's name becomes unspeakable in the school classroom (18).

The teachers call him Jones and make the other students call him Jones, too; and when the students do call him Whoreson, it is with a deliciously wicked intention of being bad and doing/saying the unspeakable. He is nameless and unnamed—yet the ambiguities he learns to confront in being at once a subjective absence and total self-presence (whore/son) comes in his trying to take on the absence of that name, the commodification of his Black body, only to later shake it off after a process of decolonization that takes place in prison. He realizes that he is unnamed and recognizes the significance of this unnaming to his present status as a pimp (159). Ironically, the rupture in Goines's narrative flow, the (un)naming of Whoreson, disturbs the rhythm of "normal" society each time someone speaks the name, or avoids saying the name. The Hip-Hop neo-slave narrative begins.

Goines exacerbates the situation later in the book by exploding the sacredness of the mother-son relationship. At the age of 14, Whoreson learns a lesson in pimping from his mother. Jessie, when asked how she is, replies, "As well as any nigger woman can hope to be." She exemplifies that there is not much a poor Black woman can hope to be outside of mother and whore; and in taking on her dual roles, she acts as Whoreson's mother and his first whore:

> "Pimping is an art, Whoreson." She told me seriously.... To prove her point she reached down in her sweater and fumbled around. When she removed her hand she held a small roll of money. She put this into the palm of my hand, then closed my fingers over the bills. "Count it," she said. "When you think I've made enough money, tell me and we'll go home" (40).

Jessie continues schooling Whoreson about the lessons of trap money for weeks until she shows him the mistakes of his ways. Jessie keeps account of all the money she has made so as to compare with Whoreson's account of the money he receives from Jessie. At the end of the day, Jessie shows Whoreson that he was not accepting enough money from her. Jessie simultaneously gives her son the tools for survival that he will need for the streets, and at the same time teaches him how to exploit herself and other women. Her duties as mother come into conflict with her oppressed body, a clear effect of the internalized subjugation of the colonized ghetto mother. The relationship between Whoreson and his mother Jessie is an interesting one because there is love there, just as love seems to exist in the community in which they live. Goines shows sympathy for the Black mother and the Black women of the streets that contradicts the misogyny his male characters represent. What is Goines saying about the Black family living in poverty? There is love there, but it suffers and is suffocated every day by the daily abuses that one must commit/submit to in order to survive.

The dilemma of the streets becomes quite clear when the mother of Whoreson's best friend dies from a heroin overdose. Jessie attempts to stop working the streets so that the courts will allow her to take care of Tony. After working at a dry-cleaning store for a week, a social worker comes to pick up Tony:

> The woman went into the cleaners and came out for a short while, followed by Jessie, who seemed to be pleading with her. It was the first time I'd seen her beg anyone.... After the woman left with Tony, Jessie went in and quit her job, but I believe in my heart that she would have stopped hustling and kept her job if it would have helped her to keep Tony. (53)

Whoreson learns very early that the actions of trying to move up, to fly, and to fly right are useless and serve no purpose in the environment he lives in. Hustling, a sometimes violent affair, is the only action that makes sense; everything else results in futile endeavors. With the inner city as a setting, Goines's narratives acknowledge the hierarchies of Black communities (enslaved and "free"), the range of experiences for middle-class/house slaves and the underclass/field slaves. The labels and morals we assign to the so-called thug, the criminal, or the hustler have no place in Hip-Hop neo-slave narratives. As Goines demonstrates, these labels assume that society is alright and that every citizen is free. However, the neo-slave context of colonialism suggests that Jessie and Whoreson, mother/son and pimp/whore, are not outlaws, but fugitives of neo-slavery struggling for freedom. Goines's Hip-Hop neo-slave narrative mirrors the voice and approach of the most radical and vilified insurrectionist, Nat Turner. Unlike the narratives of Hammon, Equiano, or Douglass, Turner's and later Goines's works show that there will be no Christian charity and forgiveness. In *The Confessions of Nat Turner*, Turner makes no apology for his actions. Further, when Thomas Gray asks for a history of motives for the insurrection, Turner replies, "To do so I must go back to my days of infancy, and even before I was born" (Aptheker 1966, 133). Clearly, Goines's narrative establishes the history of motives for what might be deemed questionable or illegal activities and intra-racial violence.

In addition, when Turner explains his decision to kill all white people, he places the discussion into the realm of power dynamics: "And on that night, and until we had armed and equipped ourselves, and gathered sufficient force, neither age or sex was to be spared" (139). Notably, Turner and his crew—in the process of moving on to another house—realize they left an infant alive and take the necessary, agreed-upon action. As Turner notes, people participating in the rebellion and insurrection have few resources, while those in power (even a white woman or infant instituted by a legacy of slavery) have unlimited resources to continuously squash uprisings. Turner's confession explores the depths and complexities of what must be done for freedom; and as prophet of rage as well as freedom, he understands that one day this same infant could hold the key to freedom he can never obtain. Turner's confession was an exchange with a white editor or recorder, and his actions are concerned with power dynamics between Blacks and whites; Goines's narrative, in its depiction of intra-racial violence, becomes an exchange between the Black middle class and the Black lower class. The complicit Black middle class symbolically becomes that white infant that Black masses must confront and ax in its own way.

Hence, Goines turns to a folk ax. Similar to Jigga and Trick Daddy, Whoreson is the revised archetype of folk character, the "bad nigger." As the bad nigger, Whoreson quickly becomes a consistent rupture in the narrative of neo-slavery. According to Daryl Dance's *Shuckin and Jivin* (1987), "the bad nigger is and always has been bad to whites because he violates their laws and he violates their moral codes... [B]lack people relish his exploits for exactly the same reason" (224). Goines plays on the bad nigger type to show that Whoreson is not the bad nigger. Whoreson is far more tragic than he is heroic. After being incarcerated for his illegal activities, Whoreson receives a visit from Janet, a childhood girlfriend who wanted to save him from his impending pimp life. Whoreson seeks to impress Janet with the knowledge that he has received while being incarcerated:

> Yes, I do have a much broader outlook on life than I had when I entered this institution, but now, back to my original line of reasoning. Now, don't misunderstand me, Janet, this is not an attempt to disguise or to palliate this widespread sickness that pervades the Black ghettos, but rather an attempt to try to understand why, why is it that so many of our generation have no higher goal in life than to be pimps. (187)

Goines demonstrates Whoreson's potential to be a leader in the revolution. Goines uses Whoreson's repentance of his past actions as a way to layer his critical flow about inner-city life. Despite the hardships, the inner city has produced some of the bravest leaders. His words resonate with a Malcolm X/George Jackson-type resiliency. However, like Whoreson himself, Goines does not wish to privilege literacy; he uses it as a means to an end. He manipulates the language. With one word, palliate, Whoreson makes the transition from one folk-character bad nigger to another, Nat Turner or Black Moses, smoothly and deftly. As he speaks, we can almost see him parting the Red Sea and guiding thousands of niggers out of the ghetto. The use of language has changed, and he possesses a new vocabulary to go with his new outlook on life. This new Whoreson can deliver himself and his people.

Of course, he is still trying to hustle Janet, but the hidden pain behind his words becomes clear as the conversation continues. When Janet tells him that she is engaged to a Jewish soul singer, Whoreson's reaction serves as a rupture of aggression and rage in the narrative of poor urban life, and a confrontation with what he sees as middle-class and white assimilation of values:

> Every time one of you black bitches get some kind of recognition with a little money to go with it, black men ain't good enough for you. Then you ask us why we want to pimp. That's all one of you funky bitches is good for, to be used (188).

Again, the transition is smooth, from Black Moses back to Pimp/Bad Nigger, and the violence is not turned towards the white man but the Black woman and all Black women, "funky bitches, to be used." Language of the street then becomes a signifying difference. It reveals pain, anger, an outpouring of rage that can only be relieved through denigration. For the Black male, then, the rhetoric and philosophies of a pimp become a violent way back to the masculinity that he does not possess in society. Pimps, hustlers, and drug dealers are modern-day models of U.S.-colonized Black bodies. They could never be as empowering as the trickster or "bad nigga," primarily because the main heroic quality of the bad nigga and trickster is their ability to get one over on the white man. The admiration of the folk character is short-lived, for the violence the bad nigga inflicts on "whitey" always seems to end up misdirected. Whoreson, who had Nat Turner potential, chooses to exact his vengeance not on the cause of his problem, white-supremacy systems or the Black middle class, but on those nearest to his wrath—the poor Black females he grew up loving. As Goines shows, the ultimate failure of Whoreson is that he does not pick up the ax and go back for the infant; he does not become that bad nigger, simply another nigger. The common and daily exploitation of one's community does not make one heroic.

As Goines's sister notes, he repeatedly demonstrates that the only person the hustler is hurting is himself and his community (Goines Interview, 15). Unlike the original slave narrative, but akin to rap narratives, escaping and running are not options for the colonized people living in the ghettos. The Hip-Hop neo-slave narrative takes its pre-generic myths from *The Wretched's* thesis concerning violence:

> . . . the last shall be first and the first last... The native who decides to put into practice, and to become its moving force, is ready for violence at all times. From birth it is clear to him that this narrow world, strewn with prohibitions, can only be called into question by absolute violence. (Fanon, 72)

Unlike Turner's actions that support Fanon's theory, Goines's narratives steadily depict intra-communal violence as unsuccessful attempts towards a desired strategy of decolonization. This is why traditional Black metaphors of freedom remain absent from his narratives. There is no migration South to North and no visions of flight, because there is no room and no hope to aspire beyond difficult circumstances. Instead, Goines replaces these metaphors of movement with modes of stifling violence and insurrection turned inward: hustling, pimping, and whoring. Though it would be all too easy to see these actions as negatives, we must not forget that the history of motives is clear; and from birth it becomes as clear as Turner's own vision that Fanonian violence and spontaneity serve a purpose. Sadly, in this case, it is a purpose misguided. Riots, the people's rebellion, in their destruction of the oppressor's lots, unite the people into a common group that must be contained via more expertly brutal militaries.

Since Goines's work thematically deals with the process of decolonization following enslavement, this situates his corpus in the genre of the neo-slave narrative. Consequently, because he chooses to utilize urban vernacular and culture to examine the process of decolonization, he becomes one of the founding fathers of the Hip-Hop narrative that both cultural and literary studies have long ignored. The neo-slave narrative itself is a complicated genre of fictional and nonfictional works. Hip-Hop changes the terrain of the genre with its own aesthetics of flow, layering, and rupture. However, just as the mode of production and use-value of rap risks corruption by mainstream commodification, so too does any written text defined as a Hip-Hop narrative. Currently, there are a number of products being classified as Hip-Hop novels and fiction. While writers such as James Early Hardy, Paul Beatty, or even rap star Queen Pen could legitimately make this claim to fame,[17] other writers or publishers are simply taking advantage of the way critics of Hip-Hop culture frequently avoid the issue of written texts. Syndicated Media Group serves as one example of benefactors, or poor imitators, of the Hip-Hop narrative, while the works of Donald Goines remind us that true Hip-Hop narratives offer a realistic representation of the ongoing process of decolonization and neo-slavery.

NOTES

1. Nas (1997).
2. Kelley (1997, 16).
3. Boyd (1997, 9).
4. In a speech for the OAAU founding rally, Malcolm X addressed the importance of the Negro myth (no history and no culture), and in doing so he explained the difference between Negro and African and its importance to Black self-empowerment. See Malcolm X (1990, 79).
5. For one of the only serious literary analyses of Goines's work, see Greg Goode (1984). Aside from small book reviews in *Village Voice* and other alternative print, in 2001 *Black Issues Book Review* (vol. 3, no. 5) dedicated an entire section to limited discussions of Goines's work.
6. Outlawzz Free Press sells artwork and writings by prisoners across the United States. The *Cell Door Magazine* is an internet magazine with all material being written by inmates for a non-prison population (celldoor.com). In addition to numerous poetry workshops like the Folsom Writing Workshops, the California Coalition of Women Prisoners publishes *The Fire Inside Newsletter*, a quarterly forum for female prisoners to express themselves in writing and art.
7. African American Images Press president and founder Jawanza Kunjufu takes issue with the violence and materialism prevalent in the fiction (Kunjufu 2001, 56).
8. See Nathan Rubin's review of *Streetsweeper in The Onion A.V. Club* newsrag and e-zine, at http://www.theonionavclub.com/reviews/words/words_s/streetsweeper01 .html [2002, p.1].
9. In Andrew Calcutt and Richard Shepard's Cult Fiction (1998), the significance of Goines's work is undermined by statements such as: "Donald Goines wrote fiction the way other people package meat. There is little point in picking any of his titles as outstanding, since they are all formulaic."
10. For a full definition of the aesthetics and elements of the neo-slave narrative, see Rushdy (1997).
11. Rose (1994) discusses the post-industrial conditions of shrinking federal funds and affordable housing, as well as shifts in blue-collar/white-collar employment. She also mentions the impact of slumlords, redevelopers, toxic-waste dumps, violent criminality, and redlining in Hip-Hop's development (30).
12. For discussions of this theory, see Henry Louis Gates, Jr.'s *The Signifying Monkey*, specifically trope of the talking book, as well as his *Figures in Black* and his introduction to *The Slave Narrative*.

13. This term refers to Black, lower-class populations and derives from Claudia Jones's "On the Right to Self-Determination for Negro People in the Black-Belt" (1949).
14. Douglass's *My Bondage and My Freedom*, the third narrative of his enslavement, reveals that abolitionists such as William Garrison attempted to dictate how and what he spoke about to white audiences. He could not appear to be too literate or too fanatical.
15. *F.E.D.S* magazine, as well as some unconfirmed sources, claim that Holloway House has sold over ten million Goines books worldwide.
16. During the late 1990s, several press releases from Black Hand Entertainment and Holloway House discussed Goines's novel, *Black Gangsta*, being adapted to film. Then, there's *Never Die Alone*, which would star DMX.
17. See James Earl Hardy's B-Boy Blues, Paul Beatty's *White Boy Shuffle*, and Queen Pen's *Situations* to see how the neo-slave narrative genre has been revamped to address issues of class, sexuality, and gender with the use of Hip-Hop aesthetics and culture.

REFERENCES

Aptheker, Herbert, ed. 1966. *Nat Turner's Slave Rebellion Together with the Full Text of the So-Called "Confessions" of Nat Turner Made in Prison in 1931*. New York: Humanities Press.

Ashraf H. A. "Neo-Slave Narratives." *In The Oxford Companion to African American Literature*, ed. William L. Andrews, Francis Smith Foster, and Trudier Harris, 533–35. New York: Oxford University Press, 1997.

Benston, Kimberly. "The Topos of (Un)naming in Afro-American Literature" in *Black Literature and Literary Theory*. Ed. Henry Louis Gates. Jr. London: Routledge, 1984.

Boyd, Todd A. *Am I Black Enough For You? Popular Culture from the 'Hood and Beyond*. Bloomington and Indianapolis: Indiana University Press, 1997.

Calcutt, Andrew; and Richard Shepard. Cult Fiction. Lincolnwood, Ill: Contemporary Books, 1998.

Cumber Dance, Daryl. *Shuckin and Jivin: Folklore from Contemporary Black Americans*. Bloomington: Indiana University Press, 1987.

Davis, Anthony C. "The New Son's Of Iceberg Slim" in *Black Issues Book Review 3*, no. 5 (13 October 2001): 56–58.

Fanon, Frantz. *The Wretched of the Earth*. New York: Grove Press, 1965.

Gardiner, Beth. *Hip Hop Books Reach For New Audiences*. New York: Associated Press (24 July 2000).

Gates, Henry Louis. *Black Literature and Literary Theory*. London: Routledge, 1984.

George, Nelson. *Hip Hop America*. New York: Penguin USA, 1999.

Goode, Greg. *"From Dopefiend to Kenyatta's Last Hit: The Angry Black Crime Novels of Donald Goines." MELUS* 2 (Fall 1984).

Goines Interview. *F.E.D.S. Magazine* 7 (June 2001): 12–15.

Goines, Donald. *Whoreson*. Los Angeles: Holloway House, 1972.

Jackson, George. *Soledad Brother: The Prison Letters of George Jackson*. Chicago: Lawrence Hill Books, 1990.

Jones, Leroi [Amiri Baraka]. "The Myth of a 'Negro Literature'" in *Home*. New York: William Morrow & Co., 1966.

Judy, Ronald T. *(Dis)forming the American Canon: African Slave Narratives and the Vernacular*. Minneapolis: University of Minnesota Press, 1993.

Kelley, Robin D. G. *Yo Mama's Dysfunktional!: Fighting the Culture Wars in Urban America*. Boston: Beacon Press, 1997.

Kitwana, Bakari. T*he Hip Hop Generation: The Crisis in African American Culture*. Boulder, CO: Civitas Books, 2002.

Kunjufu, Jawanza. Anthony C. Davis's "The New Son's Of Iceberg Slim" in *Black Issues Book Review 3, no. 5* (13 October 2001).

Light, Alan, ed. *The Vibe History of Hip Hop*. New York: Three Rivers Press, 1999.

Malcolm X. *By Any Means Necessary*. Edited by George Breitman. New York: Pathfinder Press, 1990.

Morrison, Toni. "The Site of Memory." *Critical Thinking, Thoughtful Writing*. Ed. John Chaffe, Christine McMahon. Boston: Houghton Mifflin, 2002.

Nas. "Escobar 97." *Men in Black Soundtrack*. Sony Records, 1997.

Perkins, William. *Droppin' Science: Critical Essays on Rap Music and Hip Hop Culture*. Philadelphia: Temple University Press, 1995.

Potter, Russell. *Spectacular Vernaculars: Hip Hop and the Politics of Post-Modernity*. Albany: SUNY Press, 1995.

Ro, Ronin. *Streetsweeper*. Los Angeles: (S) Affiliated Media Group, 2000.

Rose, Tricia. *Black Noise: Rap Music and Black Culture in Contemporary America*. Hanover, N.H., and London: Wesleyan University Press. Rushdy, 1994.

Smitherman, Geneva. *Talkin' that Talk: Language, Culture, and Education in African America*. New York: Routledge, 1999.

CHAPTER SIX

Diggin' the Scene with a Gangster Lean

Race as an Institutional Structure in Iceberg Slim and Donald Goines

Cameron Leader-Picone

"In our society which is white—we are intruders they say—there has got to be something inherently horrible about having the sicknesses and weaknesses of that society described by a person who is a victim of them."

JOHN A. WILLIAMS[1]

The Theory of a Hip-Hop Neo-Slave Narrative and the Trope of the Tragic Mulatto

Despite its popularity, gangster fiction has been largely ignored in the academics of African American Studies. One of the only discussions on the subject is L.H. Stallings's article "I'm Goin' Pimp Whores!: The Goines Factor and the Theory of a Hip-Hop Neo-Slave Narrative," which locates the works of Iceberg Slim and Donald Goines within the tradition of the slave narrative. Stallings's essay does an admirable job of "expos[ing] the field of African American cultural and literary criticism to its own class elitism" (Stallings 177), a project I continue in my own essay, extending definitions of slavery beyond that of chattel slavery to include economic marginalization and oppression as extensions of the slave system in the United States. In this context, Stallings describes the works of Goines as serving a similar function presently that slave narratives served in the antebellum era, namely, "exposing Black bondage" (Stallings 186) through written texts. Based on this analysis, Hip-Hop neo-slave narratives are not analogous to the "neo-slave narratives" defined by Ashraf Rushdy in his book of the same title, which return to the antebellum slave era, but instead are the literal slave narratives of the neo-slave era, an era defined no less by economic bondage.

Stallings characterizes the neo-slave narrative as arising out of the process of decolonization following enslavement, linking it artistically to a deemphasis of the written and a privileging of forms of communication that exist outside of the hegemony of the "sociological discourse of ghettoism" (Stallings 193). The inner city/ghetto, as the marginal space within which the neo-slave is forced to live, becomes the landscape in which this literature is expressed. In tying the narratives of Goines to the slave narrative, Stallings further links their artistic project to that of slave narrators, whose works, beyond playing a particular political and propagandistic role, were also formally linked to the project of self-definition:

> In its absence of conventional art, its rejection of elegance and classic form, its apparently spontaneous rhythms of consciousness, and its dependence on plain speech and empirical facts, the slave narrative exemplified many qualities of "living discourse" that transcendentalists believed were the grounds of true eloquence. (Andrews 102)

To associate these contemporary narratives with those of antebellum slaves implies that they too operate as forms of unmediated speech from the margins. The danger in such an assessment is the same as with the original slave narratives, that of denying artistic agency to the authors themselves. In claiming that the works of Slim and Goines inaugurate a cultural movement arising out of neo-slavery, both authors become subsumed by the category they supposedly help to define. While there is a definite need for serious scholarly engagement with Hip-Hop culture, a central portion of which would be the analysis of Slim and Goines, Stallings if understood correctly may underestimate the complexity of the worlds created by both novelists by deemphasizing the written form in examining their specific works. Not only do both authors engage with the African American literary tradition, their representations of African American identity and inner city communities are dependent on each novel's textual characteristics.

Both Goines and Slim have drawn on the trope of the mulatto figure that has been prominent in the African American literary tradition to provide a fascinating literary representation of the process of racial identification and its implications for defining the very communities that make up the economic margins described by Stallings. Mulattism may imply simultaneous access to both the Black community and the white community; however, it also implies a distancing from each group. This is particularly true of those figures with skin light enough to enable them to "pass." In passing narratives, it is often the psychological burden of the protagonist's departure from the racial community that dooms the characters, not any inherent inability to act white. Even given the diverse ways in which the trope of the tragic mulatto has been used in African American literature, Slim and Goines provide two distinct revisions of the theme, both of which move away from the individual existential consideration of racial identity towards an understanding of its structural roots in American racism. In his novel *Trick Baby*, Slim draws explicitly on this tradition within African American literature, crafting the tale of a "white negro" con man whose racial identity serves as fodder for both his material success as well as his awareness of its limitations. White Folks, Slim's protagonist, is ultimately forced to confront the way in which racial identifications are controlled by the institutions of white supremacy, which, despite his access to the white world, he is unable to change.

The institutional nature of racial hierarchy is explored even further by Goines in his series of novels centering around the revolutionary figure Kenyatta. While the discussion of these novels, up to this point, has focused on Kenyatta himself in an effort to outline Goines's own political ideology, a more nuanced portrait of racial identification may arise through an analysis of Ed Benson, the detective assigned to catch Kenyatta. While Kenyatta's revolutionary discourse looks backward to the Black Power era, the instability of Benson's racial identity points towards other representations of race in works of contemporary African American literature. In particular, Benson is portrayed as what I am calling an "institutional mulatto," one whose racial identity is "mongrelized" by his affiliation with the white power structure. However, as with White Folks and many figures in the tragic mulatto tradition, Benson's liminality isolates him from both the Black community of Kenyatta and the white power structure he represents, ultimately leaving him powerless to either oppose the supposed "extremity" of Kenyatta's revolution or the systemic racism of which he is acutely aware.

The mulatto figure remains prominent even in the almost exclusively Black communities portrayed in the gangster novels of Slim and Goines. By using figures whose racial identity is complicated through either their parentage (in the case of Slim) or their institutional role (in the case of Goines), these novels portray the ways in which race operates outside of the individuals and structures their interactions. Goines and Slim portray institutions as having an extreme, almost supernatural, amount of power in these novels. The characters exercise agency around their racial identities, but that agency is ultimately exerted within markedly constrained circumstances. Even in the case of a successful racial con man such as White Folks, the protagonist of Slim's *Trick Baby* who uses his light skin to bring in white marks, the ultimate con game turns out to be the one perpetrated by the white community on the Black community, which even White Folks cannot escape. The escapism arguably promised in Goines and Slim by their use of popular fiction genres is consistently undercut by a pessimism that demands revolutionary change.

"Meanwhile, back in the Ghetto. . ."[2]

When reading the works of Iceberg Slim, one cannot help but notice a tension between the sensational descriptions of ghetto life and the cautionary tone in which such descriptions are rendered. Responding to a letter from an aspiring Black writer recently returned from Vietnam, who states "I admire you, Iceberg, because you didn't grin and Uncle Tom to escape from the ghetto. You wrote your way out" (Slim, *Naked Soul of Iceberg Slim* 214-5), Slim crafts his own version of Langston Hughes's "Negro Artist and the Racial Mountain":[3]

> Watch out! Take my hand, young Brother, as we avoid that gilded glob of bullshit about the ideal of the colorless black writer and the superiority of his purely objective art. I believe that in these times a black writer is a success only when the black masses can relate to his work and to him with respect and a strong sense of kinship. I believe a black writer in these times who shuns or loses kinship with his people is early doomed to dry up and die as a writer. (Slim, *Naked Soul of Iceberg Slim* 219)

In this letter, he speaks of his desire to remain continually connected to those masses despite his monetary success, saying that while writing offers the possibility of escaping the ghettoization of Black America, as the young man who wrote to him implied, such a thing should not, and cannot, be a desirable outcome, as it serves to fundamentally undermine the relevance of the writer's art form.

Slim positions his literature as part of the evolving representation of the African American community. Through his essays, one can see that Slim feels a liminality as both an individual and as an author. He is a transitional figure, drawing on the African American literary tradition even as his marginal position creates new and unique representations of Blackness. Johnny O'Brien, also known as White Folks, the white negro con man, is both an old and new type of mulatto character. Existing within the all-Black world of the ghetto, White Folks's white skin is a tool for material gain, but one that also provides him a glimpse into the white power structure. With his absent white father supplanted by a symbolic Black stepfather in Blue Howard, who trains him both as a con man and a Black man, White Folks's racial identity is never in question. His whiteness becomes a tool of the trade and of possible revenge for white racism. However, despite his success as a con man, O'Brien is forced into the ultimate realization that the agency granted by his mixed-race heritage is contingent on a much larger and more powerful con game: the white supremacist hierarchy imposed by the American power structure.

While Slim's text partially traces a tragic arc, it does not after all fit snugly into the trope of the tragic mulatto. While many tragic mulatto narratives show their protagonists capitulating to static definitions of racial identity while mired in an existential dilemma related to their liminality, White Folks's tragedy is reflected in the access he gains to the white power structure. White Folks realizes the limited efficacy of his con, but his decision to lose himself in the white world of the long con is neither tragic nor triumphant but a nihilistic embrace of racial hierarchies he can only temporarily evade because of his light skin. Slim revises the trope of the tragic mulatto in order to emphasize the dominance of institutions in determining racial hierarchies. A figure such as White Folks, for whom racial identification is but a tool for material gain, is tragic not because of any crisis on his part as to his position within such hierarchies but because he provides an avenue through which the racist practices engrained in society can be unveiled if not challenged. His final decision in the novel mirrors Slim's own position on the margins of both mainstream culture and the African American literary tradition, mired in a simultaneous acknowledgment and critique of their power.

The Reveal

White Folks is positioned as the ultimate Black grifter; someone who can just as easily con whites as Blacks. Folks is able to use the surface instability of his racial identity as a means to profit from as well as gain access to a world that would be denied to any other African American through his relationship with the heiress Camille Costain. However, while Slim describes the structures of racial categorization in terms of the con game, this is hardly presented as an ideal situation. Indeed, the abilities of White Folks are only a temporary, and individual rather than collective, solution, and a damaging one at that. Ultimately, the process of racial identification is part of a hierarchy controlled by whites, even as Folks is able to utilize it in order to gain some individual advantage. In a scene that revises a critical moment in James Weldon Johnson's *Autobiography of an Ex-Colored Man*, Johnny's whiteness allows him access, as an insider, to a discussion of racial hierarchies by prominent white individuals.

Camille takes Folks to meet her father, and his friends, at their country club, and the subject of differing political approaches to racial issues comes up. The main conversation takes place between Camille's father, and, in a choice that has become only more ironic in the years since the book's publication, his friend, a captain in a California Police Department that bears a striking resemblance to the LAPD. As in Johnson's text, the ostensibly more liberal position, occupied by Camille's father, is characterized as ultimately more insidious than the blunt honesty of the explicitly racist but honest ideas of the captain. In this scene, Mr. Wherry, Camille's father, outlines a position similar to Cathy Cohen's "integrative marginalization,"[4] and describes the way in which it keeps Blacks in their place:

> I, and at least ninety percent of the whites in this country with so-called liberal leanings privately wouldn't care a whit if all the niggers in America were herded into one of your larger canyons out West and then bombed into oblivion. However, we realize that the niggers are with us and lamentably will always be with us. You conservatives can't resist your childish displays of hostility. (Slim, *Trick Baby* 212)

Mr. Wherry underlines the necessity of maintaining a racial hierarchy. In his conception, with the presence of African Americans guaranteed in U.S. society, there must be structures kept in place in order to maintain their position on the margins of society. Explicit racism only serves to enable the organization of a truly oppositional Black counter-public. As Slim outlines it, the white power structure is unwilling to allow African Americans equal access to the public sphere, although they depend on the presence of those same African American individuals. It is this dependence that is exploited by Blue and Folks as con men. The racist attitudes of whites position African Americans as figures to be exploited, and this imposition of stereotypes of ignorance and inferiority creates a space within which the con man can operate.

However, in this scene, the hierarchy outlined by Mr. Wherry illustrates that the space exploited by figures like Blue and Folks (and Slim himself) is contained within a larger con game over which they ultimately have little to no control:

> There are really two ghettos. One is physical, the other psychological. Now it is true that we have selected certain niggers to wear white collars. Almost all of them do make physical escapes from the ghetto, with our assistance, of course. Our motives are first to give dramatic well publicized reinforcement to our liberal image.
>
> Secondly, those niggers whom we seem to liberate are precisely those types of niggers who possess rare intellect and academic polish. We have to remove them from the seething black masses.

If we didn't they could conceivably give the mindless masses effective leadership against the white race. (Slim, *Trick Baby* 214-5)

The establishment of "hope" (213), the "convincer" in Wherry's game, doesn't simply serve as a form of brainwashing, but enables African Americans to impose their own desires onto the American system. By providing the illusion of the potential for advancement or success, whites are able to ghettoize African Americans, both physically and mentally, placing them in a position ripe for sexual and economic exploitation, while simultaneously removing those individuals who would allegedly be most capable of organizing the community to resist. In other words, the sucker has to buy into the basic terms of the con game.

Without some form of concession to the Black community, the white power structure would be unable to manipulate the group as a whole. Indeed, it is the nature of the Black/white dichotomy that allows such a thing to happen:

> The diametric differences between the nigger world and the white world afford us the devices by which we neutralize and defang the white collar escapees from the ghetto.
>
> The technique is roughly this. The freed nigger, elective and appointive as well, will face his entry into the white world with no little trepidation. His fears, his insecurity is born of the unfamiliar, unknown facets of this strange new world.
>
> Underlying all of this, of course, is his well hidden, but nonetheless strong sense of inferiority. His is an urgent, practical need, perhaps unconscious, to conform to the mores, the protocol of the new world. He has a deathly dread of conspicuous violation of these codes.
>
> His terror is that the whites who have sponsored him will take notice and hurl him back into the ghetto. He's compelled to emulate white emotional control and polished, patient conduct.
>
> We flatter him as he becomes more like us. His identity, his fiery racial resolutions, if he has any, fade and are eventually lost. If he fights the mold, we poke derisive fun at him, and make him appear ludicrous. (Slim, *Trick Baby* 215)

In the context of this conversation, the actions of White Folks take on a whole new tenor. What the reader has previously been shown as examples of Folks's agency within the confines of the ghetto now seem to feed into the power structures defined here by Wherry. The nature of Slim's lens is key because instead of simply providing the physical possibility of giving the reader a proverbial fly on the wall to reveal this plan, its setting fundamentally alters his viewpoint. As Wherry's description goes on, it becomes clear that the con that Folks believes he has been perpetrating on Camille fits snugly within the confines of Wherry's larger con, as his performance of whiteness has forced him to depart from his community and make himself more and more white in order to continue the relationship. In opposition to reputed cultural nationalist ideas of an "essentialized" Black identity, Slim here puts to lie the idea that even whites necessarily have to self-consciously believe African Americans are inherently inferior. Instead, the very structure of society is intertwined with racial identities, meaning that advancement within the system outlined by Wherry does in fact eliminate one's Blackness, not because Black biology carries with it certain essential components, but rather because the Black world is defined as existing on the margins of the white world, an idea that is elaborated by Donald Goines in the Kenyatta books.

Consequently, Folks's disgusted acts of minor rebellion, spitting in Wherry's face, and revealing his racial identity to Camille as an attempt to shame her by implying how much she enjoyed having sex with those she supposedly despises, become less important than the fact that potentially trapped within her womb is yet another White Folks, a figure both "blessed" with the awareness of the contours of the system but cursed by his own racial associations. It is at this moment that Slim returns to the tragic aspects of the mulatto trope. The mulatto, as a figure with access to both the Black and white worlds, occupies a position that can enable personal gain, but which also forces an awareness of the limited nature of those gains.

With the intimation of Camille's potential pregnancy, an image that is not raised again in either *Trick Baby* or its sequel, *Long White Con*, one can see that, while Slim does provide a strikingly entertaining adventure set in the world of the ghetto for the reader, the nature of that entertainment is inherently pessimistic. As a consequence of Wherry's outline of the white con superstructure, White Folks's decision to pass loses any potential significance because the game is already rigged. Indeed, the only potential optimism lies in the younger generations valorized in Slim's description of the Black Panthers in his essays. As Folks puts it, "I've got a mind all right. You can't imagine how sharp I am upstairs. So has dear Daddy got a mind. But he's got maggots for brains to believe that black people are going to grin and stay conned forever in their pigsties. I hope the day comes when your father crawls on his belly and begs to kiss a nigger's black ass for his worthless life" (Slim, *Trick Baby* 218).

As Folks seems to realize, his own potential as a figure who could theoretically attempt to topple Wherry's master plan has been corrupted by his willingness to participate in the con on the level he is allowed. Consequently, while White Folks maintains his Blackness at every moment of the novel, responding to any challenges to his racial identity with the self-categorization of being a "nigger," in the epilogue he chooses to submerge himself within the long con game played exclusively by whites. Folks states: "I'm going to learn all the angles of the white big con. I'm going to lose myself in the white world. I'm going to break every classy white broad's heart that gives me a second gander. I'm going to eat and sleep and fuck with nothing but white people for the rest of my life" (Slim, *Trick Baby* 266). While this would seem to be a repudiation of the possibilities suggested by his racial liminality, it actually serves to reinforce Slim's ideas. White Folks decision to pass is both the next evolution of Slim's positioning of racial identification as a form of con game, and a resignation to the racial con man's inability to change the game.

Folks's statement to Camille implies that the awareness that is required to become a hustler within the marginal Black world holds within it the key to an escape hatch. While the lumpen-proletariat of the con men, pimps, madams and whores of Slim's world do not themselves constitute an insurrectionary force, they do contain the potential for revolutionary action. By detaching, to some degree, racial identification from the individual nature of his characters and placing it within the context of larger institutional structures, Iceberg Slim opens up the possibility of racial identity itself as a tool for liberation. Just as Folks exploits both Black and white suckers by playing off their own desire to mirror their conceptions of race in his ambiguous features, his ability to manipulate such marks illustrates the utility of racial identities, even if Folks himself is ultimately unable to realize their potential. While it can be argued that his novel contains elements of an "essentialist" view of Blackness, particularly through the overt hypersexual characterization of White Folks, Slim's location of racial identification within a multi-layered con game prefigures more "postmodern" views of racial identity's simultaneous reality and construction, which run through African American literature published in the generation since Slim's novel appeared in 1967.

Black in Blue

"The Negro ceases to be Negro when he becomes a policeman."
Black in Blue[5]

While Iceberg Slim's *Trick Baby* provides a direct link between the African American literary trope of the tragic mulatto and popular gangster fiction, Slim's literary descendent Donald Goines extends and deepens the portrayal of the racial identities produced by white exploitation of the marginalized Black community. Goines was driven to write after reading Slim's books while in prison (Stone 139), and he develops Slim's idea that racial constructs exist as part of institutional structures in concert with processes of individual identity formation. These structures serve to constrain the agency of Goines's individual characters, complicating their individual choices through a narrative that leaves the reader with only an image (or mirage) of the near "supernatural" power of white supremacy. While Slim literalizes the racially ambiguous position of the Black policeman through the character of Dot Murray's splotchy black skin (Slim, *Trick Baby* 3), Goines uses his Kenyatta series, published over the course of 1974 and 1975, under the pseudonym Al C. Clark, to explore the deracinating effects of institutional cooptation of individual African Americans. In juxtaposing Benson, a Black detective, with the revolutionary Kenyatta, Goines provides an illustration of "institutional mulattism," in which Benson's status as a cop creates a liminal position analogous to that of White Folks, with a simultaneous awareness of racial power structures and an inability or refusal to change those structures.

Leaving aside the individual motivations, beliefs and self-identifications of actual African American policemen, in the Black popular fiction of the late 1960s and early to mid 1970s, the employment of Black police officers represents an actualization of the plot outlined by Slim's Mr. Wherry. Nicholas Alex describes the process in his 1969 study of Black policemen, *Black in Blue*, "the recruitment of Negroes into the department serves two diametrically opposed functions: the coopting of Negroes and their promotion to officer status serves to influence the minority community in favor of the department, while at the same time it ghettoizes the Negro policeman, and accommodates itself to use him to collect intelligence in ghetto areas" (Alex 30). While Alex describes these two functions as diametrically opposed, one sees how they become unified through the lens of Slim's articulation of the white supremacist master plan. By using African American police officers to patrol Black neighborhoods, the police department places figures who have the potential to generate sympathy from the community within the ghetto; at the same time, those same African American officers can undermine the authority of Black radical political organizations.

In an idea articulated by Alex, and elaborated upon by Goines, the institutional marker of "policeman" is a specifically white identity and thus is not racially neutral. As Alex puts it: "The Negro ceases to be a Negro when he becomes a policeman. He becomes an agent for the white society and is reminded of his special class status as a Negro by those in the Negro community with whom he deals" (Alex 133). However, while Alex may be describing the functional role played by actual Black police officers, for African American authors the figure of the Black cop becomes a fascinating figure in serving to delineate the process of racial identification in American society. While Iceberg Slim drew explicitly upon the tradition of the mulatto figure of American and African American literature, utilizing a "white negro" main character to redefine the process of racial identification, the Black policeman provides a parallel figure through which to interrogate structural racism. The Black policeman becomes an "institutional mulatto," forced to live in the liminal space between a white institution within which he or she can never be accepted and a Black community within which he or she is inherently tainted through their association with that same white institution. As the con game of white supremacy outlined by Iceberg Slim in *Trick Baby* plays out, racial markers serve to delineate roles dictated by shifting institutional contexts and displaced from either biology or individual choice.

"Mau-Mauing"

Donald Goines's revolutionary leader takes his name from a prominent member of the "Mau Mau" rebellion, and first president of an independent Kenya, Jomo Kenyatta. While most of the secondary literature on the series focuses on Kenyatta as an idealized representation of the type of figure Goines himself aspired to be (Stone 91), the novels themselves are structured as a dialectic between Kenyatta's ideals and actions and the troubled figure of Ed Benson, a Black detective trying to apprehend him. While the character of Kenyatta reads like an archetypal "Black nationalist" figure, the structural relationship between himself and Benson allows Goines to explore not just the revolutionary mechanisms of a still-fuming Black lower class community, but also the relationship between that community and those whose individual successes represent the marginal institutional changes effected by the Civil Rights and Black Power movements.

Goines outlines Kenyatta's philosophy at the beginning of the third novel in the series, *Kenyatta's Escape*:

> First, he wanted to knock off every honkie cop who had it in for Blacks. And the attacks had been smoothly calculated and swift. Many a cop had never known what had ripped his guts open before the concrete came up to meet his face.

> The second project was to rid the ghetto of all the junk pushers. The slick ones who drove the big hogs, who sometimes only fronted for the big men. Big men like Kingfisher, who sat up in a cool penthouse and raked in the money. Nickels and dimes turning into thousands of dollars. Black Dollars! (Goines, *Kenyatta's Escape* 8)

Kenyatta addresses two central threats to the stability and success of the Black community he claims to represent. First, the oppression visited upon African Americans by white cops. Second, prefiguring popular so-called "conspiracy theories" within the Black community in the 1980s and 1990s, Kenyatta attributes the scourge of drug importation and addiction to outside white influences. While Goines does not specifically levy this accusation against the government, as has been said about crack cocaine and the CIA,[6] the shadowy power structure in these novels ultimately seems to be some unholy alliance of organized crime, corporations and a corrupt government. Clement Jenkins, the top figure to whom Kenyatta is able to gain access, makes his money through legitimate sales, drugs and defense contracts from the government:

> ... he began manufacturing Christmas tree lights, then outdoor lights, and finally cornered the market on fluorescent lights.... Twenty years ago he had begun with hashish. During the fifties he had graduated to cocaine. When the sixties arrived, he had financed a young chemist in San Francisco to produce huge amounts of LSD. Then, finally, Clement Jenkins had begun selling, importing and dealing in heroin. (Goines, *Kenyatta's Last Hit* 169-170)

Jenkins ultimately stands at the intersection of multiple exploitative aspects of American culture. From his location, both literally and figuratively, atop the "American Dream" from the penthouse suite of the Sands Hotel in Las Vegas, Jenkins utilizes his position to peddle the drugs that console those who are unable to achieve the promise of that dream. The series itself gradually expands its lens from Kenyatta's individual revenge upon various individual racist Detroit police officers to his showdown with Jenkins in the Sands.

However, even as Goines establishes the necessity of Kenyatta's revolutionary discourse, he subtly undermines Kenyatta's articulation of it through strategically placed suggestions of Kenyatta's potential madness and through the dialectic relationship between Kenyatta and Benson. While Kenyatta remains a largely static character, Benson's responses to Kenyatta's action reveal the complex nature of the marginal position of African Americans. We are introduced to Benson through the lens of institutional racism. As a plainclothes detective, Benson is confronted at gunpoint by two white beat cops. However, because of his position as their superior and a Black man within a largely white power structure, he is forced to moderate his response: "No matter what you did, or what you become, the thought flashed through Benson's mind, you'd always be a nigger to some of these hillbilly bastards. The word did not disturb him but the tone of voice the speaker used did. Even though he hadn't done anything, this bastard was ready to kill him" (Goines, *Crime*

Partners 27). Benson's response is constrained by his racial identity. Despite his greater institutional power as a detective who outranks the white beat cops, their insubordination becomes possible because of their whiteness. This idea is reinforced as Goines gives the reader a glimpse into the mind of the officer: "He wished silently that he had pulled the trigger when he had the opportunity. Then it would have been just an accident. Now he didn't know where he stood" (Goines, *Crime Partners* 29). Despite Benson's status as a detective, had the officer simply shot him, it would have been excusable because the association of Blackness with the institutional status of a detective is not seen as something that the officer could have reasonably imagined. Indeed, Benson himself is both aware of, and constrained by, this knowledge. Even after his rank is revealed, his position of power within the situation is limited to its bureaucratic context. In response to the young officer's attempt at reconciliation, "we're both on the same side, right?" Benson replies, "Wrong. Your kind of man should never be allowed to wear a uniform, and I'm going to do everything in my power to see if I can't get you out of that uniform" (Goines, *Crime Partners* 31). Benson's only recourse is to challenge the white officer's own institutionally-based authority, threatening to take his badge through official channels, a threat which rings hollow, and the ineffectiveness of which is reinforced, in the immediate, by his having to look to his white junior partner, Ryan, for reinforcement (Goines, *Crime Partners* 30), and, in the long term, by the racism of Benson's own boss; this is illustrated when Benson is forced to refuse to work with these same two white deputies after his boss assigns them to aid his investigation (Goines, *Death List* 47-50).

However, while Benson is forced to withhold expressions of anger in the face of explicit (and near-fatal) racism, Kenyatta takes revenge for Benson. Following this incident, which introduces us to Benson, Kenyatta teams up with Billy and Jackie, the titular *Crime Partners*, to "rid the neighborhood of two nigger-haters that work the afternoon shift" (Goines, *Crime Partners* 46). While these killings are part of a larger scale attempt to rid the city of racist white cops, the first exercise of Kenyatta's plans with which Goines presents the reader is retaliation for the racism of the two beat cops who have just harassed Benson. Kenyatta and his organization provide an oppositional force to the official institutions and are able to act in the very ways Benson cannot. While Benson is rendered impotent by the opposition between his racial identity and the racial coding of the police department, Kenyatta is able to exert the agency that Benson lacks. On the other hand, Goines otherwise explicitly differentiates between Kenyatta's sphere and that of Benson. While Kenyatta would rather not kill Black cops, saying, "I don't want to hit no black ones if I can help it, because there's not enough black ones on the force now for us to go along killin' the few that they do have" (Goines, *Crime Partners* 58),[7] he demonstrates his willingness to do so by killing a Black and white pair who show up as backup to aid the two cops who harassed Benson (Goines, *Crime Partners* 69-70).

By detaching the process of vengeance from Benson's hands and placing it within the sphere of Kenyatta, Goines highlights the marginal position of African American police officers both from the institutional structure they represent as well as the community they are supposed to police. This process mirrors classic mulatto characters such as the "ex-colored man" who are forced to negotiate their position within the white community, regardless of whether they are passing for white or not, while simultaneously remaining aware of the potential for their detachment from the Black community.[8] As a cop, Benson can never escape the fact that his Blackness supercedes his institutional identity; while, as a Black man, he can never escape being a cop, and thus an outsider to other African Americans. Kenyatta's actions may exceed any retaliation Benson himself would have wished upon the officer who was so racist to him. However, in these early scenes, Goines establishes the restraints placed on individual agency by the relationships between official institutions such as the police department and racial identity. By having Kenyatta carry out the revenge for the actions against Benson, Goines establishes a stark contrast between him and Kenyatta that the rest of the series arguably serves to complicate.

While, as an individual, these conflicting identities limit Benson's agency within this scene, they provide Goines with a dynamic space for examining the relationship between social structures and racial identification. As opposed to Benson, Kenyatta may be said to occupy a static oppositional space. His position of awareness and willingness to take action paints him as the sort of character who is the culmination of the process described by Iceberg Slim. He is a Black man who refuses to be conned by whites any longer, mandating that any actions against the community will be responded to either in kind or with death. Even within the context of his organization, Kenyatta is unique: "there was a madness there, yet the fire that burned there was also the mark of the strong man, a leader, the kind of man the people could follow with complete trust. It was one of Kenyatta's strong points, the ability to make people believe in his dream. Whether he could make it true or not, he could make people believe him" (Goines, *Crime Partners* 49). Goines allows Kenyatta's legend to precede the events of the novels. He appears fully formed, with both his ideals and his plan intact. As opposed to Benson, who is changed through his experience of the conflict between institutional ideals and racial pride brought on by Kenyatta's actions, Kenyatta exists as a shadowy ideal, perceived always at least partially from the outside. Goines implies that even as the madness in his eyes can frighten his associates, it also provides the key to his leadership, the fact that he is willing to do whatever it takes to achieve his goals. He becomes the apotheosis of the type of figure that White Folks can never become, an individual who is the full encapsulation of racial pride, for whom nothing short of complete liberation implies his own personal failure. Consequently, the murders of the two racist cops serves as a symbolic revenge for actions taken against the African American community without resolving the conflict faced by Benson. When Benson and Ryan arrive at the scene of the killings, Benson's reactions ascribe a meaninglessness to the violence that implies that, at this point, his mindset is still tied up with its institutional commitment: "The people responsible for this must be mad. I mean, people just don't go around killing wholesale like this. What's the reason behind it? It's senseless, as far as I can see" (Goines, *Crime Partners* 81). His statement when he recognizes the faces of the men who had earlier harassed him explicitly recalls the attempted apology of the officers when they had learned Benson's identity: "He was still a police officer" (Goines, *Crime Partners* 80).

What ultimately makes the Kenyatta series a complex examination of racial identifications has less to do with the figure of Kenyatta himself, and more to do with how Goines examines the effects of Kenyatta's actions within the structures of the Black and white worlds, a dichotomy which, like Slim, Goines utilizes to describe the structure of society:

> The very air in the car seemed to become oppressive to Benson, but what his partner said was true. They would never be able to make their superiors understand. Even as Benson thought about it, it seemed foolish. What would a well dressed white man want with someone like Kenyatta, except to sell him something that would be junk a month later. They lived in two different worlds. The world of men like Kenyatta was a black world, devoid of whites. Even as Benson thought about it, he remembered that the little he was able to dig up on Kenyatta showed him to be militant, preaching against associating with whites. As he went over the possibilities in his mind, Benson quickly came to the conclusion that the fat little white man was probably just the landlord coming to collect his rent. (Goines, *Death List* 56)

This passage comes at a critical juncture of Benson and Ryan's investigation into Kenyatta. In fact, the man is not Kenyatta's landlord but a mobster selling the names of the major drug dealers to Kenyatta. Benson's misrecognition of the situation, coupled with his and Ryan's unwillingness to subvert standard procedure by pulling over a white man, prevents the cops from stopping Kenyatta's killing spree at the very moment that it is about to spill out into the white community. However, even though Benson reads the situation incorrectly, this passage demonstrates how his interactions with Kenyatta have begun to force Benson into a state of greater awareness. Earlier, Benson's actions had been limited by his racial identity within the context of his institutional one; in this moment, the opposite is true. Because of his race, Benson finds something incongruous with Kenyatta's willingness to meet with the white man. He is simultaneously aware that this knowledge would not be sufficient to justify any police action. Goines implies that, as Kenyatta is aware, there is a fundamental conflict between Benson's race and his job, as what should be a perfectly valid investigatory intuition is negated because of its origins in the Black world/white world dichotomy.

Following the massacre of Kenyatta's organization in a pitched battle with the police on his farm compound (a scene which recalls both the riots of the 1960s as well as attacks by the police and FBI on organizations such as the Black Panthers), Benson's desire to arrest Kenyatta as a criminal changes to a desire to track him down as another Black man. It is telling that while Benson blames the police department for its actions, the ultimate target of his rage is Kenyatta for creating the circumstances that enabled the massacre to take place: "The sight of so many Black bodies had done something to him… 'How the hell can they hold a whole damn race of people guilty for what a few fuckin' nuts do?'" (Goines, *Kenyatta's Escape* 80, 81). While Benson decries the actions of the police, particularly their use of excessive weaponry (such as flame-throwers and tanks) and the fact that they continue to fire even after the members of the compound had surrendered, he still lays a substantial portion of the blame at the feet of Kenyatta, of whom he says, "that will be one Black sonofabitch I'll be glad to see laying out on his back" (Goines, *Kenyatta's Escape* 85).

The novels trace a process by which Benson emerges from his position within the "white" institutional structure to oppose Kenyatta's "Black world" through an unwillingness to embrace Kenyatta's actions rather than, in his own mind, as a form of support for the flawed system of which he is clearly an agent. While it is undoubtedly true that Kenyatta is ultimately the hero of the cycle, the relationship between his actions and the responses of Benson provide the text with an ultimately pessimistic tone, reinforced by an ending that, like that of *Trick Baby*, serves to reinscribe the current power of white supremacy. Following Kenyatta's escape to Los Angeles, the narrative accelerates towards his confrontation with Clement Jenkins, who, as he is described when Kenyatta first encounters him, represents death incarnate: "Jenkins smelled of death. There was nothing about him which suggested that he had ever lived, or that he ever had any intentions of living" (Goines, *Kenyatta's Last Hit* 210). Jenkins' living dead-like quality symbolizes his participation in the drug trade and war profiteering. Like Kenyatta, Jenkins exists fully formed, more of a compilation of forces than an individual, *per se*.

The ultimate confrontation between Kenyatta and Jenkins is important not just as the culmination of the narrative, but also because it indicates the cyclical nature of power and resistance that ultimately contextualizes the lives of all of these characters. Throughout *Kenyatta's Last Hit*, Benson comes to a greater realization as to the role that race plays in establishing his position as a police officer. Benson is fundamentally troubled by what he describes as a "contradiction within itself" (Goines, *Kenyatta's Last Hit* 38), which he curiously hopes that either catching or killing Kenyatta will help to resolve. Goines uses "itself" rather than "himself" since the contradiction cannot be located within an individual, but instead the individual experiences a contradiction that takes place outside of them. However, the very process of hunting for Kenyatta serves to reinforce precisely this contradiction, which is highlighted through major events such as the massacre on Kenyatta's farm, but which also arises within the mundane details of police work. For example, in dealing with a Black informant, Benson's race serves as a key to information that a white officer may not have been able to determine: "Davis looked at the black detective, and for the first time his eyes softened" (Goines, *Kenyatta's Last Hit* 74). While his race proves an advantage in gaining the trust of the informant, it also serves to isolate him from the outcome of the work. When Benson and Ryan arrive in Los Angeles, they are met by Officer Stein, who they ultimately discover is working for the drug dealers, and who barely even attempts to excise the word "nigger" from his descriptions of Kenyatta's organization (Goines, *Kenyatta's Last Hit* 58-9).

As Benson and Ryan gain intelligence from their informant, the information serves only to widen the gap between them:

> The determination and anger was building inside Benson again, and Ryan knew it. They were both up against a strange, almost invisible block wall, trying to break through a maze of half-truths and bureaucratic jumble. Both detectives' instinct told them that something was terribly wrong. For Ryan, it was a professional sense of pride that drove him. But, for Benson, it was something else.
> *The man was black, and it made a difference.* (Goines, *Kenyatta's Last Hit* 82, italics mine.)

The relationship between Benson and Ryan has been exposed as untenable. At this point, Benson seems to realize that he is being used as a tool to defeat Black militancy (as we learn from his Captain, "by using a black detective, his chances [of catching Kenyatta] were that much greater" (Goines, *Kenyatta's Last Hit* 44)). But he has ceased to care.

Benson's individual marginalization provides Goines with his final lens into the climax of the series. Goines outlines Benson's rationale for opposing Kenyatta:

> Benson was a professional, a black who many years before had given up the right to deal with the problem of race outside the law. It was his commitment, and no one else's. At that time Benson had believed in the system. Had seen, or thought he saw, the routes through which he could make a difference.
>
> He knew that if those routes were closed to him, then all he had to do was to hand in his badge and make that journey to the twilight arena on the fringe. It was there that some of his brothers believed that out of the anarchy and chaos would come order and equality. But Benson, detective with the Detroit Police Department, and black man, did not think so. (Goines, *Kenyatta's Last Hit* 41)

Even Benson's disillusionment with the institution with which he has chosen to be associated as an individual does not provide him with a desire for the destruction of the system being attempted by Kenyatta. Through his position both within and outside the institutional structure, Benson has come to a state of disillusioned awareness. While this passage is a symbolic crossroads for Benson, a moment in which he no longer believes in what he represents but still refuses to cross over and join Kenyatta, it also prefigures the story's ending. Although he gains access to Clement Jenkins, such access only enables Kenyatta's death; though he is able to kill Jenkins, Goines implies that such a loss is of marginal importance. As Kenyatta's protégé, Elliot Stone, gazes up at Jenkins flying off in a helicopter, he realizes that even Jenkins is only a representative of larger forces: "The half-smiling, half-frightened face of the small, thin white man. It was a ghostly image that peered from within the darkness of the chopper down at Stone. The image of a man who had won again, yet who knew his time was coming" (Goines, *Kenyatta's Last Hit* 219). This final image of Jenkins recalls the earlier descriptions of him as being death incarnate.

Goines ends the novel with Benson's discovery of Kenyatta's body rotting in the Nevada desert. However, instead of offering any resolution to the contradiction contained in Benson's experience, it only implies the systemic nature of the conflict between white and Black: "Ryan looked at his partner. He knew what he was thinking, because he had been thinking the same thing. Deep inside, both men knew that the wrong man was lying on the desert. But neither man knew who the right man was" (Goines, *Kenyatta's Last Hit* 221). Goines does not explicitly resolve the complexities suggested throughout the series. Stone's escape ultimately can only imply the continuation of the struggle.

CONCLUSION

Through their shared evocations of a dichotomous structure of Black and white worlds, both Slim and Goines potentially represent an association of Black identity with criminality. Even the targeted illegal behavior of Kenyatta ultimately exists on the margins of society. In these novels, the destabilization of the marginal space of the Black world ("anarchy" for Benson) does not lead to a new order. However, through their use of characters who are capable of traversing institutional lines, Goines and Slim exemplify a trope that runs throughout contemporary African American literature. While these novels, through their use of a "pulp" genre, do provide an occasionally "lurid" and always fascinating glimpse into life in post-industrially segregated African American neighborhoods, suggesting an unmediated view of the ghetto, their narrative power is ultimately based in their textual qualities. Despite their naturalist narrative tone, and protestations as to the veracity of their stories, Goines and Slim actively participate in a tradition rooted in the slave narratives and continued through the literature of Richard Wright, gesturing outwards towards a reconsideration of racial identity not in terms of the lives of individual African Americans but through the institutions that structure American life, particularly law enforcement and the economic policies which enable the underground criminality they describe. These novels provide a necessary complement to the experimental and avant-garde works of the Black Arts Movement and other African American writers of the late 1960s and early 1970s as well as the establishment of an antecedent to contemporary Hip-Hop culture—a connection evidenced not just artistically but also through the many Hip-Hop artists who have taken their names from both Slim and Goines.

In the years since the publication of these novels, while characters like Kenyatta have become anachronistic elements of a lost activist past, a figure like Benson illustrates the troubled relationship between the growing success of some of the Black community and their relationship to the institutions that they are joining. Benson's professed benevolence and opposition to racism are limited by his role as a cop; and his struggle to navigate the conflicts between his ideals and his duties mirror the problems raised in other works of African American literature, such as: the present relationship to a troubling past of slavery; the difficult role played by African American authors in defining their art in relation to a continually shifting Black community; and, most poignantly, the search for an organizing principle around which to advocate for changes in American society even as the structures of that society seek to thwart that very search. While the image of Benson standing over the rotting corpse of Kenyatta, like that of White Folks passing as white, unable to distinguish reality from fiction, suggests the death of an emancipatory dream, characters like Benson and Stone point to the contestability of such readings and the contested space occupied by racial identification.

NOTES

1 Williams 49.

2 Goines, *Crime Partners* 119.

3 Hughes's essay is one of the central theoretical documents of the Harlem Renaissance. In it, Hughes interrogates and attempts to negotiate potential conflicts between an individual's racial identity and their art forms and role as an artist.

4 Cohen describes "integrative marginalization" as a stage in which category-based distinctions have been eliminated in the law, thus enabling certain members of marginal groups access to certain areas of the power structure. As she puts it: "To facilitate the development of this stratum, dominant elites provide schooling, jobs, and housing to certain members of the marginal group. In return, the new stratum of integrative indigenous elites are expected to promote (and enforce) compromise and conformity to dominant norms within marginal communities" (59). In other words, by allowing a token force of African Americans into positions of controlled power, dominant elites are able reinforce the continuing marginal status of other members of race.

5 Alex, *Black In Blue* 133.

6 Gary Webb wrote a series of articles about this for the *San Jose Mercury News*, which have been removed from the Mercury News website, and are available at http://www.mega.nu/ampp/webb.html (Accessed 12/21/09).

7 This is one of Kenyatta's few mentions of the advantage of having African American officers on the police force. The revolutionary potential of their position is emphasized in another classic work of popular Black fiction, Sam Greenlee's *The Spook Who Sat By the Door*, in which its protagonist's entire plan for revolution is predicated on techniques he learns as the token Black member of the CIA. In addition, his best friend, Dawson, is a high ranking officer in the Chicago Police Department; and it is Freeman's desire to turn Dawson to his cause that ultimately leads to his death.

8 For example, throughout the narration of *The Autobiography of an Ex-Colored Man*, the ex-colored man uses terms such as "them" and "they" to refer to African Americans, just as he does with whites. This serves to isolate his character from both communities, leaving him as a liminal figure continually negotiating his relationship to both whiteness and Blackness. He takes on a near anthropological perspective towards his own race, going so far as to lay out the structure of the Black community from pages 76 to 79.

REFERENCES

Alex, Nicholas. *Black in Blue: A Study of the Negro Policeman.* New York: Appleton Century-Crofts, 1969.

Andrews, William L. *To Tell A Free Story: The First Century of Afro-American Autobiography, 1760-1865.* Urbana: University of Illinois Press, 1986.

Cohen, Cathy. *The Boundaries of Blackness: AIDS and the Breakdown of Black Politics.* Chicago: University of Chicago Press, 1999.

Goines, Donald. *Crime Partners.* Los Angeles: Holloway House, 1978.

———. *Death List.* Los Angeles: Holloway House, 1974.

———. *Kenyatta's Escape.* Los Angeles: Holloway House, 1974.

———. *Kenyatta's Last Hit.* Los Angeles: Holloway House, 1975.

Greenlee, Sam. *The Spook Who Sat By the Door.* New York: Bantam, 1969.

Hughes, Langston. "The Negro Artist and the Racial Mountain." *Double-Take: A Revisionist Harlem Renaissance Anthology.* Ed. Venetria K. Patton and Maureen Honey. New Brunswick: Rutger s University Press, [1926] 2001. 40-44.

Johnson, James Weldon. *The Autobiography of an Ex-Coloured Man.* New York: Vintage, [1927] 1989.

Rushdy, Ashraf. *Neo-Slave Narratives: Studies in the Social Logic of a Literary Form.* New York: Oxford University Press, 1999.

Slim, Iceberg. *Long White Con.* London: Payback Press, [1977] 1997.

———. *The Naked Soul of Iceberg Slim.* Los Angeles: Holloway House, 1971.

———. *Trick Baby.* London: Payback Press, [1967] 1996.

Stallings, L.H. "'I'm Goin' Pimp Whores!': The Goines Factor and the Theory of a Hip-Hop Neo-Slave Narrative." *CR: The New Centennial Review* 3 (Fall 2003): 175-203.

Stone, Eddie. *Donald Writes No More.* Los Angeles: Holloway House, 1974.

Williams, John A. *The Man Who Cried I Am.* Introduction by Walter Mosely. Woodstock: Overlook Press, [1967] 2004.

CHAPTER SEVEN

"I'll Be There"

The Love and Defense Narrative
of *Black Girl Lost*

Phyllis Lynne Burns

> *I'll be there*
> *with a love that will shelter you*
> *I'll be there*
> *with a love that will see you through*
> *When you feel lost and about to give up,*
> *'cause your best just ain't good enough,*
> *and you feel the world has grown cold,*
> *and you're drifting out all on your own,*
> *and you need a hand to hold...*
> *Darlin', come on girl*
> *Reach out for me.*[1]
>
> THE FOUR TOPS (1966)

> A song drifted from someone's radio. It was "Reach Out for Me" by the
> Four Tops. The couple listened quietly to the words.
> Yes, they were reaching out for each other.[2]
>
> DONALD GOINES *Black Girl Lost* (1973)

During my M.A. studies, a course entitled "Urban Fiction" was given to the selection
of twentieth-century African American "classics." Course readings included *Invisible
Man*, *Native Son*, and *Their Eyes Were Watching God*. What I remember about the
class most was both this myopic definition of Black literature and how, as the term
progressed, the professor made the absurd pronouncement that a love story could not

emerge from an urban setting. A story of love, if it did exist in such a place, was pretty much not worth telling because the very ideal of "love," situated in this experience, would be overshadowed by the harshness of the "city."

Donald Goines, a premier author of what is called the Black experience, who is recognized as the most widely read Black author in history with more than 10 million books sold worldwide, and who wrote his first novel while incarcerated in Michigan's Jackson State Prison, devoted his genius to depicting the street and its inhabitants' battles against a network of social injustice. What makes Goines's sixteen novels so poignant is how they testify to the experience of being held captive in the central cities of Detroit and Los Angeles. Goines's writing lends authorial importance to a chorus of voices that the academy, in company with mainstream white and Black middle-class America, refuses to hear. In Goines, the task of surviving in the ghetto, or what Elaine Brown identifies as the New Age "barracoon,"[3] oftentimes requires the art of the hustle, crafted and engineered by the drug dealer, pimp, sex worker, and those transfixed by addictions to heroin and/ or money. His stories offer intricate socio-political critiques, words of caution, and general instruction regarding what it means to be alive and struggling to survive in the ghetto. And Goines makes no apologies for his characters. Why should he? The myriad experiences he tells impugn America's socio-economic structure, which feeds off of and replenishes itself through urban blight while classifying Black life as inherently heartless and predatory.

Black Girl Lost

As the title of Goines's sixth novel, *Black Girl Lost* (1973), suggests, tragedy is a central theme of the text, but the author is also interested in mapping out a war waged against this tragedy. What we witness in *Black Girl Lost* is both the tribulation heaped upon the Black female child and the strategy employed by the child to liberate herself from this tragedy.[4] *Black Girl Lost* operates as a continuation of *White Man's Justice, Black Man's Grief* (1972). Both texts offer a searing indictment of America's racist judicial and penal system, defining present-day American justice as criminal because of its reformulation of chattel slavery. But *Black Girl Lost*, written after *White Man's Justice, Black Man's Grief*, extends this polemic. Goines exposes the intersection of racism and sexism aligned to attack the girl child, and attends to the main character's war against these oppressive forces. In *Black Girl Lost*, a prism of hostility defines the very existence of the Black female child. Among other hardships, the protagonist must defend herself against a negligent and abusive mother; an antagonistic educational system; and a system of law whose passion is to deny her the legitimacy of self-definition.

What makes *Black Girl Lost* distinct and drives the narrative's momentum is, quite simply, love. The protagonist and her lover, both of whom fight to stay alive within a world that would much rather have them dead or imprisoned, wield their love for each other as a lethal weapon of defense.[5] *Black Girl Lost* is not the story where love conquers all, because Sandra and Chink's love for each does not eliminate their problems. The couple still battle racist cops. Sandra is raped and has money and drugs stolen from her. Chink is incarcerated in a facility that operates like a plantation; and, in the end, Chink dies and Sandra faces a life of imprisonment. Their life together is not a fairy tale, but as the narrator of *Black Girl Lost* informs us: "No matter what hardships life might put in their way, it would be together that they would face them" (88). Living as they do in the central city, the mean streets, the ghetto, the barracoon, their story is the ultimate "*You and Me against the World.*"

Sandra's Persistent Despair

Much like the opening of his second novel, *Whoreson: The Story of a Ghetto Pimp* (1972), in *Black Girl Lost* Goines illustrates the bondage endemic to the inner-city environment. When Goines introduces Whoreson, his protagonist recounts the story of his birth as told to him by his mother. In his retelling, Whoreson envisions the world as a place where all the elements are aligned and poised to attack him. In L. H. Stallings's analysis of Goines as the originator of the "Hip-Hop neo-slave narrative" (2003), the critic turns our attention to the first paragraph of *Whoreson*, observing: "from the snow and slush to the hidden corners or dark doorways, every descriptive element in the passage emphasizes a void and hole of oppression" (193).[6] Images of the terror that lurks in the dark, and an atmosphere of despair, also ring out in the opening of *Black Girl Lost*.

As Sandra sets out in the darkness and cold of an early morning to find her mother, who is inside a whiskey house drinking and partying:

> Sounds coming from inside the house were more than just loud and helter-skelter. "You black motherfucker!" The cuss word seemed to fill the night air whirling around the child who stood shivering in Los Angeles's early March wind. Suddenly the sound of a bottle breaking came to her. Next many voices raised at once, until another voice could be heard overriding the rest (7).

At this point in the narrative, the child is unnamed but identified by gender. Nevertheless, from this passage and other descriptions found in the very first chapter, we can glean the hostility that defines the relationship between the eight year old Sandra and her mother—a hostility then extended to include a physically brutal natural environment, a threatening cityscape, and the city's inhabitants and institutions. Sandra's predicament is organized within a world shown to be "more than just loud and helter-skelter." Thus, a distinct pattern emerges in the novel's introduction that refutes the assumption that Sandra's life is an isolated, random, inexplicable existence, as if there is no rhyme or reason to the brutal conditions she and countless others endure. Instead, Sandra's experiences as a Black child can be attributed to an intricate network of institutionalized oppression.

To begin, the cuss word emanating from the cacophony of voices is clearly heard by the child as it "fill[s] the night air whirling around [her]." Because the cuss word wraps itself around the child, joined as it is with the cold air that makes the girl shiver, the expletive becomes attached to the child. Sandra becomes the "black motherfucker" hurled. In this instance, the term is used to establish an opposition between mother and child. The girl has ventured into the darkness hungry and alone to retrieve her mother who left their apartment the day before with the promise— now a lie—to return home with food for her daughter: "Now don't go out Sandra. It's too cold out today. I'll bring back something for breakfast in a little while" (9). But as the cuss word reveals, the Black girl's needs and desires are envisioned as an intrusive disruption of her mother's plans. Any attention given in this context to Sandra, the Black child, "fucks up" the mother's plans, which directly conflict with Sandra's necessities.

Later on in the novel, we hear others call Sandra out of her name. The cuss words are always hurled at Sandra during moments when she sets herself in opposition to those who are abusing her for their own selfish gain. For example, Sandra and her mother, Sandie, fight over a cake given to Sandra by a sympathetic store owner who knows Sandra is starving. Sandie snatches the food from her daughter as she calls her daughter a "whore" (23). When Sandra confronts the heroin addict, Eddie, by calling him out for only coming around on her pay day to cop money for his fix, he calls Sandra a "[f]ool ass young bitch" (52), at the very moment Sandra has outwitted him. She receives a similar response to her defiance when she sees her love, Chink, bleeding and handcuffed in the backseat of a patrol car. Instead of allowing herself to be bullied, Sandra confronts the white cop who tries to intimidate her: "'Isn't this your boyfriend?' he asked harshly, trying to make his voice as cold as possible so that he would frighten her" (61). Sandra responds: "If you mean, honkie, do I give him pussy every now and then, that's our business. Ain't got nothing to do with no peckerwood." The cop then calls her a "[s]mart black bitch" (61). Each verbal attack erupts precisely at the moment when Sandra tries to safeguard herself from being demeaned, intimidated or exploited. The expletives are invoked to cruelly admonish the Black girl for wanting promises to be fulfilled, for not wanting to be used or bullied.

What Sandra wants is either deemed absurd or designated as criminal. The attacks are designed to remind Sandra of her place, to prevent her from overstepping the boundaries of an identity constructed by those who envision Sandra as beneath them. To be sure, Sandra is persistently locked in a vicious power struggle. This point becomes abundantly clear during her confrontation with Eddie, and even more so with the white cops, who beat Sandra mercilessly once they realize they cannot control her. A cop slaps Sandra because of her response to his question, and in retaliation against his physical attack Sandra delivers a series of devastating blows: "Sandra didn't think she could win, but she could hurt this one white bastard in front of her" (62). As the narrator explains, the police "couldn't tolerate" Sandra's retaliation, so a barrage of officers rush at Sandra with their billy clubs. The passage detailing the onslaught reads as a veritable orgy of violence: "they rushed at her with billy clubs, striking each other in their hurry to strike her" (62).

What also becomes clear from the very beginning of the novel is the limitation of Sandra's options. From the outset she is situated alone and "outside," amidst the "teeth chattering" cold. Moreover, each opportunity to rectify her situation presents potentially lethal consequences. Sandra has learned, for example, that if she goes inside the house to get her mother, her mother will become angry and beat her. She also fears what may be lurking behind the bushes, which appear before her as sinister sentries that "stood as high as or higher than a man standing straight up" (8). To make matters worse, Sandra's first approach to the house results in a "voice coming out of the darkness [that] makes Sandra jump" (9). She is confronted with a hard decision: she must either stay outside in the cold, or get into the warm car of a strange man, who she knows to be drunk from his slurred speech. However, the appearance of the drunken man, who had not "had a young girl" for "a long time" and initially plans to rape the eight year old Sandra, marks a critical turning point in the narrative in terms of its establishing a theme of love and empathy (11).

Her Sorrow Was His... and Theirs

Sandra is not raped by the man who approaches her in the darkness. He instead wrestles with his conscience once he sees Sandra's emaciated body. He becomes angered at the thought of how a mother could allow her child to go hungry while he simultaneously criticizes himself:

> "You're a sonofabitch," the man said to himself as he observed the young kid next to him. With her coat open, he could see just how poor she was. Her legs were so thin that she seemed deformed. That coat with no buttons on it couldn't possibly keep the child warm, he reasoned. What kind of a mother could the child have, he wondered, as he took his time

and examined her. The mini-dress she wore was too small, besides being a spring dress. He reached over and felt the material. The dress was stiff from being out in the cold. He pulled her across the seat and put his arm around her (12).

The interaction between the nameless man and Sandra provides our first glimpse of the protagonist from a point-of-view other than her own. This viewpoint is important in that it reinforces Sandra's vulnerability as a child, in addition to providing a critique of how poverty and neglect affect her. Goines makes a definitive statement with the inclusion of the man, who first appears as an ominous presence. Without a doubt, Goines is aware of how outsiders embrace images of the ghetto as the terrain where pathological corruption and decadence run rampant. The nameless man's response to Sandra deliberately refuses to gratify mainstream conceptions of the predatory Black male.[7] What readers are given is a man who aligns his fear with that of the starving, vulnerable child. In addition to buying her dinner, his thoughts turn to his own daughters: "He pictured them as they were when they were Sandra's age. The thought of a man attempting to do to one of them what he had started to do to Sandra filled him with rage" (14). He drives Sandra back to her home and readers are told that years later he still thinks of the eight year old. Had he raped Sandra, he believes the violence would have devastated him in equal measure: "he realized as he drove though the silent streets of L.A. that he almost committed a crime that would have filled him with so much guilt and shame that he seriously doubted if he'd have been able to live himself" (17).

This exchange between Sandra and the man foreshadows the complex emotions that drive the text, and give meaning to Sandra's relationships. Those who care for Sandra are always able to locate themselves in her suffering. Their identification with Sandra's pain emerges out of an understanding that her predicament largely results from various forms of systemic oppression. Some of these forms of oppression are more obvious, as they involve the direct action of state power, such as the police targeting of Blacks for harassment and abuse under drug laws, while hypocritically profiting from the illegal drug trade. Goines's rendition of this type of oppression registers the ironic effects of state power: while such a technique of subjugation is intended to deny its victims the possibility of fulfilling and meaningful lives, and thus put the possibility of humane and empathetic understanding beyond their reach, it instead creates the opportunity for empathy. Both Sandra and Chink are the frequent victims of this specific form of oppression, and their common situation creates the basis for a profound understanding and sympathy—for love.

Significantly, Goines introduces this aspect of power, according to which the very techniques of oppression can not only be overcome but turned against themselves, in the scene under discussion. In this case, the working of power is, perhaps, more subtle. A man finding a young girl in the ghetto on whom he'd plan to act out fantasies of rape is not, of course, part of any official government policy, but an effect of the symbolic system that sustains a social order based on racial, economic and sexual inequality. In this scene the nameless man, a potential sexual predator, must move beyond the symbolic universe in which the presumed savagery and depredations of the inner city would render them fair game (or at least obvious victims) for debauchery and abuse. In this situation a set of stereotypes, which operate to arouse the man's lust, must be overcome. These stereotypes act as a barrier between people, but as this scene demonstrates, they are not an impermeable barrier. In this case, Goines depicts not only the failure of the stereotype to create an act of sexual violence that would sustain the social order by perpetuating the stereotype— the act of rape, if registered by the police or media at all, would simply be taken as another piece of evidence of the irredeemable savagery of the inner city—but also shows the stereotype to provide the very occasion of empathetic understanding. The symbolic construction of Sandra as a victim draws the man into an encounter with her, and, as a result of his recognition of Sandra's humanity, his life is changed. Goines makes it clear that this recognition goes beyond the fact that he no longer thinks of girls in Sandra's situation as objects on which to enact sexual fantasies. Rather, he has an epiphany regarding the common humanity of such girls, based on identifying Sandra's suffering with that of his own daughters, who, he realizes, are every bit as vulnerable as Sandra.

In general, those who sympathize with Sandra do so based upon the recognition of their own vulnerability to the same forces that oppress Sandra. Common stigmatization becomes, within this novel, the basis for both empathy and, as I will discuss, passionate love. For those who empathize with or love Sandra, her life comes to signify the grotesque disparity between the normative and legal order and any defensible ethical order. She is a small human manifestation of this discrepancy, and so Sandra's allies must reach the awareness that because her suffering is not only accepted by the state or society, but on some level required by it, they must step outside the law to help protect Sandra. Sammy, the storeowner, who survived the horrors of a Nazi death camp, is able to see the look of hunger on Sandra's face because "[h]e had seen the look on too many faces when he was in a concentration camp in Germany" (20). It is significant that Sammy is the only white man to sympathize with Sandra, and he requires the lens of the genocidal horrors of the Holocaust to do so. Goines not only marks a correspondence between racial oppression in America and Nazi Germany; he also attributes this judgment to a Holocaust survivor. Sammy might be deemed properly "white" in American terms, but he has been through a horrific lesson in the provisional nature of his racial status, and in turn has acquired an awareness of his own vulnerability to racialist orders of oppression such as the one that victimizes Sandra. Sammy sees an image of his own vulnerability in Sandra, so although child labor laws prevent him from hiring an eight year old, he nevertheless gives her the small task of sweeping the floor and in exchange he routinely gives her food from his store. But whereas the nameless man and Sammy turn to a singular aspect of their life that allows empathy with Sandra, Chink relates his entire life to Sandra's and, as a result, his devotion to her is unshakable.

For starters, both Sandra and Chink are outcasts in school. The narrator explains that the two are among the "practicing illiterate children that fill the ghetto schools" (45). Sandra does not like going to school because her classmates ridicule her shabby clothes, giving her the nickname "Raggedy Ann" (24). In response to their taunts Sandra develops a "protective schizophrenia" (33) intended to redirect the attention of others away from herself: "When called upon by a teacher to stand up and speak, [Sandra] spoke in a low voice and ran her words together so that no one would really understand what she was saying. It became so exasperating that the teacher would stop calling on her" (33). Sandra deploys this strategy to make herself invisible to the teachers who think she is an illiterate "half-wit" (32). And Chink, who "suffered from the same problems Sandra had" regarding clothing (45), also makes himself invisible by pretending to be mentally disturbed. But if Sandra exasperates the white teachers, Chink elicits fear. While other students ridicule Chink because he "looked so much like a monkey" (44), the "young white teachers could not stand to look upon [Chink's] features without shivering away" (45).

Sandra and Chink also share their wherewithal to solve their problems by making the economic system work in their favor, rather than at their expense, stepping outside of the law. They learn the art of the hustle. Sandra learns how to re-appropriate goods – she becomes a skilled "thief," and her talents enable her to feed and clothe herself despite living in a world in which not even her most basic needs are recognized as legitimate. We also see evidence of Sandra turning her skills into a viable enterprise. She boosts clothes from department stores and then turns a profit by selling the clothing to prostitutes. Chink is the "school's pusher" (44); and he also uses the money from his sales to buy clothing, an apartment, and a car. Goines consistently places the choices his characters make in the context of their rational response to conscious and unconscious forms of racism and oppression, neither excusing their actions, per se, nor obscuring the system of racism and oppression. The narrator explains Sandra: "She was the product of circumstances, which had been hard and were still hard" (30). Sandra and Chink's options are limited, to say the least, and so they turn to each other for support and compassion.

CONCLUSION:
Your Life Is Mine – or Love, the Lethal Weapon of Defense

Sandra's allies ultimately understand that they must step outside the law to protect Sandra because her suffering is not only accepted, but required, by the state. Therefore, Sandra and Chink, knowing full well that no one is able to fully protect them and realizing that the state relies on its structures to attack and brutalize them, develop a love that becomes a lethal weapon which they wield to defend themselves. Rather than accede to their status as victims of an immoral legal order, they "hold court in the streets" (110). We first see evidence of their oppositional justice when Chink beats Eddie for assaulting Sandra after she refuses to give Eddie money to buy heroin. Sandra is able to attack the white cop who slaps her because Chink, after seeing Sandra beaten by Eddie, has taught Sandra how to fight. Sandra knows she will not win the fight against the cop, but she manages to spill his blood and break his nose. When Sandra is raped by the two men who come to the apartment she shares with Chink to steal money and drugs, the intruders are only able to do so because they know Chink is in jail and that the police will not intervene. But when Sandra goes to the prison to visit Chink and tells him about the rape, he immediately makes plans to escape. In the end, the men who raped Sandra and the one responsible for engineering the break-in to the apartment are both executed by Chink, "extra-legally."

In *Black Girl Lost*, oppression or the hardship of life is not a barrier to love, it is the condition of love. And, love is, at the same time, the condition of resistance. Because she is a victim of power, Sandra becomes an astute student of power, which allows her to develop strategies of resistance in order to create those small places of freedom for herself and for Chink. While the book's title leads readers to think of Sandra as losing or having been lost within a system of power, her defiance in the face of overwhelming oppression suggests a very different context for a love story: love is power turned against itself. Those who love Sandra recognize in her the effects of political oppression, and see her as a mirror of their own vulnerability and oppression. Sandra's life, and her options in life, are so clearly an effect of power that they must recognize the imperative of stepping outside the law in order to acknowledge her (and their) legitimate human needs. Love is very much the equivalent of a recognition of oppression, and it is this formulation that makes Goines's novels a frequent point of reference in Hip-Hop culture and equally anathema to mainstream academe. Denying the possibility of love to the racialized and disempowered is one way of legitimizing power over the oppressed, but acknowledging love in the context of *Black Girl Lost* can never be part of this process of legitimization.

NOTES

1 The Four Tops, "Reach Out (I'll Be There)." Written by Edward Holland, Jr., Lamont Dozier and Brian Holland (Detroit: Motown Records, 1966).

2 Goines's *Black Girl Lost*, 87.

3 Elaine Brown, former Black Panther Party chairman and author of *A Taste of Power: A Woman's Story* (1992) and *The Condemnation of Little B* (2002), examines in *Condemnation* the arrest and imprisonment of Michael Lewis, the then 12 year-old Atlanta native who now serves a life-sentence, having been tried and convicted of murder as an adult. Brown examines how America's escalating incarceration rates of Black women and men, as well as Black children tried and convicted as adults, reveals how the U.S. penal system envisions the nation's Black communities as "barracoons" (*Condemnation* 69). The barracoon, a term used during chattel slavery, is the holding space, or pen, where the enslaved were held after capture but prior to being sold at auction. Given the booming profits made via the ever-expanding prison industrial complex, the staggering numbers of Blacks held in prisons, coupled with a close reading of the Thirteenth Amendment to the U.S. Constitution that redefines "slavery" in terms of imprisonment, Brown writes that the "black ghetto is where black people have been quartered since the end of slavery" (*Condemnation*, 69).

4 According to Eddie Stone, author of *Donald Writes No More* (2003), the persona of the Black child "marked the highlight of [Goines'] emotional content. It was through the children and their mothers that the true tragedy of the black experience emerged" (77-78).

5 For another example of how love is fashioned as a lethal weapon for self-defense, see the "Prologue" and the first section, entitled "Darky," of Sherley Anne Williams's *Dessa Rose* (1987); also, see Pearl Cleage's *Flyin West* (1997).

6 Donald Goines wrote extensively about the socio-economic situation of the Black underclass in his myriad depictions inner-city life as a form of neo-slavery. And since Hip-Hop artists reference Goines extensively in their depictions of contemporary Black life, the academy must recognize the existence of a "Hip-Hop neo-slave narrative or fail as intellectual critics of contemporary Black life themselves. See L.H. Stallings's "'I'm Goin' to Pimp Whores!': The Goines Factor and the Theory of the Hip-Hop Neo-Slave Narrative" (2003).

7 Goines's refusal to repeat such stereotypes distinctly contrasts, however, with the editors at Holloway House, who make a calculated effort to appeal to the imagination of the "outsider." Their cover and selected excerpt from *Black Girl Lost* warrants our attention. On the book's cover, below the photograph selected for the text, the teaser reads: "THE DONALD GOINES STORY ABOUT A YOUNG WOMAN WHO FOUND LOVE ...

RAPE AND MURDER!" The exclamation that punctuates "RAPE AND MURDER" is troubling since it reads as if the reader should be titillated by the brutality. Similarly, the pull-quote teaser reads:

> The man glanced at her. The coat open now from the strong wind that kept blowing revealed just how thin the child was. For a moment the man hesitated, his conscience disturbed him slightly. He knew what he was about to do was wrong, but he had just enough whiskey that night not to really care. It had been a long time since he'd had a young girl.

The excerpt is taken from the scene under discussion, in which Sandra is approached by the nameless man. He initially intends to rape her, but instead buys her dinner and becomes angry with himself after reflecting on how he would react if someone raped his daughter. The editorial selection (and isolation) of the above passage strategically ignores this empathy and sensationalizes rape at the expense of the main character.

REFERENCES

Brown, Elaine. *The Condemnation of Little B.* Boston: Beacon Press, 2002.

Cleage, Pearl. *Flyin West.* New York: Theatre Communications, 1997.

Goines, Donald. *Black Girl Lost.* Los Angeles: Hollloway House, [1973] 2007.

Stallings, L. H. "'I'm Goin' Pimp Whores': The Goines Factor and the Theory of a Hip-Hop Neo-Slave Narrative." *CR: The New Centennial Review* 3:3 (2003): 175-203.

Stone, Eddie. *Donald Writes No More: A Biography of Donald Goines.* Los Angeles: Holloway House, 2003.

Williams, Sherley Anne. *Dessa Rose: A Novel.* New York: William Morrow, 1987.

CHAPTER EIGHT

Representing Prison Rape

Race, Masculinity, and Incarceration in Donald Goines's *White Man's Justice, Black Man's Grief*

Andrew Sargent

In April 1981, in the early years of what Randall Kennedy terms the racial "darkening" (134) of America's jail and prison populations, the *New York Times* reported that a New York Criminal Court judge refused to send a young, middle-class white male to the city's Rikers Island jail on the grounds that the defendant would almost certainly be sexually assaulted by the jail's predominantly African American and Latino inmate population. "We take judicial notice of the defendant's slight build, his mannerisms, dress, color, and ethnic background," the judge wrote in his opinion, "and are cognizant of the unfortunate realities that he would not last for ten minutes at Rikers Island." Arguing that "the State of New York could not guarantee [the man's] safety in prison surroundings," the judge predicted that the defendant, if sent to jail, "would be immediately subject to homosexual rape and sodomy and to brutalities from prisoners such as make the imagination recoil in horror" (Shipp B3).[1]

As the somewhat baroque language of that final sentence attests, the possibility that a white man could be raped in jail by African American or Latino inmates exerts a powerful hold over the American racial imaginary. As Ted Conover puts it, the "rape-of-the-white-guy trope" is "a fixture of how middle-class America thinks about prison" (262). At the same time, this "trope" is at least partially rooted in statistical reality: as Patricia Hill Collins notes, "male prisoner-on-prisoner sexual abuse is not an aberration," but "a deeply rooted systemic problem in U.S. prisons," and, since the 1970s, the most common form of interracial rape in U.S. jails and prisons has been committed by Black inmates against white ones (234). "White men rarely rape Black men," Collins observes. "Instead, African American men are often involved in the rape of White men who [like the above defendant] fit the categories of vulnerability" (238). It is also true that Black and Latino prisoners—particularly at urban jails such as Rikers—have outnumbered whites for decades. Indeed, by the late 1990s, ninety-two percent of the fifteen thousand Rikers inmates were Black or Latino, despite the fact that "blacks and Hispanics represent [only] 49 percent of the city's population" (Wynn 7).

What may be most striking about the above judge's opinion, however, is not its basis in "fact" but rather the troubling conclusions that it draws *from* those facts. By using a selective representation of interracial male rape to rationalize keeping a white man out of jail, the judge not only contributes to the ever-worsening problem of racially disproportionate incarceration, but also uncritically affirms a broader—and more deeply problematic—set of racial and sexual narratives that are embedded in popular perceptions of America's post-Civil Rights carceral landscape: namely that while African American males naturally belong in prison, white males do not. He also affirms that as America's jail and prison populations have become Blacker and browner since the 1970s, these institutions have become problematic not because of the damage they do to African American men and "minority" communities, but rather because of the bodily destruction they may cause to white men unlucky enough to be incarcerated.[2] By sliding past the many factors—structural racism, socioeconomic inequality, racially biased policing, and inequitable bail and sentencing procedures—that produce such populations in the first place, the judge's take on interracial rape feeds what David Savran calls "the fantasy of the white male as victim" (4), and what Auli Ek refers to as the "fantasy that black inmates control prisons" (84). In these cultural narratives, Black-on-white prison rape becomes the most extreme manifestation of how white men have been disadvantaged by the social and racial transformations in American society since the 1960s.

In what follows, I consider how this deployment of interracial rape and the reactionary narratives it authorizes were anticipated, complicated, and hotly contested by *White Man's Justice, Black Man's Grief*, African American "pulp" writer Donald Goines's prescient, neglected, 1973 prison novel. Written at the dawn of what has come to be a contemporary American epidemic of racialized incarceration—when the political fervor of Civil Rights and Black Power gave way to "law and order,"

Rockefeller drug laws, and a prison-industrial complex housing ever-expanding inmate populations—Goines's raw, naturalistic work of fiction seeks above all to expose what its front cover calls "the bigotry built into our system." Focusing on the arrest, incarceration, and eventual life-imprisonment of its Black male protagonist, the novel centers its critical project on a strategically contrarian depiction of the very thing that is, for some, the most sensational, disturbing evidence that the prison system victimizes white males: namely, Black-on-white male rape.

If it is true that certain types of white men in the late-twentieth-century prison are disproportionately vulnerable to interracial prison rape, and if it is also true that systemic racism has contributed to making America's jails and prisons disproportionately Black, Goines's novel implicitly asks how one might depict the former in order to explain the latter. That is to say, how might the literary representation of interracial rape and sodomy work as a counterintuitive heuristic for training our gaze on the "law-and-order" policies and racially biased bail, sentencing, and incarceration procedures that shoehorn so many Black men into jail and prison in the first place and, in the process, nurture the very prison rape culture decried in the judge's decision? And, finally, how might a text work to disrupt received perceptions of the "natural" criminality and sexual aggressiveness of Black men, even as it acknowledges the immorality of those who perpetrate actual sexual violence in prison?

By addressing such questions, Goines's novel fills an under-discussed gap in representations of the racial and sexual dimensions of what prison activist Angela Y. Davis calls our contemporary American "punishment industry" (x). Goines's willingness to grapple with the underlying meaning of Black-on-white prison rape differentiates him not only from the white-male-centered legal sphere embodied in the above-mentioned Rikers decision, but also from other key voices that have played a significant role in establishing prisons as a cultural battleground in the American racial imaginary: among them, radical Black prison activists of the late 1960s and early 1970s such as Eldridge Cleaver; the "grossly sensationalized" genre of Hollywood prison films (Davis x); and even the rapists themselves—all of whom attempt to evade, elide, excuse, justify, or erase Black-on-white rape. Before I say more about about Goines's novel, it is important to touch briefly on these sources in order to convey a sense of the cultural context in which Goines's transgressive project takes shape. By arguing for Goines's value as a writer and social observer, my essay seeks to contribute to the recent surge in scholarly attention paid by H. Bruce Franklin, Peter Caster, Auli Ek, and Dennis Childs, among others, to the insurgent resources of African American prison literature as a critical lens through which to view the institutional history and racially specific operations of the U.S. criminal justice system.

Prison Sociology, Radical Prisoners, and Buddy Convicts

The first major study of the racial dynamics of the American prison, Leo Carroll's *Hacks, Blacks, and Cons* (1974), appeared just one year after the publication of *White Man's Justice, Black Man's Grief*; Carroll's naming and examination of the problem of Black-on-white rape affirms Goines's prescience. By pinpointing such overlap between fiction and sociology, I do not mean to credit Goines for achieving "an unmediated real" (Caster xii) in his depiction of prison sexual violence, nor do I wish to suggest that prison sociology such as Carroll's is itself an unmediated representation of such behavior. Rather, I quote Carroll's study here to corroborate, as much as possible, Goines's case for Black-on-white rape as a salient feature of the post-Civil Rights penal institution.

In the following excerpts, for example, Carroll establishes the recurrence of what he calls "black-onto-white" sexual assault:

> In the prison, where the significance of sex is intensified by the deprivation of heterosexual contact and where black and white males live close together, the role of sex in racial conflict is thrown into sharp relief. . . . More striking than the number of sexual attacks is the extent to which they are interracial. Each of my 21 informants—black and white prisoners and staff members alike—estimated that 75 percent or more of the sexual assaults involve black aggressors and white victims. (182)

> The most common and open form of coerced homosexual behavior is the rape of young white inmates by groups of blacks. (187)

> None of the incidents involved white aggressors and black victims. (257)

Noting that such dynamics were exacerbated by heightened political solidarity among Black inmates in the early 1970s and the era's court-mandated pushes toward racial integration in prison, which fueled interracial enmity between inmates, Carroll then goes on to offer his primary explanation for this recurrence of Black-on-white rape:

> [T]he motive force behind these acts ... of violent aggression ... has its roots deep within the entire socio-historical context of black-white relations in this country. The prison is ... an arena within which blacks may direct aggression developed through 300 years of oppression against individuals perceived to be representatives of the oppressors. (184)

For the African American inmates Carroll interviews, raping white prisoners becomes a violent form of individualized payback for a history of institutionalized racial injustice, a means of asserting their own manhood through the act of robbing white victims of theirs. For Carroll, this link between the bodily realm and the historical context does not justify such violence, but it does provide a powerful explanation for its recurrence.[3]

This effort to connect individual actions to a broader history of oppression is also characteristic of the impassioned Marx-inflected critiques in Cleaver's *Soul on Ice* (1968) and George Jackson's *Soledad Brother* (1970), two touchstone texts of a Black Power-era radical prisoner movement that sought to cast African American inmates as political prisoners of an American racist-capitalist social order. Most striking about these texts is that even as Black-on-white male prison rape was becoming the most statistically common form of coercive sex in post-Civil Rights-era American jails and prisons, neither Cleaver nor Jackson openly considered it as a part of Black prison experience or as a potential act of revolutionary racial revenge. It is possible that the violence described by Goines and Carroll postdated Cleaver's and Jackson's prison writings. Yet one might also speculate that to probe the intricacies of such acts might have run afoul of the patriarchal/heteronormative worldviews of Cleaver and Jackson, Black Power activists who adhered to what Michele Wallace critiques as the doctrine of "Black Macho." To be sure, Cleaver once called the rape of white *women* "an insurrectionary act," arguing that the violation of the white female body was a form of "trampling upon the white man's law" (33). But any sexual behavior suggestive of homosexuality, even "situational" prison homosexuality, was, for Cleaver, a form of self-emasculation, a "sickness" on par with "baby rape" (136). This view perhaps accounts for the complete absence from his writings of any engagement with the social reality of interracial male prison rape.[4]

By the mid-1970s, as the radical prison movement and Black Power gave way to the Nixon era's law-and-order silent-majority backlash, Cleaver's and Jackson's efforts to situate Black inmates in the context of historical oppression were eclipsed by a more conservative, ahistorical vision of the prisoner as an independent actor victimized only by his own poor choices. As Eric Cummins summarizes, "by 1975 . . . the moral discourse of the Right on crime and the criminal had come to dominate" over "the Left's alternative vision of the convict as cultural hero and revolutionary savior, or even as cultural victim" (266). This conservative turn arguably provided an incubating cultural climate for Hollywood prison films that, in grudging deference to the increased visibility of Blacks in American life after the Civil Rights and Black

Power movements, purveyed an influential image of interracial cooperation—not interracial hostility—through the deployment of a narrative of what I would call "interracial convict bonding." In films such as *Escape from Alcatraz* (1979), *The Shawshank Redemption* (1994), and *American History X* (1998), a white male convict benefits from the friendship of a Black "lifer" inmate, a "natural" resident of the prison who helps the white inmate to survive and sometimes aids his escape as well. While prison has been "central to the oppression of black people" since at least the end of the Civil War (Franklin, *Prison* xv), these "buddy" films transform prison into a site of white male self-assertion; instead of depicting Black-on-white rape directly, they sublimate and reconstitute it into a more palatable form by positioning the Black prisoner not as a potential rapist but as a protector of the white male against a *white* sexual predator—one who is so leeringly, inhumanly white (e.g., an albino "hillbilly" or neo-Nazi skinhead) that his presence comes across as a form of narrative overcompensation.[5]

A keen illustration of these fantastic racial and sexual dynamics appears near the end of *Escape from Alcatraz*, as Clint Eastwood's white hero, convicted bank robber Frank Lee Morris, is saved by a friendly Black inmate named "English" from being stabbed by a would-be white rapist called "Wolf." As Morris, whose self-possession and muscular masculinity have already garnered him the respect of the prison's African American inmates, stands in the prison yard on the day of his planned escape, Wolf prepares to stab Morris, only to be forcibly relieved of his knife by English. English's swift-handed resourcefulness on behalf of his white friend ensures that Morris will avoid Wolf's unwanted penetration and proceed with his prison break later that night. English's action also enables the film to bolster Eastwood's racial-masculine credentials by granting his character the protection of the Black men who "rule" the prison yard while simultaneously eliminating the Black male as a sexual threat. By pairing Black and white men against a shared white homosexual enemy, the film extols an expedient image of interracial—and defensively heterosexual—allegiance. Furthermore, by erasing Black-on-white rape from its depiction of inmate relations, the film avoids placing the white hero in a situation that might undermine viewer respect for him or force us to grapple with the underlying structural realities that generate racial imbalances in the first place. In the context of such sleight-of-hand maneuvers, Goines's literary representation of interracial comity's diametrical opposite—Black-on-white rape—comes to look like an unexpected ethical tool. In Goines's hands, the "insurrectionary act" becomes not Black-on-white rape itself but rather its literary representation.[6]

White Man's Justice, Black Man's Grief

What kind of book is *White Man's Justice, Black Man's Grief?* Written in sexually graphic prose peppered with streetwise 1970s Black vernacular, the novel speaks in a denotative literary style that Greg Goode calls "ghetto realism" ("Donald Goines" 96), a mode characteristic of much of the "Black experience" fiction—or Black "pulp" fiction—first pioneered in the late 1960s by the pimp-turned-writer Robert Beck, also known as Iceberg Slim. Issued as a mass-market paperback by the Los Angeles-based Holloway House Publishing company, sold in "general stores and mom-and-pop shops in black America" (Calcutt and Shephard 109), and aimed primarily at a readership of "young, urban, and working-class African American men" (Dietzel 163), the novel has a critical status that, like that of all of Goines's sixteen novels from the early 1970s, remains marginal in scholarly circles. As Goode notes, "With respect to the standards of literature, the books of Donald Goines are not considered subliterary, for they are not even considered" ("From *Dopefiend*" 42).

The novel's minimalist plot centers on the arrest and incarceration of Chester Hines, an African American career criminal in his mid-thirties. That the name of the novel's central character is Chester Hines—almost certainly an homage to the African American writer and onetime prison inmate Chester *Himes*—suggests Goines's own self-conscious effort to situate himself in, and signify on, a literary tradition of African American crime and prison writers that includes Richard Wright, Malcolm X, and Cleaver, among others.[7] Himes, a "father figure in the urban fiction genre" (Allen 153), is best known for his mid-century racial protest fiction and hard-boiled Harlem crime novels; Himes also wrote a semiautobiographical prison novel, *Cast the First Stone* (1952), and Goines rewrites Himes's vision of inmate relationships in striking ways. As the novel opens, Chester finds himself arrested at a routine traffic stop for carrying a concealed weapon. After being assessed an impossibly high bail fee, he is incarcerated for six months in a Detroit jail. Although Chester does not participate in any sexual assaults while imprisoned, he witnesses myriad forms of sexual dehumanization in his racially integrated twenty-man jail ward. Goines—who served a combined seven and a half years during the 1960s in an inner-city Detroit jail, the federal penitentiary at Terre Haute, Indiana, and Michigan's Jackson State Prison—narrates and describes much of this sexual violence in graphic detail.

It may seem contradictory that a book that devotes considerable attention to the grisly rape of white men by Black men seeks to *challenge* the perception that white men are the primary victims of "Blackened" prisons. Based on the novel's strident six-word title and its cheap Holloway House packaging, one might conclude that

Goines is interested solely in exploiting the spectacle of interracial rape for salacious purposes or celebrating the racial payback that white men supposedly have coming to them. It seems indicative of the book's ostensibly deviant content that Franklin, the dean of prison literature scholars, intends as a compliment his description of the text as "one of the most appalling visions of prison in the terrifying pages of prison literature" (*Prison* xvii). Yet this challenge of representing the "appalling" and the "terrifying"—that is, representing racial ugliness in the service of racial protest—constitutes one of the book's most productive tensions. Indeed, Goines's deliberate focus on the roughest aspects of prison race relations enables his text to seize the reader's attention and generate deeper insights into *why* such atrocities happen in the first place. Goines's strategy of depicting the physical endangerment of white males also suggests not just a desire to practice "realism" but an awareness that in a culture that has historically privileged whiteness over Blackness, such representations might better capture the attention of readers—both Black and white—conditioned to see *white* victimization as more noteworthy than Black suffering.

How, then, can one represent Black-on-white male rape without reinforcing stereotypes of the Black man as rapist? Goines's novel manages this dilemma by relying on several techniques. First, he draws on naturalism, a literary mode characteristic of much prison fiction that casts the criminal justice system as the dominant external force in the lives of Black inmates and focuses on the underpublicized cost for *Black* men of existing in a macho prison rape culture in which Black men appear to "rule." If Goines at times drifts into what one definition of naturalism calls "sexual sensationalism," he also follows naturalism's tendency to express outrage at the injustice of human beings who suffer as "victims of natural forces and social environment" (Baldick 146).[8] It is equally important for Goines's project that the worst sexual atrocities committed by Black inmates in the novel are always seen through the eyes of Chester, the Black male protagonist, who does not commit assaults and is himself threatened in various ways by the men who commit rape. This strategy has the effect of foregrounding how Black men, even if they are only spectators to sexual violence, are themselves disciplined and punished by a prison rape culture that only *seems* to victimize white men more. In addition, even as his novel gains dramatic mileage and no small amount of titillation from depicting the act of prison rape, Goines takes care to discredit the self-justifying rhetoric of the rapists themselves, who assert that such assaults are legitimate forms of payback for historical racial oppression. Finally, Goines also juxtaposes renderings of brutal interracial assaults with at least one example of interracial male friendship, showing how the racial imbalances of jail prompt white male inmates to try to adopt the trappings of "Black" masculinity as a kind of survival technique.

"The white boys were being fucked"

Several of these narrative strategies come to the fore early in Goines's novel, as Chester, newly arrived in jail, is led by white guards down to the racially integrated, twenty-man ward where he will spend the next several months. Because this scene is rich in details central to my argument about Goines's representation of jail sexual practices, I quote and discuss it here at length:

> Chester . . . glanced into the ward and noticed that it was just as crowded as the first one, but there was one difference. The first cell had been full, but there had only been black men in it. This one had four white prisoners in it, and they all had one thing in common. Each man sported a black eye.
>
> The deputy knew as well as Chester what was happening. From past experience Chester knew. The white boys were being fucked, and their food and money were being taken. It happened on every ward. Whenever possible, the turnkeys tried to make it equal. If twenty men were in a cell, they tried to make it ten white and ten black. But it was impossible. For one thing, the whites made bond as soon as possible. Either their people were able to raise the money or their bonds weren't as high as the average black man's. Either way, whichever whitey was unfortunate enough to have to spend some time in the county jail, it was an experience he would never forget. The loss of his manhood was only the beginning. The loss of his life was a good possibility. The only ones who were ever spared were those who had done time or who knew the ropes or who could talk like a brother and fight as good as one, too. There was absolutely no two ways about it, a white boy had to fight to save his asshole. (43–44)

Here Goines advances what I would argue is his novel's most urgent thematic insight: the cause-and-effect relationship between the privileged racial position of whiteness in the institutional hierarchy of the criminal justice system (cause) and the sexual victimization of the "minority" white male prisoners in the jail (effect). Presaging the real-life consequences of the aforementioned Rikers Island case, in which a judge's short-term decision to keep a white man out of jail exacerbates the long-term racial asymmetry facing white inmates who are *not* excused from jail time, Goines observes that it is precisely because white prisoners often have more money and are granted more lenient bail amounts and sentences that they show up in much scarcer numbers in the jail itself. The resulting racial imbalances are so severe that it is impossible for the guards to, as Goines's narrator puts it, "make it equal." As a result, those particular white men who *are* jailed will unavoidably find themselves in a minority position and be vulnerable to sexual domination by their more numerous Black counterparts, who are themselves conditioned by a culture of "hegemonic masculinity" (Sabo, Kupers, and London 5) in which power and respect are attained through such acts of brutality. In this way, Goines links together the two-pronged reality that, as Carroll puts it, "the majority of sexual assaults involve black aggressors and white victims," and that "in comparison to white prisoners, black prisoners receive harsher penalties … for similar offenses" (19). Goines shows how the latter injustice *helps to bring about* the former.

Equally significant in the above passage is Goines's narrative strategy of relating the sordid details of interracial rape from Chester's point of view, so that we learn about the prevalence of rape from the narrative perspective of a Black man who is *not* involved in perpetrating such acts. In several sentences, Goines conveys that Chester "watched," "glanced," "noticed," and "knew" what was happening in the jail ward. In one sense, this emphasis on the fact that the sexual abuse of white prisoners is being witnessed by Chester enables Goines to satisfy the reader's desire to see rape while also distancing the novel's hero from any implication in rape itself. As Ek notes, this pattern of detaching the Black male from Black-on-white rape is characteristic of recent examples of Black prison autobiography such as Nathan McCall's *Makes Me Wanna Holler* (1994), in which the author wishes to avoid any hint of self-implication in homosexuality. And yet Goines's management of perspective does more than create distance between Chester and the rapists; it also prompts us to consider the impact that acts of Black-on-white sexual assault have on Chester himself. Even as it is white men who are sexually victimized in the actual jail ward, their victimization exerts a collateral impact on Black men who are disciplined to conform to this macho ethos or else risk being victimized themselves. It is telling in this regard that the back cover of the Holloway House paperback edition of Goines's novel announces that "This is the story of Chester Hines, who thought he was the baddest man to come down the street. Behind prison walls he was *nothing more than fresh meat*" (emphasis added). Even though Chester is never actually assaulted himself, the language of this summary suggests (in rhyming vernacular) that Hines is still being "fucked"—by the system, by the rape culture, and, as we discover later, by his trusted friend, Willie, who will betray him at the end of the novel.

The above-quoted passage on the jail ward also conveys the importance of style and voice in Goines's approach to capturing Chester's reality. Throughout this passage and the novel, Goines shifts deliberately between standard English and vernacular slang—"white boys," "fucked," "turnkeys," "whitey," "asshole"—in a way that suggests the importance of using the race- and class-specific argot of the jail ward to convey its ethos in an authentic manner. For Goines, it is crucial to be able to "talk like a brother" if one is to survive in the predominantly Black jail ward, and such language is equally essential—if also "essentialist"—for an author seeking to capture the lived experience of such survival. While the phrase "talk like a brother" is an arguably simplistic signifier to convey the contours of Black speech, it also evokes the 1970s working-class urban Black male vernacular of Goines's primary audience and enables him to signify on more conventional, white-centered legalistic accounts of jail life.

"An Angry Preface"

Even before we reach the jail ward, Goines has already introduced his critique of Black male victimization by starting off his novel with "An Angry Preface," a three-page polemical essay that seeks to expose how the racialized inequities of law enforcement and the bail-bonds system contribute to the overrepresentation of indigent African American men in urban jails. "Since this work of fiction deals with the court system," Goines begins in a self-conscious departure from his role as a novelist, "I'd like to direct the reader's attention to an awesome abuse inflicted daily upon the less fortunate . . . an abuse which no statesman, judge or attorney (to my knowledge) has moved to effectively remedy. I'm speaking of the bail-bond system" (7). Goines's thesis here is that urban jails—where most inmates are either pretrial detainees or convicted felons serving out a sentence of less than a year—house predominantly poor Black men because these inmates are unable to pay the bail costs that would allow them to go home. And because "the courts are glutted," Goines explains, "[t]here are cases of people (many of whom were found innocent of the charges for which they are arrested) spending more than a year in county jails simply because they couldn't raise bail-bond money" (7–8). "Make no mistake about it," Goines concludes, "there's big money in the bail bond business, and most of it is being made at the expense of poor blacks" (9). By invoking the bail-bond system here before introducing us to his characters, Goines establishes the systemic lens through which he wants us to view what follows; in effect, he argues that the individual lives of the prisoners in his novel—and the brutal acts that take place there—cannot be understood without first considering the institutional structure that ensnares them.

The sociological emphasis of Goines's preface does generate a key tension, however, as we move deeper into the novel: a tension between his preface's emphasis on Black male victimization and his novel's strategy of characterizing Chester, his lead Black male protagonist, as an unrepentant career criminal. While Goines announces that his preface "speak[s] for the people who are picked up on the streets or stopped for minor traffic violations and who are taken to jail on trumped-up, Catch-22 charges simply because the arresting policeman doesn't like their skin color" (8), we learn early on that Chester is a longtime "stick-up man and professional killer" (33) who has already served several stints in prison and who deliberately drowned his first wife in a lake only two weeks after their wedding—a crime for which he has never faced punishment. Thus while Chester is a *criminalized* figure pulled into a life-ruining undertow due to a racist judge who sets his bail at an uncommonly high "[t]en thousand dollars, with two securities" (29), he is also a cruel opportunist who deserves to pay a price for his own choices. Such details suggest that despite the novel's title, "white man's justice" may not be the only source of "black man's grief." This construction of a protagonist who is at once criminal *and* wronged signals Goines's awareness that to make one's Black male protagonist what Maria Diedrich terms a "personification of innocence" or a "black Billy Budd" runs the risk of producing a novel that is "totally out of touch with the urban realities of African America" (321) that racial protest novels have always claimed to represent. And by making it difficult for us to sympathize fully with Chester, Goines (not unlike Richard Wright with Bigger Thomas) prevents his readers from forming the kind of sentimental, individualistic attachment to his protagonist that might obscure the larger structural injustices Goines wishes to expose and indict.

The Cross-Racial Impact(s) of Interracial Prison Rape

If Goines's novel derives much of its thematic tension from this blurring of the line between criminal and victim, the text conducts a related balancing act in its presentation of the rape culture's impact on Blacks and whites. Goines devotes ample space to ratcheting up the reader's sense of dread at the white prisoners' vulnerability by describing their sexual victimization in graphic detail, but he also takes care to register the collateral cost for Black prisoners (Chester in particular) who must survive in this hellhole of hegemonic masculinity. When Tommy, the novel's most despicable character and the de facto leader of the Black gang-rapists, leads a group shower assault on a naïve white prisoner named Gene, Goines assails us with the sounds of Gene's agonized cries:

> "Wait, man, wait!" Gene screamed from the shower. Then the sound of a slap was heard. There was silence for a brief moment, then a scream was heard.
>
> "Oh my god, you're killing me. Please, man, please. It's too big. You're busting me open!"
>
> "Shut up, boy, shut your goddamn mouth or you'll get something stuck in it too."

"...Oh please, that's enough! Please, please. Help, help!" The sound of another slap could be heard, then only the sounds of grunts and moans. (54–55)

Goines's emphasis on the desperation of this young white man as he is sexually assaulted in the showers makes these lines almost painful to read. Because we only *hear* what happens in the showers, Goines compels us to reenact the assault visually in our own minds. By presenting this heinous action from Chester's point of view, Goines also emphasizes how Chester himself is affected by the violence. As the rape gets underway, we are told that Chester "gritted his teeth" with displeasure and that "[i]f there was one thing he hated it was the rape of another man" (55). Before the gang-rape even begins, Tommy, the leader of the "asshole bandits" (51), intimidates Chester and the other Black inmates into either participating in the assault or promising not to interfere with it (52–53).

Goines underscores this concept of Black men as collateral victims of the jail's rape culture by making a startling move midway through the shower rape scene: as Chester listens to the sounds of Gene being attacked, Goines suddenly shifts into Chester's own flashback to an incident from his youth in which he was nearly raped by an older Black man:

The action from the shower brought back memories of when [Chester] was just a boy, trying to make his way up from the South. He had caught a ride on a boxcar that was already occupied by an older black man. The man had tried to rape Chester later that night, after giving him some wine. It had ended with Chester getting lucky and sticking eight inches of knife in the man's chest. After searching the man's pockets and removing the ten dollars that he had found there, he had then rolled the body to the door of the boxcar and pushed it out. He had been only fourteen then, but it was an experience that he had never forgotten. (55)

By flashing away from "[t]he action from the shower" to a similar attempted rape that Chester himself endured at the hands of a Black man in an enclosed space, the novel suggests how Black men—not just white ones—are victimized by a male rape culture that is situationally "controlled" by Black men, with the space of the boxcar serving as an apt analogue for the confined dimensions of the jail ward. In effect, Chester's feverish flashback to this near-rape disallows any reading in which white men are cast as the sole victims of rape. In addition, the "eight inches" of knife that Chester forces into the Black man's chest suggests how the threat of sexual assault forces Black men to become rapists themselves; in a sense, Chester had to rape the man—putting his "eight inches" into the other man's body—or risk being raped *by* the man, a metaphor for the way the prison rape culture encourages reciprocal brutality. More problematically, the explicit reference to the length of the knife—much like Gene's aforementioned cries in the shower that his assailant's penis is "too big" and is "busting [him] open"—also signals the kind of racial and sexual machismo that Goines's novel is at least partially invested in; as Goode puts it, Goines's male characters are always "well-equipped sexual gladiators" ("From *Dopefiend*" 42), as is Chester's fellow inmate, Willie, who is "proud of the way he was hung" (134). These references to Black sexual endowment crop up in the text even as Goines reminds us that the Black male prisoner—stereotyped as a rapist and then encouraged to become one in prison—pays a steep price for that very kind of distorted sexual and racial iconography.

By offering these insights into prison rape culture's impact on Black men, Goines's novel anticipates recent work by African American cultural theorists such as Collins, who discusses how prison forces men to become predators if they want to avoid being turned into "punks." "Among . . . African American men who are incarcerated," Collins writes, "those who fit the profile of those most vulnerable to abuse run the risk of becoming rape victims. In this context of violence regulated by a male rape culture, achieving Black manhood requires *not* fitting the profile and *not* assuming the position. In a sense, surviving in this male rape culture and avoiding victimization require at most becoming a predator and victimizing others and, at the least, becoming a silent witness to the sexual violence inflicted upon other men" (239).

Goines examines the relationship between all of these positions for Black men—perpetrators of rape, spectators to rape, and victims of rape—in a key scene late in the novel in which the Black inmate Jug, another serial rapist, sodomizes Jean, his light-skinned Black "punk," first by having anal sex with him and then by penetrating him with, of all things, a candy bar. The entrance of Jean, a "light-complexioned homosexual" (164), is particularly important because the character's presence affirms Goines's effort to show that the prison culture produces raped Black bodies as well as white ones. While Jean does appear to submit to Jug voluntarily, Jug's abusive treatment of Jean suggests that even seemingly consensual homosexual relationships in the prison system center on acts of physical exploitation and humiliation. This dynamic becomes particularly evident when Jug forcibly inserts the "cylindrical shaped candy bar" (184) into Jean's rectum, prompting Jean to "beg" Jug to remove the implement because, as Jean puts it, "that stuff feels funny up inside of me" (185). Jug not only refuses to comply, of course, but goes so far as to force one of his other punks (a white inmate named Jerry) to eat the bar out of Jean's anus—publicly, in front of all the other men, as a kind of perverse macho exhibition (181–86). This emphasis on public display also enables Goines to reveal how the prison rape culture engenders conflict not only between rape perpetrators and their victims but also, again, between the rapists and their involuntary (Black) spectators. While there is little danger that either Chester or his close friend Willie will be coerced into participating in Jug's activities, we do learn that Jug has mounted this sexual exhibition largely to threaten and intimidate the two men after Chester's refusal to allow Jug to sit on his bunk bed. Indeed, Jug now "plan[s] on bringing the arrogant Chester down to his knees" (164), and, at the start of his sex show, flashes a "cold and ruthless" smile (184) at Chester and Willie before announcing his intention to "let my ladies put on a show for you sorry-ass motherfuckers" (182). Here again, Black inmates who do not participate directly in sexual assault nonetheless become what Collins calls "silent witness[es]" to the violence.

"Now we're just gettin' even": Rejecting Rape as Revenge

An equally important component of Goines's examination of the impact of prison rape on Black masculinity is his critique of Black inmates like Jug who perpetrate these sexual assaults. Not only do these men coarsen the reputation of Black manhood in the wider culture—and thus give cover to those who would seek justification for racial oppression—they also coarsen themselves in the process of defending their actions as valid payback for centuries of racial subordination. If we return briefly to Carroll's inmate interviews, in fact, we can see precisely the attitude that Goines's novel deconstructs. In response to Carroll's question about why Black-on-white rape is so prevalent, several inmates articulate their motivations:

> Every can I been in, that's the way it is. . . . You guys been cuttin' our balls off ever since we been in this country. Now we're just getting even.

> It's one way he can assert his manhood. Anything white, even a defenseless punk, is part of what the black man hates. It's part of what he's had to fight all his life just to survive. . . . It's a new ego thing. He can show he's a man by making a white guy into a girl.

> The black man's just waking up to what's been going on. Now that he's awake, he's gonna be mean. He's been raped—politically, economically, morally raped. He sees this now, but his mind's still small so he's getting back this way. But it's just a beginning. (184–85)

For these inmates, Black-on-white rape acts as an instrument for obtaining a local form of racial revenge for the enslavement and mutilation of Black male bodies that has occurred over centuries of American history. In the "ultramasculine world" (Sabo, Kupers, and London 3) of the jail, "making a white guy into a girl" is the surest way to actualize one's own manhood, to castrate the castrator. But what Goines implies in his novel is what Carroll's speakers seem inadvertently to reveal here: namely that such an attempt to force individual acts of sexual violence to work as remedies for long-standing historical injustices is, at best, misguided and, at worst, self-debasing. These acts of rape (a mere "ego thing" conjured by a mind "still small") do nothing to ensure racial redress on anything but the smallest scale. Defining one's manhood through the practice of raping another man, Carroll's speaker seems to concede, is almost pathetically inchoate ("it's just a beginning") if one's goal is to fight racism, and it only mirrors the same sort of behavior characteristic of white men who define themselves by their subjugation of Black men.

Through the character of Tommy, who repeatedly rapes and degrades his white male concubines and then strives to justify such behavior, Goines constructs a version of this revenge rhetoric that strikingly anticipates the language used by Carroll's inmates. In one particularly explicit and painful scene, after Tommy has forced Mike, one of his many white male sex slaves, to perform fellatio on him, Tommy proclaims, "I'm goin' make these honkies pay for the three hundred years of sorrow they caused us" (72–73). By placing this rhetoric in the mouth of a vengeful tyrant designed to elicit our disgust, Goines prompts us to reject the notion that rape is somehow a valid form of racial payback. I do not suggest that Goines avoids asking us to consider the notion that such rapes can be justified; nor do I deny that some readers may find Tommy's justifications compelling. It is also possible to conceive that the sheer graphic quality of Goines's descriptions might make titillating entertainment for Black and white readers alike. Consider, for example, this description of Tommy's forced fellatio: "Mike tried to pull back, but Tommy had too hard a hold on his head. Tears of frustration ran down Mike's cheeks as the black man held his head and began to come in his mouth. The boy choked on the long black penis in his mouth, but Tommy continued to hold his head tightly. Cum ran down from Mike's mouth and down the side of his chin. He choked and gagged, but it didn't do any good. Tommy held on for dear life" (72). One could speculate that for Goines's primary audience—working-class urban Black male readers— the experience of reading such zesty details might provide a frisson of revenge or entertainment. For white readers, Goines's lurid representations of emasculated white male bodies (and, again, well-endowed Black ones) might provide a source of furtive sadomasochistic enjoyment or an alleviation of racial guilt through what Ek calls the satisfaction of "private rape fantasies and desires to be punished" (109). And yet, all that being said, it is difficult to avoid the impression, based on

Goines's wholly unflattering characterization of Tommy in the text, that it is our condemnation that Goines seems most to want to elicit. Indeed, at the end of this scene, Goines has Chester express strong moral disapproval of Tommy's rhetoric in a way that Goines himself seems to endorse: "Who you trying to bullshit, man? You ain't got to worry about making [whites] pay, because everything you've did to them tonight and other nights, you goin' have to face the grim reaper for" (73). Here, Goines's startling allusion to the grim reaper—the physical incarnation of death—seems to suggest that Tommy's actions, at least as Chester sees them, breach not just his victims' bodies but a higher moral system (one that exists beyond the justice system itself) that will ultimately visit karmic payback on those who perpetrate such atrocities.

As critical as Goines's novel is of rapists like Tommy and Jug, Goines never lets us forget that although these Black inmates exert a measure of local control over the jail ward, they remain pawns on a larger grid of incarceration and exploitation. Consider the juxtaposition between Tommy's power in the ward and his impotence when white deputies, eager to punish him for his sexual activities the night before, abuse him as they lead him out of his cell for interrogation. We are told that "The sergeant kicked him in the butt as hard as he possibly could. 'Nigger,' the sergeant growled, 'when I tell you to move, I mean just that! ... Now get a move on or you'll get another taste of that!' Tommy moved, holding his backside as his face twisted up as if he was about to cry" (85). Goines's language here suggests that the guard's hard kick to Tommy's backside is analogous to the anal rape that Tommy has committed earlier; the white men's racial slurs and humiliating physical abuse bring Tommy to tears and, in effect, make him "into a girl." Thus while Goines's brand of naturalism casts the prison's Black-on-white rape culture as a deterministic force that victimizes white men, it also presents the administrative machinery of the justice system as an even more monolithic force that "rapes" Black men. This impression is reinforced by Goines's subsequent description of the "machine-like" judge who capriciously hands down sentences to a "long line of black men" who "weren't even faces to the judge . . . just black shadows that passed his way every day, shadows with folders on them, telling what they had done in the past and where they should be put in the future" (170).

"friendly with another human being": White Negroism and Inmate Friendship

For all of the bleakness of Goines's depictions of violent inmate relations, the novel offers tantalizing hope that some prisoners may find ameliorative relationships that can act as respites from the unrelentingly hostile prison rape culture. However, the stunning failure of even these "friendships" by novel's end—bonds between Black and white men and between Black men themselves—ultimately reinforces Goines's vision of the overriding hostility generated by a racially biased criminal justice system.

Perhaps most unexpected among these relationships is the interracial rapport that develops between Chester, his Black inmate friend Willie, and the white inmate Tony, a tough nineteen-year-old ex-football player who has been arrested for armed robbery and who is the only white man in the jail ward capable of defending himself against sexual assault. In one sense, the presence of Tony, "the young white boy [who] could fight" (54), is notable simply because he is one of the few white male characters in Goines's oeuvre worthy of the reader's respect. But Goines also uses Tony to examine how the white-controlled justice system and the jail's hostile rape culture paradoxically encourage white inmates to adopt the outward trappings of Black masculinity as a survival technique. If we think back to the opening jail-ward passage discussed earlier, we recall Goines's remark that "[t]he only [white inmates] who were ever spared were those who had done time or who knew the ropes or who could *talk like a brother and fight as good as one, too*" (44, emphasis added). The implication is that white inmates who avoid becoming rape victims are the ones who can successfully project a macho—and Black—image. While whiteness carries an advantage in the criminal justice system as a whole, Goines suggests, it puts white men at a disadvantage in the harsh milieu of the jail ward itself, prompting white men to enact a kind of cross-racial emulation in the hope of achieving parity with the Black men who "rule" the jail wards.

Goines illustrates this dynamic in a scene in which Tony finds himself singled out for intimidation by Sonny, a belligerent Black inmate who accuses Tony of stealing his cereal. We are told that Tony "knew what Sonny was trying to do, and it made him angry that the man had picked him out of the bunch as the weak one. All of his life he had never been ashamed of being white, but for once he wished desperately that his skin was coal black. If someone had told him a year ago that he'd one day wish that he was a Black man, he'd have looked at the man as if he was losing his mind" (104). By revealing how Tony's "possessive investment" (Lipsitz vii) in his own whiteness gives way to Tony's situational desire to be Black, the novel draws our attention to the way in which white supremacy as a social force has, in an urban American jail, helped produce an institutional space in which whiteness as a commodity holds, paradoxically, the lowest of all possible values. Through Tony's racial desires, Goines also particularizes and deconstructs a foundational move that white-male-centered prison films such as *Escape from Alcatraz* tend to make uncritically: namely, what Krin Gabbard sees as the white male's strategic "borrowing" of Black masculinity

(51). Characteristic of a whole range of U.S. culture, from nineteenth-century blackface minstrelsy to Norman Mailer's mid-twentieth-century "white Negro" (337), this borrowing tends, in its most egregious forms, to aggrandize the cultural authority of white masculinity without acknowledging the contradictions attending white men who temporarily don "Blackness" only to doff it when it no longer suits them.

These contradictions emerge later in the novel when we learn that a judge has granted Tony the lenient punishment of probation for his attempted armed robbery while Willie and Chester, convicted of slightly lesser crimes, find themselves sent directly to the Jackson State penitentiary for four-to-five-year prison sentences. As this unwelcome news chills Tony's once-warm friendship with Chester and Willie, the breakdown of their interracial camaraderie serves as a window into the structural inequalities that confront incarcerated Black men: as Tony, now having regained the advantage of his whiteness, tries vainly to "break the tension he felt but couldn't understand," Chester thinks to himself, "It's easy for a white boy to walk over to the courtroom with such an idea in his mind, probation. But for a nigger to do it was sheer stupidity" (109). Tony's temporary victimization as a white male in the jail ward, Goines suggests, is superseded by the racial privilege he enjoys as a white male in the context of the justice system as a whole.

If Goines's depiction of the severed interracial bond between Tony, Chester, and Willie undercuts the ahistorical vision of Black-white harmony at the center of Hollywood prison movies, the unhappy climax of his novel suggests that in prison, even friendship between two African American men may be vexed and fragile. Indeed, the novel's final chapter centers on the implosion of the bond between Chester and Willie, the two men who have "stuck together" (40), been "partners" (78), done "everything together," grown "exceptionally close" (199), shared cupcakes (78), and acted as each other's protectors against the Darwinian hostilities of the jail ward and the prison to which they are later transferred. When Willie gains release from prison earlier than Chester and proceeds to embark on a robbery that goes horribly awry—and that Chester begged him not to carry out—Willie cravenly attempts to reduce his prison time by implicating Chester in the botched heist. This betrayal, we learn, ultimately ensnares Chester in a lifetime prison sentence. Chester will thus spend the rest of his life in prison for a crime he never committed because "he had allowed himself to become friendly with another human being" (217). Goines invites two opposing readings of this outcome: on the one hand, Chester's misapplied punishment is cruel, even capricious; on the other, many of his other crimes had gone unpunished up to this point, suggesting a cosmic payback for his earlier misdeeds, not unlike the grim reaper's visit Chester predicts for Tommy. Furthermore, what also seems clear here is that for Goines, one of the saddest outcomes of a racist and classist justice system that facilitates interracial sexual assault is the destruction of communal bonds between Black men that might, in some small way, diminish the misery of incarceration.

This grim approach marks a pronounced shift away from the redemptive depiction of male inmate relationships offered in the prison novel that Goines, via the name of his doomed main character, seems to be signifying on: Chester Himes's *Cast the First Stone*. In that text, as well as the restored version *Yesterday Will Make You Cry* (1998), Himes offers his white protagonist a measure of happiness in a romantic relationship with an Irish-Spanish homosexual. This bond, a fictionalized version of Himes's own relationship with a fellow Black convict, has prompted Franklin to call Himes's novel "a profoundly affirmative homosexual love story" ("Self-Mutilations" 30). No such "affirmative" reading of Goines's novel is possible, of course, and one might be tempted to attribute Goines's vision—in which all homosocial bonds in prison are thwarted and destructive and all homosexual relations are coercive, violent, and deviant—to the heteronormative limitations of his worldview. Goines's choices here might also be understood in another way: as a sincere reflection of the increasingly constrained possibilities for productive male-to-male relationships of *any* orientation in a post-Civil Rights-era prison system in which race relations between inmates are, in the words of one sociologist, always already "extremely tense, predatory, and a source of continual conflict" (Jacobs 120).

Goines and "proceedings too terrible to relate"

That a prison novel penned by an African American writer often dismissed as little more than a formulaic chronicler of an urban Black demimonde can teach us about one of the key racialized institutions in American society suggests, among other things, the desirability of an energized attention to Goines's fiction, to the critical resources of Black prison literature, and to African American popular fiction's potential role as "a powerful vehicle of critique . . . [that] explicitly indict[s] the social and political forces that create and maintain racial inequalities" (Dietzel 159). For all of Goines's well-documented interest in writing mass-market fiction primarily for profit—as Andrew Calcutt and Richard Shephard assert, "Goines wrote fiction the way other people package meat" (109)—his novel's mixture of "pulpy" prurience, naturalist outrage, and analytical rigor suggests the author's own recognition that a calculated representation of the sensational can act as a potent and necessary vehicle for social critique.

By challenging competing (mis)representations of interracial prison rape operating in U.S. culture, Goines must also manage the risk of letting his own representations go awry. If, as Peter Caster puts it, "the black man accused of murder, sex crime, or assault still maintains a mythic force in the United States" and reinforces a "tacit equation of criminality with black masculinity" (xiv), how might a novelist represent Black criminal behavior in a way that fully registers the impact of racism on Black men and yet also avoids reinforcing the pernicious racial stereotypes about Black men that historically have been enlisted to justify an oppressive social order?

I revisit this question because it prompts us to consider how Goines might be situated in a continuum of modern African American writers who have negotiated this challenge. For example, we might think of Richard Wright's Bigger Thomas, who is brutally violent toward both a white woman and his Black girlfriend but is also a victim of racial oppression. We might also think of Toni Morrison's Cholly Breedlove, who in *The Bluest Eye* rapes his own daughter but also elicits our sympathy as a victim of child abandonment and white sexual terror. This challenge is equally formidable for a text such as Goines's that, as part of its effort to critique structural racism, graphically depicts Black men raping white men. As great as the risks are of representing such ugliness, Goines's novel implies that the risks of not depicting such grotesqueness are perhaps even greater: to do the latter would be to miss a key opportunity to put a recognizably ugly face on U.S. racial oppression that remains a distanced abstraction made invisible behind prison walls or trivialized in jokes about rape that are a signature of the contemporary public discourse on incarceration.[9]

In his own negotiation of this problem, in his own rough style, Goines reproduces what Morrison articulates as the primary aim of her fiction: the job of "rip[ping] that veil drawn over 'proceedings too terrible to relate,'" which she regards as "critical for any person who is black, or who belongs to any marginalized category, for, historically, we were seldom invited to participate in the discourse even when we were its topic." Morrison here refers to slave narratives—arguably the nineteenth-century precursor to late-twentieth-century prison literature—that covered up the most brutal aspects of bondage in order to appease sensitive white liberal readers whose support the authors needed. As Morrison puts it, slave narrators "shap[ed] the experience [of slavery] to make it palatable to those who were in a position to alleviate it" (191). In his own body of work, which L. H. Stallings categorizes as a Hip-Hop-inflected "neo-slave narrative" (175), Goines refuses to "make it palatable." He refuses to elide the physical ugliness that might make us want to turn away from the kinds of race relations that our ever-expanding prison system has been producing—or, worse, turn away from a chance at understanding *why* our society conceived and nurtured such a fiercely pumping heart of darkness in the first place. At a time when our prison problems seem to be worsening by the day, it would behoove us to read—and heed—Goines's insights.

NOTES

1. The defendant in question, 23-year-old David Ross, had been convicted of harassing a police officer and resisting arrest after being barred from walking his dog in a public park. The presiding judge, Stanley Gartenstein, ultimately spared Ross jail time and instead ordered him to pay a fine, perform community service, and publicly apologize to the arresting officer.

2. According to statistics from the United States Census Bureau and the Department of Justice's Bureau of Justice Statistics, African American men, though only six percent of the U.S. population, constitute over forty percent of the nation's 2.3 million inmates.

3. Carroll's findings have been amply corroborated by numerous subsequent studies—including those by James B. Jacobs, Wayne S. Wooden and Jay Parker, Randall Kennedy, William F. Pinar, and Patricia Hill Collins. While Black-on-white rape is not the only form of sexual activity in the post-Civil Rights prison, it has been the most prevalent form of coercive sex in penal institutions over the last four decades, and the most common form of interracial sexual activity of any kind.

4. Cleaver's homophobic elisions become even more striking when we consider Michele Wallace's assertion that Black-on-white male sex is the logical, inevitable outcome of Cleaver's notion of insurrectionary rape. Wallace reasons that "[i]f whom you fuck indicates your power, then obviously the greatest power would be gained by fucking a white man first … Black Macho would have to lead to this conclusion" (68). Cleaver's repression of such a possibility makes Goines's willingness to examine it so frankly (some five years before Wallace) all the more notable.

5. This buddy-convict narrative should be seen as a subset of the larger tradition of interracial male bonding in U.S. culture, first examined by Leslie Fiedler and later by Robyn Wiegman (115–78), Ed Guerrero (113–36), and Krin Gabbard (143–76). For these critics, such narratives peddle a specious image of interracial fraternity that obscures the nation's history of systemic racial oppression.

6. The singularity of Goines's project emerges even more sharply if we view his work as a critical alternative to the early-1970s Blaxploitation films that were cinematic cousins to his novels. As Guerrero argues, "Goines's novels differed from the films of the Blaxploitation genre in that the ideology of black struggle and liberation was a central consciousness in all his works, whereas this same ideology was dismissed or ridiculed in many of the films of the genre" (226).

7. No definitive account of Goines's decision to name his protagonist "Chester Hines" exists. Eddie Allen speculates that the name is either Goines's "literary tribute" to a fellow Black prison writer or an "uncanny coincidence" (152).

8. Naturalism is in fact a mode characteristic of much Black "pulp fiction," in part because it offers a powerful means of engaging in racial protest. As Susanne B. Dietzel observes, "Most Holloway House novels within the ghetto realism subgenre [which she equates with "African American pulp fiction"] draw on naturalist novels of the 1940s and 1950s" as well as "the 'protest' novel and prison autobiography" (162).

9. Indeed, as one *New York Times* reporter has recently observed, "[r]ape has such an estab-

lished place in the mythology of prisons that references to confinement often call forth jokes about sexual assault" (Lewin 1).

REFERENCES

Allen, Eddie B., Jr. *Low Road: The Life and Legacy of Donald Goines*. New York: St. Martin's, 2004.

American History X. Dir. Tony Kaye. Perf. Edward Norton, Edward Furlong. 1998. DVD. New Line, 1999.

Baldick, Chris. "Naturalism." *The Concise Oxford Dictionary of Literary Terms*. New York: Oxford UP, 1990. 146–47.

Calcutt, Andrew, and Richard Shephard. "Donald Goines." *Cult Fiction: A Reader's Guide*. Lincolnwood: Contemporary, 1999. 109.

Carroll, Leo. *Hacks, Blacks, and Cons: Race Relations in a Maximum Security Prison*. 1974. Prospect Heights: Waveland, 1988.

Caster, Peter. *Prisons, Race, and Masculinity in Twentieth-Century US Literature and Film*. Columbus: Ohio State UP, 2008.

Childs, Dennis. "'You Ain't Seen Nothin' Yet': *Beloved*, the American Chain Gang, and the Middle Passage Remix." *American Quarterly* 61.2 (2009): 271–97.

Cleaver, Eldridge. *Soul on Ice*. 1968. New York: Delta, 1999.

Collins, Patricia Hill. *Black Sexual Politics: African Americans, Gender, and the New Racism*. New York: Routledge, 2004.

Conover, Ted. *Newjack: Guarding Sing Sing*. New York: Vintage, 2001.

Cummins, Eric. *The Rise and Fall of California's Radical Prison Movement*. Stanford: Stanford UP, 1994.

Davis, Angela Y. "A World unto Itself: Multiple Invisibilities of Imprisonment." Foreword. *Behind the Razor Wire: Portrait of a Contemporary American Prison System*. Ed. Michael Jacobson-Hardy. New York: New York UP, 1998. ix–xviii.

Diedrich, Maria. Rev. of *Iron City* by Lloyd L. Brown. *African American Review* 30.2 (1996): 320–22.

Dietzel, Susanne B. "The African American Novel and Popular Culture." *The Cambridge Companion to the African American Novel*. Ed. Maryemma Graham. Cambridge, UK: Cambridge UP, 2004. 156–70.

Ek, Auli. *Race and Masculinity in Contemporary American Prison Narratives*. New York: Routledge, 2005.

Escape from Alcatraz. Dir. Donald Siegel. 1979. DVD. Paramount, 1999.

Fiedler, Leslie. "Come Back to the Raft Ag'in, Huck Honey!" *Partisan Review* (June 1948): 664–71.

Franklin, H. Bruce. *Prison Literature in America: The Victim as Criminal and Artist*. Expanded ed. New York: Oxford UP, 1989.

————. "Self-Mutilations." Rev. of *Yesterday Will Make You Cry* by Chester Himes. *The Nation* (16 Feb. 1998): 28–31.

Gabbard, Krin. *Black Magic: White Hollywood and African American Culture*. New Brunswick: Rutgers UP, 2004.

Goines, Donald. *White Man's Justice, Black Man's Grief*. Los Angeles: Holloway, 1973.

Goode, Greg. "Donald Goines." *Dictionary of Literary Biography*. Vol. 33: *Afro-American Fiction Writers after 1955*. Ed. Thadious Davis and Trudier Harris. Detroit: Gale, 1984. 96–100.

————. "From *Dopefiend* to *Kenyatta's Last Hit*: The Angry Black Crime Novels of Donald Goines." *MELUS* 11.3 (1984): 41–48.

Guerrero, Ed. *Framing Blackness: The African American Image in Film*. Philadelphia: Temple UP, 1993.

Jackson, George. *Soledad Brother: The Prison Letters of George Jackson*. New York: Coward-McAnn, 1970.

Jacobs, James B. "The Limits of Racial Integration in Prison." *Criminal Law Bulletin* 18.2 (1982): 117–53.

Kennedy, Randall. *Race, Crime, and the Law*. New York: Vintage, 1998.

Lewin, Tamar. "Little Sympathy or Remedy for Inmates Who Are Raped." *New York Times* 15 Apr. 2001, natl. ed., sec. 1: 1+.

Lipsitz, George. *The Possessive Investment in Whiteness: How White People Profit from Identity Politics*. Philadelphia: Temple UP, 1998.

Mailer, Norman. "The White Negro: Superficial Reflections on the Hipster." *Advertisements for Myself*. 1959. Cambridge: Harvard UP, 1992. 337–58.

McCall, Nathan. *Makes Me Wanna Holler*. New York: Random, 1994.

Morrison, Toni. "The Site of Memory." *Inventing the Truth: The Art and Craft of Memoir*. Ed. William Zinsser. Rev. ed. Boston: Mariner, 1998. 183–200.

Pinar, William F. *The Gender of Racial Politics and Violence in America: Lynching, Prison Rape, and the Crisis of Masculinity*. New York: Lang, 2001.

Sabo, Don, Terry A. Kupers, and Willie London. "Gender and the Politics of Punishment." Introduction. *Prison Masculinities*. Ed. Sabo, Kupers, and London. Philadelphia: Temple UP, 2001. 3–18.

Savran, David. *Taking It Like a Man: White Masculinity, Masochism, and Contemporary American Culture*. Princeton: Princeton UP, 1998.

The Shawshank Redemption. Dir. Frank Darabont. 1994. DVD. Castle Rock, 2007.

Shipp, H. R. "Refusing to Jail a White Is Called Racist by Koch." *New York Times* 10 Apr. 1981: B3.

Stallings, L. H. "'I'm Goin' Pimp Whores!' The Goines Factor and the Theory of a Hip-Hop Neo-Slave Narrative." *CR: The New Centennial Review* 3.3 (2003): 175–203.

United States Census Bureau. "Overview of Race and Hispanic Origin." By Elizabeth M. Grieco and Rachel C. Cassidy. *Census 2000 Briefs and Special Reports*. U.S. Census Bureau, Mar. 2001. 15 July 2009. <http://www.census.gov/prod/2001pubs/c2kbr01-1. pdf>.

————. "Race and Hispanic or Latino Origin by Age and Sex for the United States: 2000." *Census 2000 Briefs and Special Reports.* U.S. Census Bureau, 25 Feb. 2002. 15 July 2009. <http://www.census.gov/population/www/cen2000/briefs/phc-t8/index.html>.

————. Department of Justice. Bureau of Justice Statistics. "Prison Inmates at Midyear 2008—Statistical Tables." By William J. Sabol and Heather C. West. *Bureau of Justice Statistics.* Bureau of Justice Statistics, 31 Mar. 2009. 13 Jan. 2010. <http://bjs.ojp.usdoj.gov/index.cfm?ty=pbdetail&iid=839>.

Wallace, Michele. *Black Macho and the Myth of the Superwoman.* 1978. New York: Verso, 1999.

Wiegman, Robyn. *American Anatomies: Theorizing Race and Gender.* Durham: Duke UP, 1995.

Wooden, Wayne S., and Jay Parker. *Men Behind Bars: Sexual Exploitation in Prison.* New York: Da Capo, 1984.

Wynn, Jennifer. *Inside Rikers: Stories from the World's Largest Penal Colony.* New York: St. Martin's, 2002.

CHAPTER NINE

Beneath the Law

Donald Goines and America's Sliding Scale of Criminality

Quincy T. Norwood

Donald Goines's *White Man's Justice, Black Man's Grief* contradicts the racist and classist notions of criminality and justice extolled in America. This book was published nearly four decades ago, but it could just as easily be describing 2010, as "race relations" and the balance of power in the United States remain virtually unchanged. Race and class persist in being determining factors in defining criminal behavior and the laws designed to curtail said behavior, which in turn saturates prisons with people of color. Chattel slavery, the "Black Codes," and "Jim Crow" laid the foundation for the prison industrial complex and the mass incarceration of people of color. In light of current ideas of "change" and "progress," justice for the dominant culture is indeed grief for people of color in the United States because of this country's unwillingness to address "race relations" or race and racism in a meaningful way. Donald Goines communicates the sentiments of those who have been on the wrong side of American justice with no solace to be found.

Goines's novels provide a voice for those who have been marginalized due to racial or economic standing, in addition to revealing the sanctimonious character of America's culture and institutions. *White Man's Justice, Black Man's Grief* uses the life of its antagonist Chester Hines to expose the discrimination intrinsic to the United States's social structure, particularly the U.S. justice system. The novel, a deft critique of America's courts and prisons, begins with a seemingly routine traffic stop in which Chester makes the initial "mistake" of "driving too carefully," one which causes him to run a red light. Before the police stop his black Ford, Chester contemplates attempting to elude them, but he quickly concludes that escape is not a viable option and decides to comply when the cops signal for him to pull over. Chester pulls to the curb and does his best to appear as non-threatening as possible when handing the officer his license. However, Chester's "honest-John smile" is all for naught as the police decide to "call in on him." In response, Chester reasons that had he been white, the chances of their doing this would be small—they would have written him a ticket, instead, apologized for detaining him and sent him on his way. The police officer's "calling in" indicates that in the officer's mind Chester has already been deemed suspicious based on the cop's preconceived notion of what a criminal profile entails. What's even more interesting about Chester's traffic stop is the subtle way in which Goines articulates the looming threat of violence at the hands of police. After exiting his vehicle Chester moves very deliberately. He doesn't dare make any quick movements, so as to avoid giving the officer an excuse to commit an act of brutality. Goines is undoubtedly aware of the prevalence of police brutality, and his depiction of Chester's interaction with the police illustrates an antagonistic relationship between Blacks and police that persists in the present day.

White Man's Justice, Black Man's Grief was originally published in 1973, to be precise, a mere six years after the Detroit Rebellion of 1967, which resulted in over 40 deaths, almost 1,200 injuries, and approximately 7,000 arrests. The catalyst for the upheaval was a raid on an after-hours drinking establishment in a predominantly Black neighborhood in Detroit where the police attempted to arrest over 80 citizens attending a party for two Vietnam veterans. However, the seeds of racial tension had been germinating for quite some time, as police brutality in Black communities was commonplace. The strained relationship between Blacks and the police in Detroit was exacerbated by the advent of the "Tac Squad" or the "Big Four" (or the "Big Fo'" as they were often referred to), groups of four police officers who patrolled the streets of Detroit targeting young Blacks, making them produce identification, and frequently calling them "boy" or "nigger," beating and in some cases outright murdering them. The extent of police brutality in Detroit prior to the rebellion is typified by the shooting death of Shirley Scott, a Black prostitute who was shot in the back while attempting to flee a police car. Further, there was the case of Howard

King, a Black teenager who was severely beaten by police for "disturbing the peace." Bearing in mind the rampant police violence of the times, it is easy to understand Chester's overly cautious movements when he was apprehended by the police in *White Man's Justice, Black Man's Grief.* As with many other Blacks, one false move could very well have cost him his life.

Chester's traffic stop sets the tone for the remainder of the novel, as Goines explores the duplicitous nature of ideas of criminality and justice as they are applied in the United States. Chester migrates "up South" to Detroit seeking an escape from his native "Jim Crow" Georgia, only to discover that injustice and racially motivated violence are not confined to states below the Mason-Dixon line. Goines displays a keen awareness of history in relating Chester's life, as his migration mirrors that of many Blacks across the country.

Throughout American history, the law has been used as a tool of racial subjugation, as the legislatures that create laws and the courts that interpret them have served to advance an agenda of social control and Black disenfranchisement. Officially sanctioned segregation in the form of restrictive covenants continued the legacy of "Jim Crow," as the law precluded from Blacks from purchasing homes in white communities, for example. Though restrictive covenants became law in 1917 in response to the *Buchanan v. Warle*[1] court ruling, the 1926 case of *Corrigan v. Buckley* legitimized them. In the *Corrigan* case, a white woman attempted to sell her property to a Black person which resulted in a lawsuit to enforce a restrictive covenant from 1921 to block the sale of this property. The District of Columbia's federal court system upheld the ruling to enforce the covenant, and later the Supreme Court unanimously dismissed any challenge, essentially validating the covenant.

The consequences of restrictive covenants were far-reaching for Blacks. Detroit, Goines's hometown and the setting of *White Man's Justice, Black Man's Grief,* saw an influx of Blacks beginning in the years after World War I, and continuing for decades after as Blacks migrated to northern cities in hopes of creating better lives for future generations. However, migrant Blacks in Detroit were met with great hostility, and opportunities for housing and employment were scarce. Restrictive covenants forced Blacks into sections of the city in which living conditions were abominable. Moreover, because Blacks were only allowed to live in legally designated sections of the city, competition for housing was high, a fact which afforded landlords the luxury of charging unjustifiably high rent. Restrictive covenants generated a vicious cycle that was used to justify their enforcement. There was no law in place to ensure that whites who rented to Blacks maintained their rental properties, which were often dilapidated or altogether unsafe. What's more, there was a limited amount of space with many people in need of a place to live, so overcrowding was a consequence. In fact, by the 1940s most of the city's Black residents were crammed in the space of 60 square blocks on the east side of the city, an area that would clearly come to belie its moniker, "Paradise Valley."[2] The aforementioned living conditions, combined with low wages and a high cost of living gave way to poverty and crime, which gave credence to those who argued the need for restrictive covenants and repressive policing.[3] Anger at these restrictive covenants, discriminatory laws that reduced both Black employment and opportunities for education, and rampant police brutality in Black neighborhoods would eventually result (before the Detroit Rebellion of 1967) in the 1943 Detroit "Race Riots" in which approximately 25 Blacks were killed and more than 1800 were arrested.[4]

White Man's Justice Black Man's Grief sees Goines replacing the mobs of the South with law enforcement officers and judges, as Goines conveys in a passage recounting Hines's arraignment on a weapons charge:

> [Chester] had been in and out of courtrooms all his life, but he never got over his fear of them. The black-robed men who sat up high on the benches dispensing "justice" filled him with awe. It was not a feeling of reverence or of wonder caused by something sublime. It was a feeling of terror, inspired by the raw power these hypocrites held over the helpless black men who came before them.... He feared the power of life and death these men held in their hands.[5]

The "feeling of terror" that Chester feels as he enters the courtroom and witnesses the judge's intimidating posturing stems from the knowledge that, despite his guilt or innocence, his fate will ultimately be left to the judge's discretion, which is often marred by racist attitudes transferred from one generation to the next. Goines continues, "they tried to beat down the complexities of the seventies with their gavels, with their twenties- and thirties-spawned attitudes, with raw power."[6] The portrayal of Chester's initial encounter with the judge reflects the sentiment of myriad Black persons ensnared by a legal system that has yet to address its own institutionalized racism. Through Chester, Goines speaks to a historical precedent of legal discrimination grounded in racist notions of "Black criminality."

It is the legacy of lawful means of oppression that registers with Chester as he enters the familiar surroundings of the courtroom. In addition to the judge, Chester also makes note of the disproportionate number of Black folks present: "The line that Chester was in seemed endless as he stared over the heads of most of the black men in front of him. He started counting. There were thirty men in front of him, and out of that thirty, only three were white."[7] Chester observes that the majority of those being arraigned are Black, and even notes that two of the white men he sees "had the look of the derelict," meaning they were of "low" social standing.

In Goines's novel, as in life outside the novel, the Black and the poor saturate the criminal justice system to an alarming degree. No small contributors to America's incarceration frenzy are politicians wishing to gain favor by appearing tough on crime and the unwinnable "War on Drugs" which has wreaked havoc on Black and poor communities. The disparity between the laws concerning sentencing for possession of "powder cocaine" and "crack cocaine" (which is cheaper and made more readily available in Black communities) has helped facilitate the expanding prison population. Deplorable socio-economic conditions create the climate that spawns addiction and violence. Goines depicts poverty as an impetus for crime when describing Chester's inner thoughts as he counts $50 he relieved from an inmate: "A few nights ago, if he had had this much money in his pocket, he wouldn't have been pressed to go out into the streets and commit a crime."[8] The conditions that often cause crime rarely receive the same attention as the act itself, or the punishment. The willful ignorance of America's dominant culture and assimilation-minded Blacks allows for the survival of the myth of "Black criminality," which fosters public policies that disproportionately targets communities of color. Legally, anti-loitering and "anti-sagging" ordinances, gang injunctions, and other ambiguous mandates provide police with excuses to harass young people of color simply for living.

As America's "War on Crime" flourishes, so does the prison industrial complex. There are close to two and a half million people locked down in the vast network of American prisons and jails, with 70 percent of those incarcerated being people of color.[9] This would lead one to believe that Blacks have a virtual monopoly on crime, yet a study released by The Justice Policy reports that while whites and Blacks sell and use drugs at a similar rate, Blacks are more than ten times more likely to be incarcerated for drug offenses. The study also revealed that over half of the approximately 175,000 people incarcerated in 2002 were Black.[10] Goines draws attention to the fact that race is used as a determining factor in sentencing by citing the futility of many defendants' attempts to make favorable impressions on judges and juries by wearing a suit to court: "They could appear in sacks, for all the judges cared. The only thing that mattered was the color of the man."[11] Undergirding the disparity in the sentencing of Blacks and whites is the racist rationale that Black folks are predisposed to criminal behavior and beyond redemption, so issuing longer sentences gets construed as a matter of preserving public safety. Goines displays an acute understanding of the criminal justice system in his portrayal of the different handling of the nearly identical cases of two cellmates in *White Man's Justice, Black Man's Grief*, Willie and Tony; who are Black and white respectively. Both Willie and Tony are awaiting trial for armed robbery. Tony is naively confident that either they both will receive probation or he will receive a tougher sentence because a gun was used in his crime. After listening to an exchange in which Tony is attempting to convince Willie that he may be able to get his charge reduced to one that would warrant probation, Chester discloses his thoughts: "It's easy for a white boy to walk over to the courtroom with such an idea in his mind, probation. But for a nigger to do it was sheer stupidity. All he would be doing is fooling himself, looking for something that wasn't about to happen, unless he was an informer or something."[12]

Chester and Willie are intimately familiar with the inherent racism of the criminal justice system; and they know that unlike Tony, they have no chance of receiving probation. Willie and Chester's fates mirror those of scores of imprisoned persons of color and poor people whose existence has been criminalized in the name of social control and profits for the few. For as with most ventures in the United States, the prison industrial complex is fueled by the drive for capital. William Upski Wimsatt notes in *No More Prisons*: "Prisons are a $100 billion dollar industry. A lot of money is being made. The beds must be filled."[13] Fashionable "hard on crime" politics, based on racist perceptions of criminality and bolstered by media imagery, justify mass incarceration in the public mind. Incarceration bolsters the illusion of public safety as it is championed as a viable solution to crime. However, punishment has proven to be more profitable than strategies of "rehabilitation," creating in turn a soaring rate of systematic recidivism. This along with a callous application of laws and the handing out of longer sentences all serves the economic interests of contractors, vendors, architecture firms, Wall Street investment banks and others groups that profit from erecting new prisons and providing essential services in existing ones. It is in the best interest of the prison industry to keep the number of inmates high, causing special interest groups representing organizations that stand to gain from mass incarceration to lobby for the passage of laws that will guarantee a return on their investments. The law, whether in the form of "Jim Crow," restrictive covenants, or the "War on Crime," has historically been employed as a mechanism to remove 'undesirable' (Black and/or poor) elements from society while generating capital at their expense.

The formal abolition of chattel slavery did not spell the end of all slavery or coerced labor, as Section 1 of the Thirteenth Amendment of the U.S. Constitution states: "Neither slavery nor involuntary servitude, *except as punishment for a crime whereof the party shall have been duly convicted*, shall exist within the United States, or any place subject to their jurisdiction."[14] Prison labor and convict leasing have become a sort of cottage industry in the United States, with big businesses reaping the benefits of having a non-unionized and extremely cheap labor force at their disposal. Prison laborers have no rights and make little to no wages, yet they are as popular as ever. As Chester makes the acquaintance of another young inmate in

White Man's Justice, Black Man's Grief, he remarks, "It looks like the judges wanted to make sure they had plenty men. They must need some help up at the prison for pickin' and shit." Goines demonstrates the direct correlation between the demand for cheap labor and incarceration:

> Some sacrificed their whole welfare checks to buy suits. They sacrificed everything under the misguided belief that it would help. How could it? What could help against the poisonous pus of double-standard justice, racial bigotry, and the demand for black men to fill the work quotas? Many men were needed at a certain time of the year to help pick the fields.... These things couldn't be left to rot; they had to be picked.[15]

The commodification of prison labor is by no means a new phenomenon. The chain gang has undergone a makeover to better suit the modern age, as prisons have rapidly joined the Third World as a major source of cheap labor for capitalist corporations. Government-managed and privatized prisons are thriving as more businesses realize that it is more cost-effective to have prison laborers rather than private citizens as workers. Victoria's Secret, Starbucks, and many others have utilized prison labor to assemble products, field phone calls, and perform other tasks once performed by paid employees.[16]

For Goines, the ideological trappings of racism are not some relic of a distant past, but serve as the foundation for the establishment and interpretation of law. "Well, that's one good nigger down the alley now. He won't be bothering anyone any damn more," exclaims a cop in *White Man's Justice, Black Man's Grief,* after shooting a young Black man in the back while he ran away. The only "crime" the young man and his associates were guilty of was participating in consensual sex with a white woman. The cops act as judge, jury, and executioner for the young man; his partner, David Walker, is lynched in the courts. Though David was in an alcohol-induced slumber while the alleged "rape" occurred, he still feels the full brutal wrath of the cops, and later the judge. Since he refuses to plead guilty, having committed no crime at all, David is prosecuted to the full extent to the law. He relates to Chester, "Oh, hi, Chester ... them motherfuckers gave me twenty to twenty-five. Years man, years! Can you imagine that? Twenty-five years for something I'm not guilty of."[17]

The rhetoric of "change" and America's notion of "progress" have reached the height of popularity with the election of its first "Black" president. However, a closer examination of these concepts will reveal their hollowness as they apply to people of color and those on the lower rungs of America's economic caste system. While the United States touts itself as "The Land of the Free," those who have endured the exploits of American capitalism have been forced to bear witness to an America that refutes such a lofty claim. It is writers like Donald Goines and other torchbearers of his Black literary tradition who provide perspectives of those whose labor and suffering have been the actual catalysts for American socio-economic "progress" while simultaneously being excluded from benefiting from it in any meaningful way. As long as America's basic climate of racist and classist hostility persists, there can only be justice for the few, and grief for the many.

NOTES

1 *Buchanan v. Warley*, 245 U.S. 60 (1917) is a unanimous United States Supreme Court decision ruling declaring racially biased zoning unconstitutional. But *Buchanan* only applied to legal statutes, not private agreements, which popularized restrictive covenants.

2 Rashid, Frank. "Paradise Valley/Black Bottom." Marygrove College. 12/9/09 <http://www.marygrove.edu/ids/Paradise_Valley.asp>.

3 Martin, Elizabeth Anne. "Detroit and the Great Migration." Bentley Historical Library, University of Michigan. 1/10/10 <http://bentley.umich.edu/research/publications/migration/ch1.php>.

4 Baulch, Vivian. "The 1943 Detroit Race Riots." *The Detroit News*. 12/14/09 <http://apps.detnews.com/apps/history/index.php?id=185>.

5 Goines, Donald, *White Man's Justice, Black Man's Grief* (Los Angeles: Holloway House, 1973), 26.

6 Goines 26.

7 Goines 27.

8 Goines 36.

9 Giroux, Henry A. "Racial Injustice and Disposable Youth in the Age of Zero Tolerance." *Qualitative Studies in Education* 16.4 (2003): 553-65. Web. 3 Dec. 2009.

10 Beatty, Philip, Amanda Petteruti, and Jason Zeidenberg. *The Vortex: The Concentrated Racial Impact of Drug Imprisonment and the Characteristics of Punitive Counties* (Washington, D.C.: The Justice Policy Institute, 2007), 3.

11 Goines 124.

12 Goines 109.

13 Wimsatt, William Upski, *No More Prisons* (New York: Soft Skull Press, 1999), 8.

14 U.S. Const. amend. XIII.

15 Goines 125.

16 Scwartzapfel, Beth. "Your Valentine, Made In Prison." *The Nation*. 3/14/09 <http://www.thenation.com/doc/20090302/schwartzapfel>.

17 Goines 197.

REFERENCES

Goines, Donald. *White Man's Justice, Black Man's Grief.* Los Angeles: Holloway House, 1973.

Stone, Eddie. *Donald Writes No More: A Biography of Donald Goines.* Los Angeles: Holloway House, 2003.

Wimsatt, William Upski. *No More Prisons.* New York: Soft Skull Press, 1999.

16 Novels on the Microphone

For 'Cultural Guerilla Resistance,' Now

Greg Thomas

"Deep"
"A hell of story"
"My life"
"[A] few tips"
"My father figure"
"Supafly"
"About the business of this shit!"
— Critical reviews of Donald Goines's novels from the secondary literature of Hip-Hop
(1990-2010)

One of Sylvia Wynter's dopest early essays is entitled "Novel and History, Plot and Plantation" (1971). Her insights there apply directly to Donald Goines. An elder Black Studies powerhouse, she disrupted a bourgeois academic conference with questions—radical questions, from the grassroots. Somewhere in the Caribbean part of Africa's Diaspora, she charts a clash between "those who defend the 'autonomy' of the 'civilized' highly educated artist" (or "those who justify and defend the system") and "those who defend the claims of the community and the folk" (or "those who challenge" the system) (Wynter 1971, 99; 102). And, promoting "cultural guerilla resistance" (100), she begins with these potent lines: "First, let us define our terms. What, in our context, is the novel? What, in our context, is history? What *is* our context?" (95). Academic business-as-usual generally proceeds without such questioning. After *Word Hustle*, however, we could be so inspired ourselves to ask a series of related questions in closing—radical questions, from the Pan-African grassroots: *"What did Donald Goines do to the novel, for our context?"* In battle still against neo-slavery and neo-colonialism in "Plantation America," we might ask: *"What did he do not only to or through 'literature' (if by this we simply mean writing), but to the very notion of literacy, when we define each of these terms on our terms in the context of our history and all history?"*

His is not Fred Douglass's literacy, to be sure. Writing-wise, Goines assimilates no Victorian ethic of "respectability" for ruling-class eyes. He has no white father(s) to please, or appease, or to bewilder him. More like Martin Delany, you might say, or Frances Ellen Watkins Harper, he is just not torn. The face of his audience is absolutely his own. The "man" is neither an uncritical masculinist nor "benevolent patriarch" in his words, as L.H. Stallings would demonstrate time and time again with her vanguard work in *Word Hustle* and elsewhere. He writes to the masses from among the masses, physically and metaphysically, not merely about them from a spiritual distance. He is no advocate of Anglo-European "humanism" or Americanism, at bottom, like the antebellum figure whose texts are taught *ad nauseum* in U.S. academia. In point of fact, if Goines were to "write his way to freedom," as it were, this writing would be of a *very* different kind and function, without a doubt. As detailed well by this collection, his literacy calls the writings of (Field Marshal) George Jackson (of the Black Panther Party) and the anti-colonial "Kenyatta" (of "Mau Mau" country or "African Revolution" on the continent) explicitly, militantly to mind.

Finally, *Word Hustle* recognizes.

In conversation, Acklyn Lynch of *Nightmare Overhanging Darkly: Essays on Black Culture and Resistance* (1992) would compare Goines to Henry Dumas, the Black Arts word sorcerer who, besides poems and novels, penned short stories such as "Fon" and "The Circle Will Not Be Unbroken" in *Ark of Bones* (1970), before getting shot down by New York City Transit Police in what they had the gall to call "a case of mistaken identity." The name of Donald Goines is thus added to the long list of those (Black artist-writer-activists) who died too early; the list of those who were killed; the list of those whom, when read, may likely be studied or consumed with little critical attention to the "mysterious" circumstances of their unnatural deaths or outright murders. Yet when he died on October 21, 1974, at the young age of 37, his mother put him to rest with copies of his books in his casket.

Ironically, most writers who are more conventional objects of intellectual study cannot lay claim to so many of Goines's creative claims to fame. The hegemony of novels now a historical fact, his have never gone out of print—as a rapacious publishing house pitches him repeatedly as "America's #1 Best Selling Black Author," in bold print on each cover, nearly 35 to 40 years after their original publication. His speak the supposedly unspeakable in a number of ways as they also reflect or refract key historical contexts and environs, which is to say, current and recent historical circumstances often studiously avoided by most novels of "the Norton anthology" literary type. His mesmerize a devoted non-middle class readership with Goines's own renegade class authorship or Black communal practice of incredibly scrupulous writing. For his dedicated if elsewhere unfathomable readership, his are beyond memorable; their imprint is indelible. His are popular cultural rather than more or less campus-bound phenomena—hence Goines's ever-increasing cinematic and videographic shelf life in the form of feature films and documentaries (none of which are "Harpo" productions). For this very reason, his shelf full of books may never go out of print, at least not in the foreseeable future. And who but his beloved Chester Himes could rival Goines's prolific output, even by the end of their careers, let alone in the course of the short period of time (1971-1975) during which he published?

Who else can put 16 novels on the microphone?

The Black masses are not supposed to "read" or "write"—according to the standard constructions of literacy and literature in North America and elsewhere. Yet what could be more absurd? For this is despite writing's ancient African origins as well as Donald Goines and Hip-Hop's world-renowned, self-described lyricists of the present day (cf. Grant 2001), among many others. Thankfully, theirs would be a 'literacy' and 'literature' of another sort, traditionally antithetical to the literacy and literature of Western bourgeois empire.

Indeed, emcees write about their reading of *Word Hustle*'s author of note far more than any literary critic of the elite. As Grand Puba rhymes on Brand Nubian's *One for All* or "Who Can Get Busy like This Man… " (1990): "The skills go back to the days of flippin' coins / Passed time reading books by my man Donald Goines." Common rhymes on *Resurrection* or "Orange Pineapple Juice" (1994): "I'm the act to follow / housing kids like Ronald / Mac like Donald / Goines / Flows I change like coins." E-40 rhymes on *Tha Hall of Game* or "Record Haters" (1996): "Boost up my coins / Proceed to spit mo' *Supafly* / than Donald Goines." Ghostface Killah rhymes on his *Supreme Clientele* or "Child's Play" (1999): "Lines from Dolemite / Few tips from Goines / Birthday / Gave her two fifty-cent coins." And Ludacris rhymes on *Chicken & Beer* or "Eyebrows Down" (2003): "I was still makin' demos, perfectin' the craft / Some said I wouldn't make it, they would giggle and laugh / So I picked up a couple books by Donald Goines / about the business of this shit, how to flip a few coins."

Not that his profundity goes unremarked in the economics of struggle. As AZ rhymes on *Doe or Die* or "Rather Unique" (1995): "…Too hard to follow / You took a bite but couldn't swallow / Your mind's boggled / But I'm as deep as Donald Goines's novels." More famously, 2pac rhymes on *All Eyez On Me* or "Tradin' War Stories" (1996): "Niggaz whisper when they mention / Machiavelli was my tutor / Donald Goines, my father figure / Moms sent me to go play with the drug dealers." No less famously, perhaps, Nas rhymes for "Escobaro '97" on *Men in Black: The Album* (1997): "Kinda hard bein' Escobaro / Eldorado Red, sippin' Dom out tha bottle / My life is like a Donald Goines novel." Nas wrote his own "Black Girl Lost" opus for *It Was Written* (1996); Foxy Brown records an officially unreleased song with the same title herself (*circa* 2003); and Papoose joins Nas with the help of Dirty Harry and DJ Kay Slay on a tribute-remix, "Black Girl Lost 2005," which appears later on *Unfinished Business: The Best of Papoose* (2009). In *Word Hustle*, this clearly captivating novel is critically engaged by Phyllis Lynne Burns's "I'll Be There," at long last.

The Queensbridge emcee is not alone in making multiple Goines references in rhyme. As a soloist, Jadakiss of The Lox returns to mic-check the same sixth novel as Nas on *The Last Kiss* or "Smoking Gun" (featuring Jazmine Sullivan) (2009), rhyming: "And that's why I feel for you / That's why I'm ready to kill for you / That's a Black girl lost for you / Call me, I'll come through and let it off for you." This is after he rejoins The Lox to cite Goines's fourteenth novel on Sheek Louch's *Walk witt Me* or "Mighty D-Block (2 Guns Up)" (2005), rhyming: "Yo, the revolver or the matty's cool / Knife game like Daddy Cool / since Bally shoes / This is tha real life street shit / truest and the deepest." Dennis Chester is on the same page, so to speak, when he writes on "masculinity" and *Daddy Cool* (1974) for *Word Hustle* in "By Certain Codes." A "graphic novel" edition of this Goines narrative would appear for a new generation of audiences in 2006.

Some emcees are sure to pinpoint certain novels, beyond *Black Girl Lost* (1974) and *Daddy Cool*, whether as their personal favorites or as a specific lyrical creation demands. Wu-Tang Clan's RZA rhymes with Gravediggaz on their *6 Feet Deep* or "Defective Trip (Trippin')" (1994), for example: "The wine / it fucks up my mind / every time / I'm goin' / and all I wanna be doin' is bonin' / but like a *Dopefiend* character / of Donald Goines." And Memphis Bleek rhymes on Jay-Z's *Reasonable Doubt* or "Can I Live II" (1999), as well: "That credit, you dead it / I know heads gettin' annoyin' / Knew all about a dopefiend before readin' Donald Goines."

The New York City underground's MF Grimm rhymes on "Take Em to War" or his *Scars & Memories* compilation (2005): "If Donald Goines wrote my life, my name would be Kenyatta." He has been further identified as both a "comic book writer" and "audio graphic novelist," himself. It is the sum total of Goines that is ordinarily, meticulously appreciated in Hip-Hop, nonetheless. Cam'Ron rhymes on the mix-tape circuit's "'Fetti" (featuring Vado) (2009): "Like Donald Goines / you write a hell of story." The San Francisco Bay Area's Andre Nickatina rhymes (with Equipto) on *Gun Mouth 4 Hire: Horns & Halos #2*, or "Cottoncandyland" (2005): "You know the way I keep it flowin' / is like that life of Donald Goines."

Maybe most impressively, nevertheless, Cru (or Rhythm Blunt Cru) from the Bronx could recall The Notorious B.I.G., or Lil' Kim's "Dreams" from her classic *Hard Core* (1996), when they compose "Goines Tale" for *Da Dirty 30* (1997) by building a composite storyline around the titles of each and every one of Goines's

16 novels. They open by rhyming, for instance: "Black Girl Lost, cuz Pops is Daddy Cool / former Dopefiend, now a pimp: damn fool! / He's a Black Gangster, Inner City Hoodlum / phat prankster, must admit, a pretty good one / But little do he know he on a Death List and shit / This'll be Kenyatta's Escape, Kenyatta's Last Hit...." In a sense, Donald Goines controls the mic like he's a live emcee himself. Cru may be especially engrossed by the Kenyatta series explored in *Word Hustle* by both Terrence T. Tucker in "Revolutionary Hustler" and Candice Love Jackson in "The Paradox of Empowerment." Their "Goines's Tale" closes by evoking another iconic novel, *White Man's Justice, Black Man's Grief* (1973). It is examined by both Quincy T. Norwood's sober contribution here in "Beneath the Law" and Andrew Sargent's "Representing Prison Rape."

What other 'novelist' has such an artful mass appeal, anywhere, at any time in the novel's history, on or off the plantation, per se, within the Americas or without?

The list will go on and on, too, as Kelvin Williams directs *Donnie's Story: The Life Story of Donald Goines* (2008) with a host of Hip-Hop lyricists providing the bulk of impromptu commentary for this independent documentary:

"He had a record deal back then ... with a book company."
"The words never die."
"He left no room for a misunderstanding in his books."
"God sent."
"The most appreciated ... [His] work is what bars and weights are to the body."
"Books in motion."
"Something they can feel ... This man really gave us something back."
"The book of the jail ... like *The Bible*."
"Great author."
"Definitely one of the masters of the urban street novel."
"A brilliant brother."
"Records in the form of a book ... The reeling off of experiences."
Etc., etc., etc...

The artwork and album concept of Bilal's *Airtight's Revenge* (2010) also combines a classic reference to Malcolm X and, according to the artist himself, a nod to Goines as well as Iceberg Slim who is read or juxtaposed with Goines in *Word Hustle* (in an effort to think "race" as an "institutional structure") by Cameron Leader-Picone's "Diggin' the Scene with a Gangster Lean." We see how Goines and the revolutionary Kenyatta's live on, all attempts to eliminate them aside. The Brooklyn group Pitch Black includes an emcee known as D.G., who rhymes on *Pitch Black Law* or "R U Ready 4 This" (featuring Busta Rhymes) (2004): "I *Defy* Gravity on *Devil's* Ground, simple and plain / It's *D.G., Donald Goines,* spittin' *Digital Game.*"

Another emcee from New York (and not Detroit, significantly, given Goines's trans-local, international reach) has named himself Donny Goines, while Lady Goines emerges from Brooklyn as well to release her debut album, *Black Girl Lost* (2006); it's described as R&B mixed with Hip-Hop, Jazz and Spoken Word. This is the perfect culmination of any chronology of the Donald Goines bibliography of Hip-Hop's discography.

Having read Goines's Kenyatta novels and *Cry Revenge* (1974), among others, thanks to Common, Bilal informs *Vibe* that "Airtight" is the alias-persona he assumes as a producer, the executive producer of all his sonic work (C. Writes 2010). Enthusiastically, and slyly, D.G. of Pitch Black urges listeners to cop *Dopefiend* (1971) and *Inner City Hoodlum* (1975)—the very first and the very last of the narratives—then "the whole catalog" once they are surely hooked on Goines's writing (Spence D. 2004). And, sharply, Donny Goines tells Okayplayer.com, as an emcee, after the release of *The Breakfast Club* (2009): "I felt like the moniker made sense. I speak on my community's struggles and real life situations…. And we share a lot of similarities. We were both in the armed services, we're from the streets, and we had run-ins with the law. I felt like if I was going to name myself after anyone, why not after an author? I'm an author in my own right" (Silas 2009).

A Black renegade class readership confirms renegade Black authorships, in Hip-Hop lyricism, despite standard constructions of 'literacy' and 'literature' (e.g., "poetry" as well as "the novel") and the mis-education of elite literary critics of the Western bourgeoisie. Where is the renegade criticism, where in the world has it been?

When Amiri Baraka as LeRoi Jones wrote "The Myth of a 'Negro Literature'" (1966), it was to condemn the "impressive mediocrity" and "spectacular vapidity" of basically Black middle class writing that is at bottom imitative of white middle class models of art, literature and culture in North America (165). Wickedly, unafraid of Blues and Jazz "Negritude" at the height of civil rights-oriented assimilation, he would ask why there was no Duke Ellington, Louis Armstrong, Charlie Parker, Ray Charles or Lightnin' Hopkins of "Black literature," in lieu of Phyllis Wheatley and Charles Chesnutt, on the one hand, *and*, on the other hand, Jean Toomer, Richard Wright, Ralph Ellison and James Baldwin (165; 166). In a pointed subversion of the normal class politics of literature, Baraka would define "High Art" in a manner which does not privilege middle class modes of expression, or even writing in particular: "by this I mean any art that would attempt to describe or characterize some portion of the profound meaningfulness of human life with any finality or truth" (167). He would conclude that it is historically found by and large in "only the 'popular traditions' of the so-called lower class Negro" rather than those middle class Negroes tutored by middle class "America" and its "middlebrow"

"Academy" (167; 170); and so of the school of "Negro poet" once lamented by Langston Hughes, he says: "It would be better if such a poet listened to Bessie Smith sing *Gimme A Pigfoot*, or listened to the tragic verse of a Billie Holiday, than be content to imperfectly imitate the bad poetry of the ruined minds of Europe" (170). The untutored poet-critics of Hip-Hop in the "*post*-civil rights" era of assimilation must agree. If, as Amiri Baraka, the former LeRoi Jones would paradoxically and unfortunately retreat from *some* of the unfettered heresy of "The Myth of a 'Negro Literature,'" it was this sort of heresy that could make Donald Goines's organically and indisputably Black art of "literature" conceivable in theory before it would hit Hip-Hop with no middle class pretensions whatsoever—which is nothing short of extraordinary given the conflicted bourgeois-capitalist origins of the contemporary novel of North America and European cultural imperialism. Overall, *Word Hustle* concerns a body of writing that is *neither* bourgeois literature *nor* "pulp fiction," which is an elite category itself, the only conceptual tag imaginable by most critics for writing with an audience beyond bourgeois elitism (cf., Calcutt and Shepherd 1999; Nishikawa 2008). Such a stigmatizing classification stigmatizes not only the writer of this stigmatized audience, but it also stigmatizes relevance. It stigmatizes the popular, as in the popular masses. In other words, anything too popular or anyone too productive just can't be that good ("He could write a book in a week," says Joan Goines-Coney of her brother); anything that good, it just shouldn't be too popular—*literary damnation*. Unimaginable for this kind of aestheticism is Goines's non-elite/anti-elite writing, therefore, to the precise extent that it is scrupulously crafted indeed *without* historically bourgeois orientations as regards, apart from audience, its form or content; narrative; style; characterization; language, discourse or lexicon; cultural ethos; morality or moralism; socio-historical consciousness; and literary as well as "extra-literary" (or "non-literary") politics, for example, novel after novel after novel—or (we could say, with Stallings), narrative after narrative after narrative?

Speaking of the Americas at large, and real-life scripts of empire (i.e., geopolitics; CIA-interventionist coups; government propaganda, etc.), Sylvia Wynter stated in "Novel and History, Plot and Plantation," provocatively: "It is clear, then, that it is only when the society, or elements of the society, rise up in rebellion against the external authors and manipulators that our prolonged fiction becomes temporary fact" (Wynter 1971, 95). The point was to note an opposition between the values of the imperialist market system born of the plantation and the traditional values of the "indigenous, autochtonous" African (or "Indian") structure of the "plot" (96). This was before she invoked Nas as a guidepost herself in "Un-Settling the Coloniality of Being/Power/Truth/Freedom" (2003). For, "from early on, the planters gave the slaves plots of land on which to grow food to feed themselves in order to maximize profits. We suggest that this plot system was … the focus of resistance to the market system and market values." This is the system of "those who defend the 'autonomy' of the 'civilized' highly educated artist." By contrast, "African peasants transplanted to the plot all the structure of values that had been created by traditional societies of Africa" (99). The consequent folk culture of the Black masses would provide to this day, across the hemisphere and beyond, "a point outside the [dominant imperialist] system where the traditional values can give us a focus of criticism against the impossible reality in which we are enmeshed" (100). It is source, or resource. This plot outside the novel has its own narrative of history with its own folk songs (101-102), global African music that morphs in form over time as the "basic system" of "Plantation America" remains intact with "the city" coming to operate as "the commercial expression of the plantation" and the marginalized masses "disrupted from the plot" (102). Thus enters "Hip-Hop Revolution" on the world historical stage after Donald Goines to constitute one set of urban African Diasporic examples of what Wynter's "Novel and History, Plot and Plantation" promotes as "cultural guerilla resistance to the plantation system," past and present (100).

Ayi Kwei Armah also makes a crucial intervention in the established critical discourse on the novel more recently in *The Eloquence of the Scribes: A Memoir on the Sources and Resources of African Literature* (2006). His aim is to consider African "verbal art throughout the ages," and to detach or free such considerations from "the facile and false notion of a European genesis of African literature" (145-46). He disputes the canonical history of the novel as an "invented" history of Western chauvinism, Occidentalism, or European narcissism. For neither Daniel Defoe of 17th Century England or Cervantes of 16th Century Spain in fact begin the actual history of the novel as such in Armah's sweeping literary historical research.

Heretically, Wynter had asked questions: "*What, in our context, is the novel? What, in our context, is history? What is our context?*" As if in response to her call, Armah directs heretical critical attention to other texts, other *novels*: Lo-Kuan-Chung's *Romance of the Three Kingdoms* and Shih Nai-An's *Water Margin* of 13th or 14th Century China as well as Murasaki Shikibu's *The Tale of Genji* of 10th Century Japan, apart from "The Hieroglyphic Record" of Egypt and the long historical continuity of verbal art all across Africa (143). The author of classic novels himself, such as *The Beautiful Ones Are Not Yet Born* (1968) and *Two Thousand Seasons* (1973), Armah as critic writes to reject the role of the "conformist traditionalist" in favor of the "artistic innovator." This is to say, he writes for the ("grassroots") "base" as much as Pan-Africa's whole "continent" (Armah 2006, 151). He writes *The Eloquence of the Scribes* not to reinscribe epic hierarchies, but to recover "old" art as sources or resources for "new" art, for "future thinkers, artists and writers" (154). In rewriting the colonial-imperial history of the novel, re-appropriating verbal art history in general and novel-writing historicity in particular, for every colonized people, Armah could rewrite its historical present no less than its future. Could Donald Goines in his narratives lay claim to *a novel ancestral*—one propagandistically obscured by colonial historical fictions that canonically privilege the novel of England (i.e., Defoe) or Spain (i.e., Cervantes)? And if the text of "a just society" is for Armah "more beautiful than any work of art" (11), then might not the "novel" or the *new* in Goines (travelling accessibly well in translation throughout the Francophone empire in Africa, at least) factor in considerably when "African literature" is reconsidered globally as "an evolving body of interconnected works from the beginnings of writing in ancient Egypt to the latest publications today" (19), interestingly enough?

In closing, as the first collection of critical essays to be published on Goines, *Word Hustle* hopefully marks a beginning. It is just a beginning. It breaks rank with "literary criticism" as usual (or literary criticism of "the system"), in effect, to join forces with Hip-Hop – Hip-Hop's "verbal art." As Hip-Hop articulates both "primary texts" of its own and, therein, a groundbreaking "secondary literature" on Goines that is at least two full decades old, if not quite as old as Hip-Hop lyricism itself: "16 Novels on the Microphone." What terms of our discourse are not in joyful dispute? The "novel" may merely reference the marvel of the "new," even the newly renewed or a renewal of the "old," beyond the noun form and novel form of Europe and its artful bourgeoisie. The need for novel forms of "cultural guerilla resistance" is no less manifest now, as of the 40th anniversary of the assassination of George L. Jackson. Hardly to be confused with an Eldridge Cleaver, in terms of sexual or any politics, he was the revolutionary inspiration for Goines's *Swamp Man* (1974). He'd relocate the theatre of physical guerilla warfare to "neo-slavery's" cities and concurrently theorize the need for a revolutionary culture in "Plantation America" and across the globe. With "revolutionary love," these were the hallmark features of his unrestricted *Blood in My Eye* (1972) in particular. In effect, *Word Hustle* highlights Goines's contributions to this culture, or "guerilla cultural resistance." *"What did Donald Goines do to the novel, for our context?" "What did he do not only to or through 'literature' (if by this we simply mean writing), but to the very notion of literacy, when we define each of these terms on our terms in the context of our history and all history?"* He inscribes a crafted, indigenizing 'literature' of the Black masses in defiance of Western and Westernized, academic and non-academic elites. He inscribes a 'literacy' of revolutionary resistance to neo-colonial regimes of assimilation and accommodation. He inscribes a practice of revolutionary writing that does not dichotomize or hierarchize the written over the oral in Western bourgeois fashion— or alienate the practice of writing from its ancient African origins, while U.S. society offers more the same brand of middle class books "on tape" for the consumer status-quo. Politically and intellectually, artfully, *Word Hustle* affirms this much and more with much respect due to Hip-Hop's microphone.

REFERENCES

Armah, Ayi Kwei. 2006. *The Eloquence of the Scribes: A Memoir on the Sources and Resources of African Literature.* Popenguine, Senegal: Per Ankh (The African Publishing Cooperative).

Calcutt, Andrew, and Richard Shephard. 1999. "Donald Goines." *Cult Fiction: A Reader's Guide.* Lincolnwood: Contemporary: 109.

D., Spence. 2004. "Pitch Black Interview: Brooklynites Bring the Crew Concept Back to Rap" *IGN* (February 6): http://music.ign.com/articles/490/490685p1.html.

Dumas, Henry. [1970] 2003. "Ark of Bones and Other Stories." *Echo Tree: The Collected Short Fiction of Henry Dumas.* Ed. Eugene B. Redmond. Minneapolis, MN: Coffee House Press: 9-127.

Grant, Tracy. 2001. "Why Hip-Hop Heads Love Donald Goines." *Black Issues Book Review* (September 14): 53.

Jackson, George L. 1972. *Blood in My Eye.* New York: Random House.

Jones, LeRoi. [1966] 1994. "The Myth of a 'Negro Literature.'" *Within the Circle: An Anthology of African American Literary Criticism from the Harlem Renaissance to the Present.* Ed. Angelyn Mitchell. Durham, NC: Duke University Press: 165-70.

Lynch, Acklyn. 1992. *Nightmare Overhanging Darkly: Essays on Black Culture and Resistance.* Chicago: Third World Press.

Nishikawa, Kinohi. 2008. "Donald Goines." *Encyclopedia of Hip Hop Literature.* Ed. Tarshia L. Stanley. Westport, CT: Greenwood Press.

Silas, M. Antonio. 2009. "Donny Goines: What's Behind a Name?" Okayplayer: http://www.okayplayer.com/interviews/latest-interviews/donny-goines:-what_s-behind-a-name%3F-200905268079/

Writes, Civil. 2010. "A Long Convo with … Bilal." *Vibe* (June 10): http://www.vibe.com/content/long-convo-bilal.

Wynter, Sylvia. 1971. "Novel and History, Plot and Plantation." *Savacou* 5 (June 1971): 95-102.

———. 2003. "Unsettling the Coloniality of Being/Power/Truth/Freedom: Towards the Human, After Man, Its Overrepresentation—An Argument." *CR: The New Centennial Review* 3, no 3 (Fall): 257-337.

THE DONALD GOINES BIBLIOGRAPHY

Dopefiend. Los Angeles: Holloway House Publishing Co., 1971.

Whoreson. Los Angeles: Holloway House Publishing Co., 1972.

Black Gangster. Los Angeles: Holloway House Publishing Co., 1972.

Street Players. Los Angeles: Holloway House Publishing Co., 1973.

White Man's Justice, Black Man's Grief. Los Angeles: Holloway House Publishing Co., 1973.

Black Girl Lost. Los Angeles: Holloway House Publishing Co., 1974.

Eldorado Red. Los Angeles: Holloway House Publishing Co., 1974.

Swamp Man. Los Angeles, CA: Holloway House Publishing Co., 1974.

Never Die Alone. Los Angeles: Holloway House Publishing Co., 1974.

Crime Partners (as Al C. Clark). Los Angeles: Holloway House Publishing Co., 1974.

Death List (as Al C. Clark). Los Angeles: Holloway House Publishing Co., 1974.

Cry Revenge (as Al C. Clark). Los Angeles: Holloway House Publishing Co., 1974.

Kenyatta's Escape (as Al C. Clark). Los Angeles: Holloway House Publishing Co., 1974.

Daddy Cool. Los Angeles: Holloway House Publishing Co., 1974.

Kenyatta's Last Hit (as Al C. Clark). Los Angeles: Holloway House Publishing Co., 1975.

Inner City Hoodlum. Los Angeles: Holloway House Publishing Co., 1975.

NOTES ON CONTRIBUTORS

Phyllis Lynne Burns is Assistant Professor of English at Otterbein College. Her areas of research and teaching include African American literature, Black film, and Black feminist theory.

Dennis Chester is Associate Professor of English at California State University-East Bay, where he is also Chair of the English Department. His areas of research and teaching include African American Literature, Post-Colonial Literature, Film Studies and Twentieth Century American Literature.

Candice Love Jackson is an Assistant Professor of English at Southern Illinois University at Edwardsville. Her research interests include African American and southern literatures, film, and popular culture. Her current book project, *The Literate Pimp: Reclaiming and Revisioning the Pimp Authored Text*, examines the works of Robert Beck (Iceberg Slim), Donald Goines, and the Bishop Don Magic Juan as well as interrogates the contemporary embracing of the pimp image in African American culture. Her work has appeared in the *Cambridge History of African American Literature*, *New Essays on the African American Novel*, the *Companion to Southern Literature*, the *Ethnic American Encyclopedia*, *A Gift of Story and Song: An Encyclopedia of African American Literature*, and the *Richard Wright Encyclopedia*.

Cameron Leader-Picone is Assistant Professor of English at Ithaca College. He received his Ph.D in African American Studies from Harvard University in 2009. A recent Fellow at Harvard University's W. E. B. Du Bois Institute for African and African American research, he is currently working on a book on representations of racial identity in contemporary African American literature.

Quincy T. Norwood has an M.A. in English from Michigan State University and is currently an instructor in the Oakland Community College English Department. He has contributed work to *Mainstream Press, Proud Flesh: New Afrikan Journal of Culture, Politics, and Consciousness,* and *The Michigan Chronicle*. He has also worked with various non-profit community-based organizations in Detroit.

Andrew Sargent is Assistant Professor of English at West Chester University, where he teaches courses in African American, American, and Civil Rights-era literatures. His essays and reviews have appeared in *MELUS, College Literature, Great Lives from History: African Americans,* and *The St. James Encyclopedia of Popular Culture*. He is currently at work on a book-length study of race, masculinity, and law enforcement in twentieth-century African American literature and film.

L.H. Stallings is a native of Durham, NC. She is Associate Professor of AAADS and Gender Studies at Indiana University-Bloomington. She is the author of *Mutha Is Half a Word!: Intersections of Folklore, Vernacular, Myth, and Queerness in Black Female Culture* (Ohio State University Press, 2007), which critically engages folk and vernacular theory, Black cultural studies, and Queer Theory to examine the representation of sexual desire in fiction, poetry, stand-up comedy, Neo-Soul, and Hip-Hop created by Black women. She is currently completing work on *Funky Erotixxx: Funk, Sex Work and Black Writers.*

Greg Thomas is a native of Southeast, Washington DC. He is Associate Professor of Black Studies (African & African Diasporic Literature and Culture) in the English Department at Syracuse University in New York. The founding editor of *PROUD FLESH*, an electronic journal, he is also the author of *The Sexual Demon of Colonial Power: Pan-African Embodiment and Erotic Schemes of Empire* (Indiana UP, 2007) as well as *Hip-Hop Revolution in the Flesh: Power, Knowledge and Pleasure in Lil' Kim's Lyricism* (Palgrave Macmillan, 2009). He is currently at work on a study of the intellectual politics of George L. Jackson, "The Dragon.

Terrence T. Tucker received his M.A. and Ph.D. degrees in English literature from the University of Kentucky. He is Assistant Professor at the University of Arkansas. His work focuses on African-American literature, particularly works after World War II to the present. His teaching interests include African American literature and drama, American drama, 20th and 21st century American literature, and popular culture. He has published articles on Walter Mosley, Black superheroes, *The Boondocks*, and Ernest Gaines. His book *Furiously Funny: Comic Rage in Late 20th Century African American Literature* explores the comic expression of Black rage across 20th century African American literature, drama, and popular culture.

INDEX